GAY TOURISM:
CULTURE, IDENTITY AND SEX

Also available in the series:

Gay Tourism: Culture, Identity and Sex

Edited by Stephen Clift,
Michael Luongo and Carry Callister

continuum
LONDON • NEW YORK

CONTINUUM

The Tower Building, 11 York Road, London SE1 7NX

370 Lexington Avenue, New York, NY 10017-6503

www.continuumbooks.com

First published 2002

British Library Cataloguing-in-Publication Data

A catalogue record for this book is available from the British Library

ISBN 0-8264-6696-6

Typeset by CentraServe Ltd, Saffron Walden, Essex

Printed and bound in Great Britain by

MPG, Bodmin, Cornwall

Contents

CONTENTS

CONTENTS

List of Figures

List of Tables

Contributors

CARRY CALLISTER worked for a number of years on health education research projects in the Centre for Health Education and Research, Canterbury, UK. She has worked on projects to produce information resources on sexual health education for young people and teachers, and most recently worked as part of the Europeer Project on the role of peer education for HIV prevention among young people. Currently she has her own shop selling beautiful things in the charming English seaside town of Deal.

STEPHEN CLIFT is Professor of Health Education in the Centre for Health Education and Research, Canterbury Christ Church University College, UK. Since 1995 he has pursued research interests in the area of international tourism and health, and has undertaken research on malaria prophylaxis and the sexual behaviour and risks of gay men on holiday. He is co-editor of three books on tourism and health: *Health and the International Tourist* (Routledge, 1996), *Tourism and Health: Risks, Research and Responses* (Pinter, 1997) and *Tourism and Sex: Culture, Commerce and Coercion* (Pinter, 2000). He has recently acted as consultant to the Living for Tomorrow Project concerned with gender, youth culture and sexual health, in Estonia and co-ordinated from the Nordic Institute for Women's Studies and Gender Research. He is also currently involved in research on the health benefits of active participation in music-making.

MARTIN COX was a PhD student in the department of geography at University College London. His research into gay holidaymaking aimed to advance the mapping of the geographies of gay people and to contribute to the queering of geography as an academic discipline.

MARK GRAHAM lectures in Social Anthropology at Stockholm University and is Visiting Fellow at the School of Sociology, University of New South Wales. He has written and published on the topics of refugees in Sweden, immigrants in the Swedish labour market, migration, male leather culture in Stockholm, queer theory and spatial relations. He is currently writing two books: one on male embodiment and leather culture and another on queer theory and anthropology. His next major project is an ethnographic study of gay and lesbian consumption in Sydney, Australia.

HOWARD L. HUGHES is Professor of Tourism Management at Manchester Metropolitan University, UK. He is the author of an internationally used economics textbook for hospitality and tourism management studies and of *Arts, Entertainment and Tourism* (Butterworth–Heinemann, 2000). The relationship between the arts and tourism has been a longstanding research interest, and a substantial number of papers have been published in this field. Recent research interests have also included the diversity of tourism experiences: ethnic minorities, economically disadvantaged families and gay men. Research in the field of gay men's holidays has focused on the contribution of the holiday to the construction of homosexual identity and on the influence of gay tourism on the spatial transformation of destinations.

MATTHEW LINK is the publisher of the *Rainbow Handbook Hawaii*, the first gay travel almanac to the islands, which *Our World* magazine called 'one of the most entertaining gay and lesbian guides ever produced'. He is an editor at *Out & About*, the prestigious gay travel newsletter, and he has contributed to the Access guides by HarperCollins, Ferrari's gay travel guides, and Fodor's guides. He has also written travel and other pieces for *Frommer's Budget Travel*, *Advocate*, *MetroSource*, *Our World*, *Hero*, *Genre* and others, including publications in Australia, Germany and Italy. Growing up on his father's sailboat as a youth, he has at various times called Hong Kong, the Philippines, Papua New Guinea, Palau, New Zealand, Hawaii and California home (in addition to having travelled extensively in twenty other countries). He has also produced award-winning video documentaries on HIV-positive Christians and male prostitution that have been shown on PBS stations and at film festivals.

MICHAEL LUONGO has a Master's degree in Urban Planning from Rutgers

University, and co-authored one of the first academic journal publications on the gay tourism industry while there. He has worked for a number of HIV-prevention projects with gay men and other populations in different parts of the United States. He has a particular interest in the geography of gay tourism and issues of HIV risk and prevention in tourism contexts. He had worked at the Centre for Health Education and Research, Canterbury, UK, to help develop the Terrence Higgins' Trust HIV-prevention campaign targeting gay tourists. He has also undertaken fieldwork on gay tourism in Ibiza. He was until recently, the Communications Manager for Columbia FunMaps, the gay travel map company. Michael currently resides in New York, working as a freelance writer and photographer on travel and other subjects. His work has appeared in various publications and websites in the United States and Europe, including *Our World, Out & About, Genre* and *GayHealth.com*.

CLAUDIA MILLER is the Managing Editor of *LesbiaNation.com*, the leading lesbian portal on the web, and a columnist and contributing writer for *WHERE*, the Miami tourist magazine published by ABARTA Media.

THOMAS ROTH has a background in both tourism and marketing. In 1992 he founded Community Marketing, Inc., which produces the International Gay & Lesbian World Travel Expo and other research, marketing and educational services for travel and tourism entities wishing to reach and serve the gay market. Community Marketing's Travel Alternatives Group (TAG) is the first consortium of travel agents serving the gay and lesbian community. The Community Marketing team organizes and produces the International Conference on Gay and Lesbian Tourism, now in its third year, and develops gay and lesbian journalist media trips for destinations as diverse as Sweden, Quebec, Peru and South Africa.

DOUGLAS SANDERS has been a professor in the Faculty of Law, University of British Columbia, Vancouver, Canada, since 1977, with earlier academic appointments at universities in Ontario. His primary academic work has been on the rights of indigenous peoples, and on international human rights law. He was the first 'out' gay man to speak in a UN human rights meeting, the Sub-commission on Prevention of Discrimination and Protection of Minorities (Geneva, August 1992). He was on the executive board of the International Lesbian and Gay Association from 1997 to 1999. Much earlier, he was the second president of the Association for Social Knowledge, the first lesbian and gay rights organization in

Canada, founded in 1963. He teaches law one month a year in Bangkok, Thailand, where he lives part of the year.

RICHARD SCHOLEY has worked in the field of HIV-prevention for gay men since 1994 and since 1997 in the Health Promotion Division of the Terrence Higgins Trust, the UK's leading HIV and AIDS organization. He is editor of *ISSUE*, the Terrence Higgins Trust's quarterly bulletin on HIV prevention with gay men and was co-developer of the Terrence Higgins Trust's gay men's travel campaign spanning the four years between 1998 and 2001.

MICHAEL STUBER holds a degree in Industrial Engineering and Management from the University of Karlsruhe. He is currently an independent Diversity Management and Marketing Consultant based in Cologne, and has been involved in European projects since 1989. Among his fields of expertise are gay/lesbian workplace and marketplace issues. He provides services in market research, brand consulting, marketing strategy and planning, networking, communication and training. He regularly writes articles and speaks at conferences and universities on his work. His clients include Kraft Foods, the British Tourist Authority and Hamburg Tourist Board.

PHILIP WANT is a senior lecturer in Tourism Studies at South Bank University, London, and is currently involved in research concerning global tourism and sexual minorities. His specialized teaching areas include Tourism Policy and Politics, and Tourism and Transportation. Recent publications include articles in *Tourism Concern* and conference papers presented at the International Association for the Study of Sexuality, Culture and Society at Manchester Metropolitan University, the seventh Annual Hospitality Research conference in Glasgow and 'Sexuality and Space: Queering Geographies of Globalization' in New York. Other publications include a chapter in *Radical Records* (edited by Bob Cant). In 1997 he was employed as a consultant to undertake research at the 1997 London Gay and Lesbian Pride Festival. Prior to his current university post, he was employed in the tourism industry for a number of years, working for both tour operators and airlines in the UK and the United States.

Introduction

STEPHEN CLIFT, MICHAEL LUONGO AND CARRY CALLISTER

GAY TOURISM: YESTERDAY, TODAY AND TOMORROW

Among the earliest documented examples of what we might now call gay travel is from the Victorian period, when homosexual men from northern Europe went on grand tours of the Mediterranean region. Such men visited Italy and Greece, and other locations seeking culture and importantly, the companionship of young men. Here, away from their families and strict northern mores, their sexuality could be more freely expressed (Aldrich, 1993).

This type of travel was usually confined to a wealthy, highly educated elite with the aim of seeing works of art and historic sites. There was also the pretence of an intellectual connection to ancient Greek and Roman culture – societies where homosexuality was more accepted. Van Gloeden's photographs from this period of boys with togas and urns in Taormina, Sicily, were essentially examples of pornography in the guise of classical reinterpretations. Yet even these trips and relationships were not without their sad side, as captured in Thomas Mann's *Death in Venice* (Aldrich, 1993).

During this seemingly repressed period, however, there was evidence of a developing gay urban subculture available to the traveller. One of the most striking examples of this is in the 1877 guidebook, *Pictures of New York Life and Character*. A book of illustrations showing what visitors might see on New York City streets, it includes a drawing of a foppishly dressed, limp-wristed man standing under a street sign. Highly caricatured, he is clearly meant to be homosexual (Averell & Co., 1877).

Chauncey discusses the further development of New York's gay urban infra-

1

structure from the beginning of the twentieth century through to the Second World War. Greenwich Village and Harlem were the neighbourhoods most known for their gay-popular venues (Chauncey, 1994). The same type of moderately openly gay and lesbian culture was also evident in Europe in the salons of Gertrude Stein and her fellow writers in Paris, and in Berlin's pre-Nazi Weimar Republic era. Ironically, Berlin had perhaps the most advanced homosexual subculture in existence at that time, and it was not confined to the cafés and cabarets immortalized by Christopher Isherwood in *Goodbye to Berlin*. A visit to the Schwule Museum or Gay Men's Museum in Berlin gives an indication of the variety of publications and institutions available to homosexuals just prior to the Nazi takeover. Still, gay travel as it were remained elitist. It was primarily for the rich intellectuals and artists who could afford to travel between the cities of London, Berlin, New York and Paris at a time when international travel was not yet affordable to the middle classes.

The Second World War and the urban social upheaval which came in its wake helped to give rise to the greater growth of gay neighbourhoods. During the war troops movements through New York City and San Francisco, (both important ports) allowed homosexual men and women from the provinces to sample the gay urban subculture. This may have contributed to the rise of both of these cities as major gay centres after the troops returned to the United States (Wright, 2000; Kissack, 2000). Further social changes in the postwar period present largely in the United States, but also to some degree in Britain, of de-industrialization and an abandonment of the urban inner-core, helped contribute to the growth of gay communities. In the United States this was due in large part to both car culture and racial tensions, as large numbers of blacks moved north seeking jobs. White-flight devalued entire neighbourhoods, creating space in cities to be adopted by artists, creative people and, importantly, gays and lesbians for their own spheres of safety away from the greater world. This same de-industrialization and abandonment pattern is most obvious in Manchester, England. Decentralization in London had also contributed to the degrading of Soho, resulting in a neighbourhood known for pornography and its tolerance of alternative sexualities. Many of London's gay venues settled in this part of Westminster on and around Old Compton Street. Later studies point to under-utilized urban housing as a primary location point of gay neighbourhoods (Bailey, 1999).

That homosexual subcultures in New York, Los Angeles and San Francisco had developed into important communities even by the 1950s and 1960s is evidenced by gay milestones that occurred prior to Stonewall. Los Angeles saw some of the earliest gay and lesbian publications, from the 1950s *Physique*

Pictorial and *One* magazine, to the late 1960s (and still-published) *Advocate*. In 1961 San Francisco female impersonator Jose Sarria was the first openly gay person ever to run for political office in the United States (he lost). Stonewall was not even New York's first public gay protest. In 1964 the New York League for Sexual Freedom held what might have been the first public gay and lesbian rights demonstration in the United States (Romesburg, 2001). While these events do not necessarily indicate travel between these major cities, they do demonstrate that the communities which would eventually become major gay tourist destinations were already in place by the mid twentieth century.

By the late 1960s and early 1970s, the neighbourhoods now embedded as legendary in the psyche of gays and lesbians had developed. These areas, particularly the Castro in San Francisco, West Hollywood in Los Angeles, and Greenwich Village, New York (which was a gay neighbourhood long before) and eventually Miami's South Beach became the most important gay neighbourhoods. Coupled with these were remote smaller beach cities, which became gay resorts with large year-round gay populations. These were often difficult to access, but were still within a few hours of major metropolitan regions. Provincetown in Massachusetts, Key West, Florida and Fire Island, New York, were the most important of these resorts in the United States, with some indication of their popularity as early as the 1930s (Newton, 1995). In the UK, the royal resort of Brighton has served a similar role for Londoners, and Blackpool for residents of the industrial North.

Gay travel at this time might be described as a case of chosen, and necessary, segregation within this small handful of gay-safe spaces. The neighbourhoods were like tourist bubbles, and gay chains developed within them such as A Different Light bookstore or All-American Boy clothing in New York, San Francisco and West Hollywood, or easily recognizable bars such as the leather-oriented Eagle. Many gay and lesbian vacations consisted of trips from the gay enclaves in which they lived to another in a different city or resort. For rural and suburban gays and lesbians, vacations allowed them to leave behind their mainstream daily lives and enter into completely gay environments. In light of the times (it was the Stonewall era), it was the safest way for gays and lesbians to travel. The very existence of such spaces was important to gay and lesbian identity, even for those who could never travel to them. As Bailey (1999: 92) comments, 'a subject need not physically inhabit such an identity space . . . to be influenced by it'.

Early gay guidebooks suggest the importance of these few destinations and urban centres. Two important guidebooks were created during this time and still continue to be basic building-blocks of gay travel information. *Damron's* was first published and distributed in the years 1964 and 1965, and was started by Bob Damron, a San Francisco gay bar-owner and avid traveller. The book first concentrated on the largest US cities, 'expanding over the years to cover everything in between', according to Gina Gatta, the current president of the company. Still, it was not the earliest publication of its type, she explained. 'There were early hand-made guidebooks passed around as early as 1954, that we know of', produced by the Mattachine Society. In 1963 Damron's business partner and lover Hal Call had also printed the guidebook *Lavender Baedeker* for the society, but that was the only edition (Gatta, 2001, personal communication). Similarly, *Spartacus*, started in Germany in the late 1960s, served a similar function. It covers many more countries than the present *Damron's*, which concentrates on North America. Still, the United States represents the largest section of this European guidebook (Bedford and Rauch, 2000).

The creation of these books is an indication that a more formal structure was developing in gay travel. By the 1960s, gay travel clubs such as the Mattachine Society's One Travel or the New York Islander Club for trips to Fire Island led all-gay outings for their members. However, Hanns Ebensten's gay travel company, opened in New York in 1972, is considered by many to be the first tour company to sell directly to the gay public. Significantly, he also conducted all-gay tours to destinations as remote as the Galapagos and Easter Island. At the time, he explained, 'Everyone said this is all so audacious and daring. I never thought that it was. I just thought, let's do it' (Ebensten, 2001, personal communication). It seemed to him a natural extension of his mainstream travel work. The company did not call itself gay in the beginning, but by having all-male tours, it was well understood even by straight clients who recommended the tours to friends. Most clients were from big US cities, but a number were from small Midwestern towns, who, he recalls, felt, 'maybe this is something I can try without getting into trouble', as it was too dangerous where many came from to meet other gay men. A detailed history of Ebensten's trips is available in his book, *Volleyball with the Cuna Indians* (Ebensten, 1993).

Even with tour companies like Ebensten's, most gay vacations were exclusively within a handful of centres. This segregation of travel was necessary for the creation and reification of gay identity (White, 1980; Hughes, 1997; see also Cox, Chapter 6, this volume). However, it also lead to an unfortunate situation, allowing the spread of HIV throughout the United States and abroad. Early discussions of HIV point to Gaetan Dugas, a French–Canadian flight attendant, as a conduit of infection for men in Los Angeles, New York and San Francisco with the then as yet unknown virus which causes AIDS (Shilts, 1987; Rotello, 1997). Named Patient Zero, there were undoubtedly many other men like him.

Still today, twenty years after the advent of AIDS, San Francisco, Los Angeles, Miami and New York are among the US cities with the highest rates of HIV infection. Similarly, in the UK, the important gay centres of London and Brighton exhibit high HIV prevalence. A more detailed discussion of the link between travel and HIV is available in Randy Shilts' book, *And the Band Played On* (see also Clift and Carter, 2000).

Gay travel through the 1980s continued to remain separate from mainstream travel. Many gays and lesbians who came of age after Stonewall still vacationed in exclusively gay destinations, resorts and hotels. By 1986 there was even an exclusively gay cruise company, RSVP (Grant, 2001). This was to change by the 1990s when there was a noticeable shift from previous trends, particularly for the generation coming of age after the HIV epidemic's initial outbreak. Some of the reasons for these changes were social; others were economic.

By the mid 1990s, both the UK and the United States had liberal governments, aiding social equality. As gay and lesbian rights progressed, the new generation no longer seemed to feel the need to confine itself strictly to all-gay environments. Gay and lesbian rights demonstrations also became high-profile and, importantly, lucrative tourist events. Among these were the 1993 March on Washington, New York's Stonewall 25 and Gay Games in 1994, and Sydney's Mardi Gras, which grew to become Australia's largest tourist event (Stubbs, 2000). Coupled with increasingly positive media images of gays and lesbians, the mainstream corporate world took notice. Significantly, the early 1990s economic slowdown fuelled a search for 'recession proof' market niches (Holcomb and Luongo, 1996).

Economic necessity was not the only adversity helping to fuel mainstream interest in the gay and lesbian travel market, but rather improving a company's public image as well. In 1993 American Airlines saw itself under siege when staff asked for the removal of all blankets and pillows from a plane because of the risk of AIDS, after flying a group of gay people from New York to Dallas (see Roth and Luongo, Chapter 5, this volume). Under threat of a boycott, the airline created a gay liaison, the first of the top 50 corporations to do so, and began intense promotion work within the gay community. These efforts included sponsoring gay and lesbian Pride events, circuit parties and other AIDS-related functions. The airline is today regarded as the most popular airline among American gays and lesbians.

This mainstreaming trend caused the International Gay and Lesbian Travel Association (IGLTA) to grow tremendously. It was created in a bar in Hollywood, Florida, in 1983. Then known as the International Gay Travel Association (IGTA), there were originally only twelve members. The organization has grown to include more than 30 airlines, nearly 400 travel agents, and dozens of other companies, over 1100 members in 42 countries. With its headquarters in Key West, Florida, there are regional offices planned throughout the globe. According to Robert Wilson, Executive Director, the membership is approximately 60 per cent gay and 40 per cent straight. 'We encourage the straight community to become involved' (personal communication, 2001). The international reach of the organization is reflected in the varied locations for their gatherings, including Lima, Peru – not usually thought of as a gay destination. According to Wilson: 'That's a perfect reason for us to be there that will only enrich both sides of the picture.' While acknowledging that homophobia exists in some of the places where they hold meetings, he explained: 'It's a totally different story when you are talking with a professional person about business.' The organization thus serves to bridge a gap between the mainstream world and a once exclusively gay one, allowing local tourism boards and businesses throughout the world to see the power of the gay market.

Two important gay travel publications were also born in this mainstreaming period. The magazine *Our World* was the first gay and lesbian travel monthly and was created by Wayne Whiston in 1989. Over the years, the number of mainstream advertisers has increased significantly. The newsletter *Out & About* was launched in 1992, created by Billy Kolber-Stuart and David Alport. Both provided gay and lesbian travellers with near monthly updates on gay travel destinations. According to Kolber-Stuart: 'one of the reasons we started the newsletter was that guidebooks were too slow and outdated'. Kolber-Stuart had been an employee of American Express, which became his first major mainstream client. The company first used *Out & About* as a diversity tool within their corporation, purchasing copies of the newsletter for distribution in their travel centres. Another publication milestone of this period was the 1996 *Fodor's Gay Guide to the USA* by Andrew Collins. This was the first time a mainstream publisher had produced a guide of this type. The book has been republished several times, and extended into a city series. Other books have followed suit; for example the 1997 *Frommer's Gay & Lesbian Europe* by David Andrusia.

While it might be expected that cities with large gay populations such as Miami Beach, Key West and West Hollywood would actively court the gay and lesbian travel market, through the early 1990s few other destinations were doing the same. Often, it was the gay community itself doing the promotion work through business guilds, and then city governments began to utilize some of this information (Holcomb and Luongo, 1996). New York City, for instance, distributed gay and lesbian information provided to it by the now defunct New York City Gay and Lesbian Visitors Center (Goldstein, 1993). This would change by the end of the decade. In 1998 London became the world's first major city actively to campaign internationally for the gay and lesbian market. Other cities around the world have since followed suit (for more on this, see Stuber, Chapter 4, this volume).

This mainstreaming of gay and lesbian travel has also changed the nature of its advertising and promotion. While indicative of other changes in gay culture with the advent of AIDS and civil-union rights, gay travel has become de-sexualized. In the early 1990s, a US-based gay-owned travel agency once touted a trip to London as a chance to 'bang Big Ben', a play on words calling to mind sexual opportunity abroad and a 'phallic' national symbol. In complete opposition, yet including Big Ben for place-setting, the London Tourism Board's advertisements focus on couples, tea on the Thames and shopping. Even famously permissive Amsterdam uses a picture of a loving male couple surrounded by tulips and dreamy canals on the cover of its gay guide. France is perhaps the only government tourism board involved in this market, which directly uses flirtation and the possibility of casual sex as a selling-point.

At the opposite end of sexual mainstreaming was the development of the North American circuit-party system. These huge, extravagant events originally begun to raise money to fight AIDS, helped to create the image of a gay destination. This is perhaps most evident with Miami's White Party, among the earliest circuit parties. In Signorile's book *Life Outside*, one interviewee credits the White Party with making the city an important gay destination: 'If you go back a few years ago to the beginning of the Vizcaya [mansion holding the White Party] event, that was the beginning of the scene in Miami' (Signorile, 1997: 98). Cities as diverse as Philadelphia, Washington and Phoenix use these parties to spur gay travel. Montreal's 1999 Black and Blue Ball was credited with placing $35 million Canadian (approximately $23 million US) into the local economy, 'one of the highest return [*sic*] of any organised tourist event in Canada' (BBCM Foundation, 2000).

Yet, many of these events have come under criticism. Originally AIDS fundraisers they are accused of promoting unsafe sex and illegal drug-use – the very behaviours they were meant to combat. This situation has created a dilemma for some mainstream financial supporters. A highly publicized drug overdose also led New York's Gay Men's Health Crisis (GMHC) to discontinue its Fire Island Morning Party, once among its largest fund-raisers (see Miller, Chapter 9, this volume).

Whether it is a Phoenix circuit party or an all-gay cruise, the amount of vacation spots welcoming the gay and lesbian market is nearly impossible to count. Gay groups now travel to far-flung destinations such as Egypt, India and even Transylvania for Halloween. This is an astonishing change from only twenty years ago, when with few exceptions gay and lesbian vacationers rarely travelled as openly gay to all but a handful of urban districts and shore resorts. This trend has come about partly because of marketing interests as tourism boards and travel agencies seek to increase profitability, as well as with civil rights advances throughout the world. At the same time, new technologies such as the Internet have allowed any destination or travel company to market itself to a wider audience.

One might also throw aside all these trends, however, and state that perhaps the increases in gay and lesbian travel are simply one extension of a larger trend in travel. Over the past several years one aspect of globalization is that international travel has become cheaper, and more people are willing to visit what were once considered exotic locations. Thus coming full circle, like any kind of travel, gay travel has become more affordable, less obscure and accessible to middle-class gays and lesbians, fuelling a boom in a very visible niche. Only the future will show whether gay and lesbian travel becomes less lucrative and visible as lesbian and gay civil rights and assimilation progress, so helping to fulfil the World Tourism Organization's commitment to 'freedom of movement of people', in a new way.

Still, what travel means to today's gay men and lesbians might have also changed in this mainstreaming process, so distinctly different is it from the experience in years past. There may once have been a secret thrill to travelling to a remote out-of-the-way place, such as a small all-gay hotel on the last island of a chain, or a club hidden on the backstreets of an emerging gay neighbourhood. Today, one can check into the most luxurious five-star hotel, where it is no problem for two men to share a bed, and become blended in with the rest of the world as just one more market sector for a commodity.

THE PRESENT VOLUME

Over the period 1992–8, a group in the Centre for Health Education and Research,[1] developed a programme of research exploring the interconnections between international travel and health. This included projects on:

- tourist health preparations and health problems experienced on holiday (Page *et al.*, 1994);
- holiday behaviours and their positive and negative health implications (Clift and Clark, 1996);

- tourists' experiences and compliance in using malaria prophylaxis (Clift, 1996; Clift et al., 1997; Abraham et al., 1999);
- sexual behaviour abroad among attendees at clinics for sexually transmitted infections (Black et al., 1995).

As this programme of research progressed, consultations took place with public health and health-promotion professionals across southeast England, to identify priorities for research and health-promotion initiatives. One issue identified concerned the sexual behaviour of gay men on holiday abroad, and whether this involved increased risk of HIV infection. A review of the existing literature revealed that little research had been undertaken on travel and sexual activity among gay men (Clift and Wilkins, 1995), and suggested the need for further work. This led to a substantial survey of gay tourism and sexual-risk behaviour, focused on the south coast resort town of Brighton, which has the largest resident gay population of any town in the UK outside of London (full details of the findings can be found in Clift and Forrest, 1999a, b; 2000a, b). Further research followed at the London Freedom Fairs (gay and lesbian leisure and travel) (see Clift et al., Chapter 10, this volume), and work was undertaken to support the development of a national HIV-prevention and sexual health campaign aimed at gay travellers, organized by the Terrence Higgins Trust in London (see Scholey, Chapter 11, this volume). Together these studies provide evidence on the diversity of gay men's holiday motivations, the destinations they visit for holidays, and their experiences and sexual behaviour in holiday settings. Compared with the picture emerging from studies of the sexual behaviour of heterosexual travellers/tourist gay men are undoubtedly more sexually active on holiday (Clift and Carter, 2000), but it is certainly not the case that all gay men are looking for sex on holiday. Furthermore, while some gay men reported unprotected sex on holiday, the incidence of unsafe sex appears to be lower than that found among heterosexual tourists.

The studies undertaken by the CHER team were primarily concerned with sexual behaviour and risks, and were motivated by a concern to inform further practical work in HIV-prevention and sexual-health promotion. The theoretical work undertaken was limited to the development of predictive models (see Clift and Forrest, 1999a), and the methodology was primarily survey-based and 'quantitative' in character, although some interviews were undertaken to explore gay men's experiences of holidays and sexual behaviour in greater detail (see Clift and Forrest, 1998). The limitations of this work and the need for more contextual qualitative studies were apparent. A small-scale feasibility study for an ethnography of gay tourism and sexual behaviour was undertaken in Ibiza Town in 1998, which demonstrated the value of such an approach. This work served to identify a worrying lack of safer-sex promotion in a popular gay holiday resort, the difficulty of obtaining strong condoms and lubricant, and some of the barriers and difficulties involved in mounting a proactive campaign in resort settings (Clift *et al.*, 1999). The need for wider historical, economic and cultural perspectives on gay tourism as it has developed since the mid 1950s also became apparent, addressing such issues as the development of 'gay destinations'; the commercialization of 'gay tourism' as a niche market; and reactions and resistances to gay tourism in specific places. Some research on some of these issues has appeared in the academic literature (e.g. Holcomb and Luongo, 1996; Hughes, 1997), but it is notable how little attention has been given to them to date. Hence the rationale for this book: to bring together contributions from leading practitioners in the business of gay and lesbian tourism, and from academic researchers – both to provide an overview of current issues and to act as a stimulus for further research.

Part 1 of the book considers the historical–cultural contexts of gay and lesbian tourism. Mark Graham provides a valuable overview and extends the historical perspective provided above. He distinguishes three forms of tourism – homosexual, gay and queer – and discusses them in relation to ideas of 'place' and 'space' and the challenges they have offered to dominant 'hetero-normative regimes' in Western culture. Matthew Link and Douglas Sanders then provide two case-studies of gay tourism in Hawaii and in Thailand – non-Western societies which have their own distinctive historical/cultural traditions of sexual/gender categorizations and roles, but which are similar in their normative prohibitions on open communication about sexuality. Both Link and Sanders highlight that the image gay visitors may have of lesbian and gay life in Hawaii and Thailand may not correspond with the social realities which exist there. They also highlight the significance of tourism for the economies of both Hawaii and Thailand, and also the dilemmas that result if certain kinds of tourism or categories of tourist are considered undesirable. This has been an issue of particular political significance in both societies – for Thailand with respect to its reputation for sex tourism, and the political need to play down this image and discourage tourism for sex – and as Link explains, for Hawaii, in relation to the political and legal controversies over 'gay marriage'.

From a very different perspective, Tom Roth and Michael Stuber provide an account of current developments in the business of gay and lesbian tourism and issues in marketing – in the United States and in Europe. Both contributors have played a leading role in development of tourism services for gay men and lesbian women, and in working with commercial interests inside the wider travel and tourism industry, in encouraging the development of services and products, which are 'gay-friendly'. The scale of the lesbian and gay 'niche' in the travel and tourism market is made very clear by their accounts – and not least by the illustrations of marketing material and advertising included in their chapters. (There can be no more graphic demonstration of the way in which gay men are regarded as a lucrative body of consumers in the tourism market, than the advertisement put out by the Toronto Tourism Board: 'You're here, you're queer, let's go shopping!') All travel and tourism businesses draw heavily today on the Internet, and even a cursory use of search engines to find sites devoted to 'gay travel/tourism' will provide an indication of the recent growth and current scale of gay tourism business in recent years. For more focused surfing, Michael Luongo's Appendix, provides a selective review of sites that are particularly worth visiting. Sites of relevance to individual chapters are also listed throughout the book.

Part 2 of the book goes on to focus more on the personal dimensions of lesbian and gay tourism, and explores issues of identity development in relation to travel and holiday experience; motivations for travel and processes of decision-making; and experiences of homophobic resistance and hostility in tourist destinations. Martin Cox provides a fascinating account of the challenges that tourism can present to gay men at the level of identity – when they travel for the first time from a 'smalltown' setting, to one of the major metropolitan gay cities, or resort destinations. Howard Hughes also argues for the significance of holidays in relation to gay identity formation and development, but explores further the factors that influence the decisions gay men make about travel destinations. The issues of risks associated with travel, particularly to countries which have a reputation for being non-accepting of homosexuality is particularly explored in developing a model of tourism decision-making. This theme is further explored by Philip Want, who provides an overview of the many anti-gay and anti-lesbian incidents that have arisen in tourism destinations in recent years. He goes beyond documenting these occurrences, however, in presenting an analysis of the legal, cultural and commercial factors which underpin hostility and resistance to gay and lesbian tourism. Interestingly, while he highlights the positive stance that a number of national tourism boards or authorities in Europe have taken in promotional work to gay and lesbian markets, it is clear from their Internet sites that a marked segregation of materials and messages has been maintained between the general travelling 'market' and the gay and lesbian 'niche'. Finally, in this section, Claudia Miller provides a first-hand account of the development of a circuit-party network among lesbian women in the United States. Drawing on her personal knowledge and contacts in this scene, she highlights its significance for changing patterns in lesbian culture and personal identity. Also of considerable importance is her discussion of the patterns of risky drug-taking and sexual behaviour in circuit parties among gay men, and the reactions this has provoked among sponsors of events and charitable groups that potentially benefit from fund-raising. This issue leads well into the final part of the book in which Stephen Clift, Michael Luongo and Carry Callister consider the sexual behaviours of gay men in holiday settings, and Richard Scholey describes a major UK initiative in HIV-prevention targeting gay holidaymakers.

The present volume is the first of its kind in focusing specifically on gay and lesbian tourism, and in bringing together contributors involved directly in the business of gay tourism, and academics interested in theoretical analysis and research. Gay and lesbian tourism is a relatively new and growing economic and social phenomenon, which clearly has substantial cultural and personal significance for gay and lesbian travellers themselves, for their countries of origin and for the destinations they visit. As editors, we hope that this volume both informs and enlightens – but perhaps more importantly, stimulates further research on gay and lesbian tourism at all levels.

NOTE

1. Stephen Clift, Stephen Page, David Stears, Nicola Clark and Paula Black were part of the original team. Others joined as projects developed: Lynnette Thomas, Vicky Madden, Simon Forrest, Adam Tidball, Carry Callister and Michael Luongo.

REFERENCES

Abraham, C., Clift, S. and Grabowski, P. (1999), 'Cognitive predictors of adherence to malaria prophylaxis regimens on return from a malarious region: a prospective study', *Social Science and Medicine*, 48: 1641–54.

Aldrich, R. (1993), *The Seduction of the Mediterranean: Writing, Art and Homosexual Fantasy*. London: Routledge.

Andrusia, D. (1997) *Frommer's Gay & Lesbian Europe*. New York: Frommer.

Averell & Co. (1877), *Pictures of New York Life and Character*. New York: G.W. Averell & Co.

Bad Boy Club Montreal (2000), *2000 Black and Blue Festival 10th Anniversary Press Packet*. Montreal: BBCM.

Bailey, R. (1999), *Gay Politics, Urban Politics: Identity and Economics in the Urban Setting*. New York: Columbia University Press.

Bedford, B. and Rauch, R. (2000), *Spartacus International Gay Guide*. Berlin: Bruno Gmünder Verlag.

Black, P., Clift, S. and Wijesurendra, C. (1995), 'Sexual behaviour abroad: a study of genito-urinary clinic attenders', *Travel Medicine International*, 13 (6): 66–9.

Chauncey, G. (1994), *Gay New York*. New York: HarperCollins.

Clift, S. (1996), 'Malaria prophylaxis: concerns, choice and compliance among British tourists to The Gambia', *Travel Medicine International*, 14 (16): 1–6.

Clift, S. (2000), 'Tourism and health: present issues and future concerns', *Tourism Recreation Research* 25 (3): 55–61.

Clift, S. and Carter, S. (eds) (2000), *Tourism and Sex: Culture, Commerce and Coercion*. London: Continuum.

Clift, S. and Clark, N. (1996), 'Dimensions of holiday experiences and their implications for health: results from a survey of British tourists in Malta', in S. Clift and S. Page (eds), *Health and the International Tourist*. London: Routledge.

Clift, S. and Forrest, S. (1998), *Gay Men, Travel and HIV Risk*. Canterbury: Centre for Health Education and Research, Canterbury Christ Church College.

Clift, S., Callister, C., and Luongo, M. (1999), *A Feasability Study for an Ethnography of Gay Tourism in Ibiza Town*. Canterbury: Canterbury Christ Church University College.

Clift, S. and Forrest, S. (1999a), 'Factors associated with the sexual behaviour and risk of gay men on holiday', *AIDSCare*, 11 (3): 281–95.

Clift, S. and Forrest, S. (1999b), 'Gay men and tourism: motivations and holiday destinations', *Tourism Management*, 20: 615–25.

Clift, S. and Forrest, S. (2000a), 'Tourism and the sexual ecology of gay men', in S. Clift and S. Carter (eds), *Tourism and Sex: Culture, Commerce and Coercion*. Leicester: Pinter.

Clift, S. and Forrest, S. (2000b), 'Gay tourism, sex and sexual health promotion', in J. Horne and S. Flemming (eds), *Masculinities: Leisure Culture, Identities and Consumption*. Eastbourne: Leisure Studies Association.

Clift, S. and Grabowski, P. (eds) (1997), *Tourism and Health: Risks, Research and Responses*. Leicester: Pinter.

Clift, S., Grabowski, P. and Sharpley, R. (1997), 'Health precautions and malaria prophylaxis among British tourists to The Gambia', in S. Clift and P. Grabowski (eds), *Tourism and Health: Risks, Research and Responses*. Leicester: Pinter.

Clift, S. and Page, S. (eds) (1996), *Health and the International Tourist*. London: Routledge.

Clift, S. and Wilkins, J. (1995), 'Travel, sexual behaviour and gay men', in P. Aggleton, P. Davies and G. Hart (eds), *AIDS: Sexuality, Safety and Risk*. London: Taylor & Francis.

Collins, A. (1996), *Fodor's Gay Guide to the USA*. New York: Fodor's.

Ebensten, H. (1993), *Volleyball with the Cuna Indians: And Other Gay Travel Adventures*. New York: Penguin.

Ebensten, H. (2001), former owner of Hanns Ebensten Travel Company, personal communication.

Gatta, G. (2001), Damron company editor and publisher, personal communication.

Goldstein, J. (1993) Co-founder, The New York City Gay and Lesbian Visitors' Center (now defunct), personal communication.

Grant, T. (2001), 'Cruising with RSVP', *Our World Magazine*, May.

Holcomb, B. and Luongo, M. (1996), 'Gay tourism in the United States', *Annals of Tourism Research*, 23 (2): 711–13.

Hughes, H. (1997), 'Holidays and homosexual identity', *Tourism Management*, 18, (1): 3–7.

Kissack, T. (2000), 'New York City', in G. Haggerty (ed.), *Gay Histories and Cultures: An Encyclopedia*. New York: Garland.

Kolber-Stuart, Billy (2001), Managing Editor, *Out & About*, personal communication.

Newton, E. (1995), *Cherry Grove, Fire Island: Sixty Years in America's First Gay and Lesbian Town*. Boston, MA: Beacon Press.

Page, S., Clift, S. and Clark, N. (1994), 'Tourist health: the precautions, behaviour and health problems of British tourists in Malta', in A. V. Seaton (ed.), *Tourism: the State of the Art*. Chichester: Wiley.

Romesburg, D. (2001), 'Innovation through the ages: Los Angeles', *The Advocate*, 14 August.

Rotello, G. (1997), *Sexual Ecology: AIDS and the Destiny of Gay Men*. New York: Penguin.

Roth, T. (2001), *The 6th Annual Gay & Lesbian Travel Survey – A Place for US 2001*. San Francisco, CA: Community Marketing.

Shilts, R. (1987), *And the Band Played On: Politics, People and the AIDS Epidemic*. New York: St Martin's Press.

Signorile, M. (1997), *Life Outside*. New York: Harper Perennial.

Stubbs, P. (2000), Sydney Mardi Gras organizing committee, personal communication.

White, E. (1980), *States of Desire: Travels in Gay America*. New York: Dutton.

Wright, L. (2000), 'San Francisco', in G. Haggerty (ed.), *Gay Histories and Cultures: An Encyclopedia*. New York: Garland.

PART 1

History, Culture and Commerce

CHAPTER 1

Challenges from the Margins: Gay Tourism as Cultural Critique

MARK GRAHAM

INTRODUCTION

Mention tourism and most people's thoughts turn to travel. Tourism is usually understood to involve moving from the familiar to the unfamiliar, from home to abroad and from being a potential host to being a guest. In the anthropological collection *Hosts and Guests* (Smith, 1978), hosts are distant 'others' and the guests are 'westerners' who visit them from elsewhere. While the distinction certainly applies to much of today's tourism, it none the less deflects our attention from the presence of 'guests' at home. In societies structured by hetero-normative regimes whoever does not conform to the hegemonic form of gender/sex will at some time experience the feeling of being out of place, marginalized and assigned to the social and cultural periphery. They will feel like guests at home. The feeling of being out of place is directly related to how 'place' is produced within hetero-normative regimes, which aim to keep locations heterosexual by suppressing displays of same-sex eroticism in all but a few spaces. In this way the marginality of homosexuality is maintained while its importance for the stabilization of heterosexuality can be denied. Within recent queer studies much labour has gone into arguing the centrality of homosexuality within Euro-American culture contrary to the dominant opinion that it is morally, culturally and socially marginal. A central contention is that the category 'heterosexual' is constructed in relation to devalued sexualities, including homosexuality, which then act from their marginal position as its constitutive outside. If the category of homosexual ceased to exist, then the category heterosexual would have nothing with which to stabilize its boundaries (see Sedgwick, 1990; Butler, 1990; Fuss, 1991; de Lauretis, 1991; Warner, 1994).

The spatial practices of hetero-normative regimes aim to ensure that bodies, gender and sexuality coincide with each other in agreement with heterosexual norms. Lefebvre (1991) sees the production of space as the result of capitalist relations of production (however, the hetero-normative regime cannot be reduced to the workings of capitalism and while I find Lefebvre's model useful, I do not adopt its Marxist assumptions). The process involved conforms to Lefebvre's tripartite distinction between 'spatial practice', 'representations of space' and 'spaces of representation' (1991: 33). Challenges to the dominant, in this case hetero-normative, representation of places emerge from within spaces of representation. Lefebvre writes that these spaces embody 'complex symbolisms, sometimes coded, sometimes not, linked to the clandestine or underground side of social life' (1991: 33). It is these spaces of representation, linked to gay tourism, tourists and tourist events, with which I am mainly concerned.

Writing largely from within an anthropological framework I shall be looking at tourism in terms of three broad overlapping categories: homosexual tourism, gay tourism and queer tourism. I address how each of these types contributes to maintaining or disrupting the heterosexual–homosexual dichotomy, and, in particular, the forms of marginalization – geographic, social and cultural – it generates.

Homosexual tourism, which is structured around a sharp distinction between the homophobic home and a destination that affords relative sexual freedom, will largely be examined in the context of the nineteenth-century travel by northern European men to the Mediterranean region. The more recent phenomenon of gay tourism will be explored by drawing on examples from Amsterdam, Stockholm and the 2000 Sydney Olympic Games – places and events which provide contexts for the celebration of gay culture, but which at the same time contribute to forms of marginalization in which a clear homosexual–heterosexual dichotomy is maintained. I return to Sydney to consider the queer dimensions of the 2000 Olympics and events associated with it that undermine this dichotomy. Other instances of the same queer challenge are taken from New York and the 2000 World Pride celebrations in Rome.

HOMOSEXUAL TOURISM

Sexual licence in connection with travel is an old phenomenon. The works of Chaucer and Boccaccio among others bear eloquent witness to how the medieval pilgrimage combined faith and piety with bawdiness and licentiousness. What I here refer to as homosexual tourism made its appearance in eighteenth-century Europe and has continued until this day. Homosexual tourism refers to a form of travel, which comes close to resembling flight. Homosexuals left their own country to find sensual and sexual release elsewhere, in less repressive environments. Of course, heterosexuals, too, seek sexual places elsewhere, but this usually means going from one kind of heterosexual context to another (e.g Brighton, as described by Shields, 1991).

Aldrich (1993) has described the attraction of the Mediterranean for eighteenth- and nineteenth-century men in terms of the yearnings that forced them to flee to another place. He terms it the 'Aschenbach phenomenon' after Thomas Mann's character in *Death in Venice*. Visits to the south by northern Europeans, which developed out of the tradition of the Grand Tour, were for reasons of architecture, renaissance art, classical landscapes, the sun and sexual attraction. As Aldrich notes, 'cultural interest and sexual longings went hand in hand, and in the Mediterranean the British [and many other northern Europeans] could try to satisfy both appetites' (1993: 69). Many of the men who had the money and time to make the visit were educated and familiar with classical texts which they could read in the original Latin or Greek. This gave them access to a world of homoeroticism that had often been suppressed in translation. Knowledge of the 'unknown' in texts reinforced the desire to visit the 'unknown' sexual landscapes of Europe's southern periphery (ibid.: 166).

Visiting these 'familiar' places could result in a kind of shock brought on by the uncanny familiarity of what was found. Palpitations, laboured breathing and vertigo were common symptoms of the 'Stendhal syndrome' named after Stendhal's own reactions to visiting the tombs of Michelangelo, Galileo and Machiavelli in the church of Santa Croce in Florence in 1817 (ibid.: 169). The reaction was a sign of a sensibility and an appreciation of the significance and beauty of what one was witnessing. The sexual experience of the homosexual tourist was, then, closely bound up with an artistic and aesthetic experience. A particular kind of homosexual role was available to those who could position themselves within classical Greek and Italian tradition. Homosexuality was a dimension of art.

The homosexual figures in the margins included the German Winckelmann, one of the founders of the discipline of Art History. British travellers included Symonds, who shaped the British view of the Renaissance, and literary figures such as Lord Byron, Oscar Wilde and E. M. Forster. In France the same was true of the author Verlaine. All of these men were central figures within European culture, but they often realized their visions in the spatial and sexual periphery from which they then infused the centre. In the wake of the Wilde trials in 1895 a steady stream of British men crossed the Channel. For some it was an enforced and sometimes permanent exile in countries which had previously served as an escape for the homosexual tourist. In the Catholic countries of southern Europe the Church retained considerable control over public morals. The state kept its distance. By contrast the sectarian nature of northern Europe left the secular authorities with responsibility for morals. In Catholic countries homosexuals could do very much as they pleased as long as it was in private and did not disrupt public life by challenging orthodox views on sexuality (on the history of different sexual cultures in Europe see Eder *et al.*, 1999).

Homosexual tourism, then, involved travel to distant or relatively distant places. It can be said to leave the homophobia of the home country intact in that it does not pose a challenge that emanates from within the country itself. There are borderline cases, however. Cherry Grove, located on Fire Island a few miles off the east coast of the New York metropolitan area became a refuge for homosexuals in the 1930s. But it was to become an integral part of the gay urban scene of New York in the coming decades and as such part of its challenge to American homophobia.

GAY TOURISM

The emergence of gay tourism has not automatically entailed the disappearance of tourist sites on the margins. On the contrary, sites such as Fire Island's Cherry Grove, described in Esther Newton's (1993) historical ethnography, and Key West in Florida are still flourishing destinations. These geographic margins, unlike the sites of homosexual tourism, are part of a wider network of gay tourist destinations that are not confined to peripheries. Gay and lesbian tourism has its main point of anchorage in the major urban centres of Euro-American countries. These centres are highly reflexive and made mutually aware of each other's existence through media connections. They can be seen as part of a growing global gay connectivity in which tourist visits to the major cities contribute actively to this awareness (for a general overview of increasing global interconnections and their cultural implications, see Tomlinson, 1999, and Friedman, 1994). A recent example is the 2000 celebration of World Pride in Rome, to which I return below. The places in question are usually familiar to most gays and lesbians, if only by reputation, and may even be inspirational for gays and lesbians who do not live in them. Many major lesbian and gay tourist events such as national gay pride celebrations, EuroPride and World Pride are also politicized. Unlike homosexual tourism, they do not cater for a narrow homosexual male role but also encompass the social, cultural, economic, political and health dimensions of life. Homosexual tourism does not necessarily imply a total lack of specialized facilities. Local people in the Mediterranean destinations of the nineteenth century catered for the needs of the north European gentlemen who visited them, much as locals do in sex tourism destinations in different parts of the world today. But there was nothing approaching the infrastructures found in gay resorts.

Yet, despite their prominence within the collective imaginary of gays and lesbians these sites are still often peripheral in the sense of being separate from the surrounding society. The spatial settings of gay tourism in Amsterdam, for example, are distinct from the heterosexual space of the 'Wallen', and tend to be focused on the areas of Kerksstraat, Warmoesstraat, Rembrandtplein and Reguliersdswarsstraat. Despite the importance of gay tourism for the city, and some efforts to attract North American tourists by the Amsterdam Tourist Office in 1992, the overall response of the tourist authorities and Amsterdam's City Hall and Chamber of Commerce has been lukewarm. For the policy-makers who prefer Rembrandt, Van Gogh, Anne Frank and the diamond-cutters, Amsterdam's status as the 'gay capital of Europe' is a peripheral feature of the city (Duyves, 1995: 55).

Another example of marginalization, this time self-imposed, can be found in Stockholm. Since it hosted EuroPride in 1996 the main focus for the Pride Week has been the Tantolunden Park located on central Stockholm's southern island. An area with stalls and marquees, a large stage for the live performances and dozens of portable toilets are enclosed by a double wire fence two metres high with security personnel posted at various points to ensure that nobody sneaks in. Entry is through a gateway at which officials check to see if celebrants have the dog-tags, which they must buy in advance from selected gay outlets. The enclosure itself is located deep in the park and is easy to miss completely if you do not know its exact whereabouts. While organizers defend the enclosure as the only way to ensure that costs are covered, others complain that it feels like being in a zoo. Anyone not wishing to buy a dog-tag can sit on the grass outside the enclosure and look in at the people inside. The location of the site has also been criticized from a security standpoint because once people leave the immediate area of the event they are easy targets for gay-bashers. Several cases of vicious assaults by skinheads are reported each year. There have been calls to relocate the event to ensure greater visibility throughout the entire week rather than confining it to the march through the centre of Stockholm, which rounds off the Pride celebrations.

Gay and lesbian enclaves are not hermetically sealed neighbourhoods. Worries among gay community groups in Sydney surfaced in the weeks preceding the 2000 Olympics. There were fears that heterosexual tourists might inadvertently stray into the major gay districts of Darlinghurst and Newtown. The possibility that confrontations might ensue was discussed and information brochures for tourists informing them of Sydney's large and prominent lesbian and gay population planned. But gay and lesbian neighbourhoods can also attract heterosexual tourists who want to observe the sexual minorities in their natural habitat. Busloads of Japanese tourists make a stop in the Castro on their tour of San Francisco. Given the number of lesbians and gays who can be found throughout the city there is no need to visit the Castro to see them. Such visits by tourists reinforce the assumption that sexual minorities are separate from the majority and that they are localizable (Bailey, 1999).

But tourists are not localizable. They do not stay for long and they return home. Hence the commonplace idea that tourists are ambassadors and that their actions will reflect on their home countries. Tourists also take home with them impressions of the host country. Events that attract huge numbers of tourists also usually attract the mass media. The hosts may thus find themselves under scrutiny by the tourists in their midst and by the international community. Those in a position to do so may attempt to control the image of the host nation or city in a way they feel is appropriate. Tourist events, as we shall see, can become occasions for very public controversies over national image and freedom of assembly and expression. In the cases considered here, the mixture of heterosexual tourists and homosexuals triggered the conflicts.

Sydney 2000 Olympics

It is an obvious but significant fact that gay tourists are not only present at explicitly gay events such as Pride celebrations. The Olympic Games, for example, attract many thousands of gay and lesbian tourists to the host cities. The 2000 Sydney Olympics was the major media event of the year. As one of Sydney's largest gay newspapers put it:

> There is no way this five-ring circus will make a detour around our part of town. It's coming, so we'd better be ready for action! In fact, for thousands of visitors, tourists and athletes included, a visit to the southern hemisphere's gay and lesbian Mecca will make their Olympic experience all the more memorable (*Capital Q*, 2 June 2000).

Sydney's two major gay newspapers, *Sydney Star Observer* and *Capital Q*, published regular pieces about the gay and lesbian contribution to the organization of the Games. These included profiles of the senior manager and the technology manager of the Olympic co-ordinating authority, which had responsibility for ambulance, fire and police services, the medal-ceremonies manager, the producer of Sydney's official website for visitors, the Cluster Staff Supervisor responsible for the 1800 chauffeurs who drove members of the national Olympic Committees around town, and one of the designers of the costumes worn by performers in the opening ceremony.

During the weeks prior to the start of competition, the Olympic torch was carried throughout the length and breadth of the country. The torch relay received massive media attention, including the many attempts by members of the public to put out the flame. The question for many gays and lesbians was who would carry it through Darlinghurst, the centre of gay and lesbian life in Sydney? The torchbearers are usually people who have done something for the local community through which the torch passes. A representative from Darlinghurst's very large gay and lesbian population would have been appropriate. On the day, the torch was carried by 86-year-old Lola Harding-Irmer, who helped organize the opening ceremony at the 1936 Berlin Games. However, Darlinghurst's gay community was not to be left out of the picture. Lola was joined by a bevy of drag-queens when she reached Oxford Street's Taylor Square in the very heart of the gay district. The ladies had been holed up in the basement porn shop Toolshed putting the finishing touches to their make-up. When the torch appeared, they clattered up the stairs in high heels and were greeted by a huge roar from the enormous crowd of locals and tourists outside. Striking poses for the cameras, they made a colourful splash of synthetic fibres and gaudy wigs as they ran alongside the torchbearer in their outrageous and flamboyant costumes, each carrying her own silver torch with orange cellophane flame. Maude Boat, whose headpiece in the shape of a cathedral was entitled St Peter's in London, was particularly striking. Informed that St Peter's is in Rome and St Paul's is in London, she airily replied: 'All those boys are the same to me dear.'

The sexuality of people involved in the Games is not always as obvious as drag-queens in frocks. Guessing whether or not someone is gay is a favourite pastime among gays and lesbians and the Olympics were no exception. The avid collection of queer rumours and snippets of gossip about who is or is not gay were all part of the Sydney Olympics. The gay press, which was the main source of information on matters of relevance for gay and lesbian residents and tourists alike, ran several articles on gay and lesbian Olympians past and present. In some cases the sexuality of the person was common knowledge, such as Canada's Mark Tewksbury, gold medallist in the 100 metres backstroke in Barcelona, who was interviewed in the *Sydney Star Observer*. He talked of receiving many telephone calls from other elite gay athletes since his own coming out. Swedish diver and European Champion Jimmy Sjödin was featured, as was French tennis player Amelie Muresmo. An article entitled 'The Out Elite' (*Sydney Star Observer*, 24 August 2000) addressed the virtual invisibility of gay and lesbian competitors within sport, listing pressures from team members and the fear of losing sponsors as factors keeping people in the closet. The article also included the names of known or rumoured-to-be gay or lesbian competitors.

Speculation about the sexual preferences of prominent athletes was not confined to the press. The following piece of gossip was told in the bar of the Beauchamp Hotel on Oxford Street. It was about two male swimmers, who were reportedly caught with their pants down in the changing room of the Sydney Aquatic Centre, the venue for the swimming events. When one of the parties to the gossip asked where the news had come from, the man telling the story told him that he had heard it from someone who worked at the Sydney Aquatic Centre who had heard it from someone else who also worked there. A discussion ensued about the reliability of the gossip and whether anyone had harboured suspicions about the sexual preferences of the two swimmers in question. The people who were directly involved in the conversation or who were able to eavesdrop included three Australians (all Sydney residents), two British visitors, myself (British but resident in Sweden), one Swede, and one American. Apart from the Australians all would be leaving Sydney and taking the gossip with them.

It matters not for present purposes whether the rumours are true or false. What this gossip does is to attempt to penetrate the opacity that surrounds same-sex sexual desire. Homophobia is a very effective device for creating and sustaining opacity in social relations and culture by excluding the topic of homosexuality from public settings. At the same time it is able to establish a spurious transparency in social and cultural relations in that everyone is assumed to be heterosexual until proven otherwise. One aim of gossip is to attempt to ferret out what is hidden but suspected. It reveals the presence of what ought not to be there and deflates hetero-normative pretensions to universality. In this respect gossip is a queer kind of phenomenon. Gossip also helps in the gathering of information and the creation of boundaries between those who know and those who do not and can contribute to strengthening group belonging and cohesion (Gluckman, 1963). It is often a device of the excluded and the relatively powerless who attempt to make sense of their world without access to privileged information. It is from snippets of gossip like this that rumours about a prominent person's reputation get under way and can be communicated rapidly throughout a network of social relations (Paine, 1967) which is sometimes transnational in its scope.

Without doubt the most high-profile gay component of the games was in the closing ceremony. Rumours had been flying for some time prior to the event that drag-queens would be taking part. They proved to be correct. As part of a tribute to Australian cinema, well-known actors paraded past the crowd, including Paul Hogan of *Crocodile Dundee* fame. A bus surmounted by a giant silver stiletto and fronted by an enormous pink wig drove around the stadium. The bus was a reference to the hugely successful film *The Adventures of Priscilla, Queen of the Desert*, which tells the tale of three Sydney drag-queens in the Australian outback. Alongside the bus paraded 42 female impersonators. Some drove motorized high-heeled shoes while others strolled by in full drag.

By all accounts the final ceremony was well received by the spectators from home and abroad, and the television audience. The controversy that preceded it suggested that there might be trouble. In order to calm the waters, the Sydney Organizing Committee for the Olympic Games (SOCOG) denied that the Priscilla tribute was a tribute to drag *per se*. The Olympic Minister hastened to assure people that the section was *not* a celebration of homosexuality prompting one gay columnist to reply: 'He's absolutely right. It's quite possible to be an accomplished, well-balanced fag without any expertise in cross-dressing at all' (*Sydney Star Observer*, 31 August 2000). The New South Wales Council of Churches fulminated that drag-queens were not representative of the majority of Australians. Clearly, the Church Fathers were worried that a misleading picture of Australian culture was being presented for foreigners. But as several columnists in the mainstream press noted, drag is an integral part of Australian popular culture. Mainstream television programmes like 'The Footy Show', which, as its name suggests, features football stars and personalities and is largely aimed at a heterosexual male audience, regularly include drag sketches, and straight audiences flock to the drag shows on Oxford Street. But some of the critical voices came from within the gay community itself. The main objection was that drag packages male homosexuality as something humorous, frivolous and non-threatening, and thereby reinforces the common association between male homosexuality and effeminacy for a worldwide audience. Any suggestion that homosexuality and sport can go hand in hand was avoided.

Past actions by national Olympic committees have also made it abundantly clear that the true Olympics ought not to be associated with homosexuals. In 1981 San Francisco Arts and Athletics (SFAA) began to promote the Gay Olympic

Games. To finance the event they sold T-shirts, buttons and bumper stickers. The United States Olympics Committee obtained a lawsuit to prevent SFAA from using the term 'Olympic'. The preliminary injunction became a permanent injunction and the SFAA was forced to pay the legal costs of the wealthy Olympic Committee. Dissenting from the appeal bench, Judge Kozinski noted that the Committee was using its control over the term 'Olympic' to reinforce the image of homosexuals that participation in sports was meant to dispel. In 1987 the Supreme Court upheld the exclusive rights of the Committee to the term 'Olympic'. Justice Brennan dissented from the majority verdict and noted that over 200 organizations listed in the New York and Los Angeles telephone catalogues alone used the term 'Olympic' in their name. He feared that the verdict threatened free speech (Coombe, 1998: 137).

The 2000 Olympics were exploited as an opportunity to advertise the Gay Games to be held in the city in November 2002. The Gay Games are expected to attract many more visitors than the annual Sydney Gay and Lesbian Mardi Gras. Present estimates suggest that 14,000 athletes will compete, 2300 people will participate in the various cultural events and 20,000 visitors will attend as spectators. Although the Gay Games are to take place in the same city as the Olympic Games, it is possible to see the event as a confirmation of the exclusion of gays and lesbians from elite competition. The Gay Games provides the arena in which queers 'play' at sports without really 'playing' sports. The Olympics is the arena for 'real' sports. The great majority of tourists who visit the Gay Games are likely to be gays and lesbians even though the Games welcome everybody, including heterosexuals.

QUEER TOURISM

Efforts to inject same-sex eroticism into contexts where it is normally absent are not confined to sports. Visitors to Amsterdam's Artis Zoo can join tours that reassure them of the naturalness of homosexuality. The tour visits gay monkeys and geese, a lesbian chimp and flamingos that have same-sex orgies. According to zoo director Maarten Frankenhuis: 'Many visitors are surprised. They realise that they themselves or their sons and daughters are not strange at all, they just belong to a minority' (*Capital Q*, 1 September 2000).

The surprise of finding 'gay' animals in places where their presence is not usually signposted reminds us that most tourist-markers only ever focus on selected aspects of the attraction in question. A simple distinction between gay tourism and queer tourism is that while gay tourism tends to leave the hetero–

homo dichotomy in place, queer tourism reveals that the marginal, the peripheral and the excluded are in centres where they do not at first appear to be present. Moreover, the sexual marginals are not a clearly circumscribed and easily identifiable group or minority. Put simply, queer tourism involves the search for what others have not 'seen' before but which are co-present. Queer tourism exhibits some of the central features of a queer relationship to place (Bell and Valentine, 1995; Ingram *et al.*, 1997; Beemyn, 1997; Graham, 1998), namely the realization that places are not heterosexual by default and that even ostensibly heterosexual places conceal a queer presence, such as queer animals at the zoo. However the zoo tour is only ambiguously queer because although it signposts the unexpected presence of lesbian chimpanzees and the like, its main aim is to reassure people of the naturalness of a minority. That is, queer animals comprise a separate segment of the general population of animals (on the scientific fascination with queer animals, see Terry, 2000). A queer dimension becomes much more apparent when this kind of minoritizing is difficult to sustain.

The Queer Olympics

If we look more closely at what tourists at the Olympic closing ceremony were watching, we find examples of just such a queer subtext in addition to the more obviously gay elements described above. A common thread that bound together the ceremony's segments was Australian icons. In one segment, pop singer Kylie Minogue, an icon among many gay men in Australia, was carried into the stadium on a giant thong (a rubber beach sandal) by male lifesavers. Lifesavers are one of the great symbols of Australian manhood and beach culture. Decidedly homoerotic greetings cards that depict these bronzed and muscular saviours of the surf wearing Speedos pulled up tight to expose the maximum amount of their buttocks are favourite purchases by gay male tourists. But their displays of life-saving skills on Sydney's Bondi Beach are also favourite spectacles among heterosexual tourists, including the men who can gaze admiringly at the flesh on display without any suspicion of homoeroticism falling on them. Kylie Minogue's performance on stage backed by a camp dance routine choreographed by a gay male choreographer reinforced the queerness of the segment. The entire spectacle was a stunning combination of gay icons and queer intrusions into what Juan Antonio Samaranche, President of the Olympic Committee, praised as 'the best Olympics ever'. His compliments evoked immense national pride among Australians who were already very pleased with how well the Olympics had gone and the positive feedback from competitors and visitors alike.

To be able to recognize the queer elements in the closing ceremony, as did many gays and lesbians who saw it, demands knowledge of gay signifiers, and an ability to read between the lines of ostensibly heterosexual spectacle. Recognition of the queer dimension is an acquired skill. It is unlikely that heterosexual males understand their own admiration of lifesavers as evidence of queer leanings or pleasures, given that any such insight is systematically denied and suppressed within a hetero-normative ideology. It is perhaps not surprising that the presence of professional drag-queens (who are a fairly unambiguous indicator of homosexuality) sparked off the controversy about the closing ceremony, and not the queer signifiers, which seem to have gone unnoticed by most of the heterosexual audience. Queer readings require an ability and willingness to question what is hidden and masked in representations of space as heterosexual by default, and access to the alternative spaces of representation that are co-present. In short, they require a re-education of the tourists in the subtleties of queer co-presence. The next two cases were about helping tourists (and locals) to see what was not immediately apparent.

The Sisters of Perpetual Indulgence

During the Sydney Leather Pride Week in April, a number of guided tours for locals and visitors alike are arranged by the Sisters of Perpetual Indulgence. The purpose of these tours, which are free of charge, is to reveal something about local history. One such tour is the Leather and Bondage tour of Darlinghurst.

Anyone who wanted to join the tour was welcome to gather outside the Post Office on Crown Street at 12.00 p.m. Actually, only two nuns, the boyfriend of one of them and a mutual acquaintance were there on time. We were soon joined by two more nuns, one carrying a mysterious doctor's black bag and the other a bottle in a brown paper packet, the contents of which could not be seen. One of the nuns, Sister Agnes Mother of Pearl, carried a small placard on which was written 'Leather and Bondage Tour'. The Sisters, all members of the Order of the Sisters of Perpetual Indulgence, gay male nuns who have been in action in Australia since 1981, looked much like nuns do, except that they were men ranging in age from their thirties to their fifties and one had a beard and all wore Doc Marten shoes. Small details such as a belt toggle in the shape of a phallus and the fact that one of the Sisters was carrying a riding crop took a little longer to notice.

As we waited outside the Post Office, I must have looked the worst for wear after all the leather week festivities because Sister Agnes asked me if I was feeling ill. I explained my tiredness to her and received a blessing; there were to be many blessings that afternoon. By quarter-past twelve the group had grown to fifteen people, including the Sisters, and it was time to set off. Our group consisted of our guide David in his early forties, four Sisters, the boyfriend of one of them, two young lesbians in their early twenties, myself and my partner (in our late thirties and early forties respectively), a large and as it turned out know-it-all man in his late thirties, a male couple in their early sixties, and one short leather clone in his early forties.

David led us a block down Crown Street to Headquarters, a sex-on-premises club. We all trouped into HQ past the cashier into the lounge area where there are armchairs for patrons. A large curtain covers the back wall and behind it is another room with a large video screen where films are shown. Our visit started with a talk from one of the owners about the history of the establishment, including how the building had been bought and renovated. We then continued downstairs to the various sections of the club. These included a dungeon, private cubicles, a sling room, shower room, a bridge across to the playpen and several cruising areas. During the evening most of the club is dark or dimly lit, but for our benefit the lights had been turned on so that we would be able to see our way around and admire the mural depicting construction workers that covers the doors to the private cubicles. Each stage of our exploration was carefully chaperoned by the Sisters who ensured that no one disappeared into the cubicles to do anything untoward and to make sure than no one got left behind in the labyrinthine interior of the club. Our visit lasted about twenty minutes and then it was time to leave HQ and return to Oxford Street.

Back on Oxford Street we slowly made our way past the various shops and business establishments of today and were told of what had existed on the same sites in the past. One noticeable fact about the earlier, now defunct bars was how many had an entrance hidden away down a back lane. The doors were often locked and a bell had to be rung to gain entrance, or a flight of rickety stairs climbed to reach the door. The places were part of a growing gay and to a lesser extent lesbian presence on Oxford Street.

We crossed over to Oxford Square on the other side of Oxford Street where we paused for ten minutes or so. From Oxford Square it was possible to see the entrances to what had been two bars. Two of the older nuns had very fond memories of them. At some distance from the square lies William Street. The street itself was not visible but it was possible to see a multistorey hotel, which stands on the site of what used to be Club 80, a popular bar of the late 1970s. Before leaving Oxford Square and making our way back up Oxford Street, the Sisters paused to bless its Victorian wrought-iron drinking fountain.

Our first stop on our way back up Oxford Street was a leather and fetish shop where we were encouraged to look around and perhaps buy something. This caused some consternation among the customers when a burly, bearded nun over six-foot tall started to browse through the harnesses and whips. The window display in the shop was of two mannequins dressed in leather harnesses and various leather straps and headwear. By present standards they were fairly innocuous, but as our guide pointed out they would have been unthinkable only a decade earlier. Sydney is after all a city in which the religious right regularly pray for bad weather to ruin the Mardi Gras. One of the best known examples is the Revd Fred Nile who tried to take the credit for the bad weather in 1990. He claimed: 'We have no option but to ask God's intervention to stop Mardi Gras with something like thunderstorms or hailstones – but of course not big hailstones, not large enough to actually hurt people' (Carbery 1995: 125).

The information we were provided with was frequently interspersed with the reminiscences from one Sydneysider whose only reason for being on the tour seems to have been the opportunity it afforded him to display his knowledge about the area. His version of history did not always agree with that of our guide or the older Sisters – although the latter tolerated his interruptions with impeccable Christian patience. Another Sydneysider, a man in his sixties, had his memory jogged on several occasions and added his recollections to the unfolding story. The Sisters too had plenty of reminiscences. One of the Sisters told us how she had been arrested while demonstrating against the Pope when he visited Sydney in 1986. The police had dragged her to the psychiatric wing of a local hospital in an attempt to have her committed. The hospital is run by nuns who, on seeing the Sister, explained to the police in no uncertain terms, that wearing a nun's habit is most definitely *not* a sign of psychiatric disorder! Other, less amusing stories included accounts of beatings by the Darlinghurst police and being locked in cells. Even though the Sisters told everything with a humorous tone, their stories revealed the deep seriousness of the history that was being recounted on what was apparently a fun walk.

The reactions of people on Oxford Street were almost as interesting as the tour itself. For some people, usually local gays and lesbians, it was just another tour. A number of people – presumably tourists, judging by their cameras – took photos. When the Sisters stopped to bless a dog, it raised a laugh from several pedestrians. Car drivers strained to see what the motley group was up to and several didn't notice when the traffic lights changed. They were brought rudely back to reality by the honking of horns from behind them. But not everybody was amused. Oxford Street is a major road artery in and out of central Sydney and by no means all the pedestrians are gays or lesbians. Some men, presumably heterosexual, seemed a little flustered by the sight of nuns, leather men and tourists bearing down on them accompanied by the guide's monologue about the fetish bar that used to be located in the premises on the left. In another example of how national icons should not be associated with homosexuality, a planned tour by the Sisters of Sydney's Opera House during the 1998 Mardi Gras was cancelled because of pressure from religious groups.

Pink plaque guides

In 1994 a multimedia artist collective in New York put up signs at nine locations in lower Manhattan. The inverted triangles in pink masonite marked important sites in the history of gay and lesbian New York. They were part of attempts to make visible gay and lesbian space in the city, and to support public memory. The border text that framed each sign read 'Queer Spaces' at the top and 'places of struggle/places of strength' along the two sides (Hertz *et al.*, 1997).

The project looked at recent gay activism and its roots around the Stonewall period. The plaques were erected at the same time as the 25th anniversary of Stonewall, the Gay Pride Parade and the Gay Games and the influx of enormous numbers of tourists, and the massive media attention this attracted (Hertz *et al.*, 1997). However, this attention was mainly on the events taking place rather than the history behind them. Sign 6 reads:

> Bonnie & Clyde's, a lesbian bar, stood at 82 West 3rd Street from the early seventies through the mid-eighties. Bars were one of the few places where people could be open about their sexuality. But bars were not only about meaning and mating. In the early seventies Bonnie & Clyde's was a hangout for politically active lesbians as well as a place where women socialized across racial and class lines. Often women would gather here after meetings at the Gay Activists Alliance Firehouse to continue discussions, arguments or strategy sessions begun earlier in the day.

One of the ambitions of the project was to cover the entire city for although the area of the Village, Chelsea and Soho are central to the history of gay New York, they are not the only areas of importance. The project had ambitions to queer place because its aim was to make people aware of same-sex eroticism outside of the sites most often associated with it. It was not unearthing a history that is confined to contemporary gay and lesbian neighbourhoods. However, limited resources made this unfeasible as so few signs would have been set up that the message would have been diluted (Hertz *et al.*, 1997). The organizers claim that 'The signs proved to be a powerful intervention in the routine lexicon of the street. As indicators, they formed a dialogue among history, place, and community and reminded the viewer of a particular site's value' (Hertz *et al.*, 1997: 368). Here we might want to argue with 'remind' as it is unlikely that the vast number of tourists in New York at the time were even aware of the particular value of any given site. It is also far from certain that many New Yorkers were any better informed, as the authors who were also involved with the project recognize later in their article.

Walks like the Sisters' guided tours and the pink plaque guides in New York and elsewhere bring into the open the submerged histories and presence of queer sites. The tourists include people who want to know about the local history of the places they are visiting. It also attracts the local people who do not know their local history. Conversations with the younger Sydneysiders during and after the tour of Darlinghurst revealed that it had provided them with information that was almost entirely new. They had no memories to evoke of the period in question. Like tourists, they visit a familiar place only to find it made slightly unfamiliar when its hidden past is revealed. Most of these sites are conspicuous by their sheer ordinariness. MacCannell's distinction between 'marker involvement' and 'sign involvement' (MacCannell, 1976: 112–13) is relevant here. The tourist sites themselves may not amount to much as sights. The bondage tour, for example, involved looking at shop fronts, doorways, even an empty lot. Sight involvement, which refers to the reaction to physical places such as these, may lead to disappointment. But the marker, that which explains the significance of the site/sight, can more than make up for this.

World Pride in Rome 2000

The spiritual centre for the world's Roman Catholics (and not least in the year 2000), Rome is also the centre of the Catholic Church's globally orchestrated homophobia. Yet World Pride suddenly revealed queers near the Vatican (historically, there has, of course, been no shortage of them inside the Vatican) (see Figure 1.1: World Pride Roma 2000).

The Catholic Church, with support from the Italian far right, put pressure on the authorities to deny permits for the 2000 World Pride Festival in July. The Church had consistently opposed World Pride, among other things, because it coincided with its own celebrations of two millennia of Christianity. The Pride organizers showed some consideration by moving the planned march through the city from 28 June to 8 July to avoid the feast of St Peter and St Paul on 29 June, and by cancelling a drag-queen contest. But the choice of Rome for 2000 was a considered one. The decision to host it in the Eternal City was made in 1997, even though some in the World Pride organization felt that a city like

Figure 1.1 World Pride Roma 2000. *Source*: Andrea Giuliani, General Manager, Mario Mielli, organizers of World Pride Roma 2000.

Amsterdam would have been more appropriate. However, the opportunity to challenge the homophobia of the Roman Catholic Church on its home ground proved too compelling. The president of the event, and former president of the San Francisco Gay Pride Association, Deborah Oakley-Melvin, said: 'We know that visibility is the first step to change in society. We knew this would be a perfect opportunity to highlight the problems of gays and lesbians and transgender people' (*Washington Post*, 4 June 2000). This visibility was due to the large influx of foreign and domestic tourists. Under pressure from the Vatican, funding promised by the city of Rome was withdrawn. The International Gay and Lesbian Human Rights Commission (IGLHRC) and Amnesty International threatened protests against the city's decision. When Italy's Prime Minister Giuliano Amato said that the event was 'inopportune' and that 'unfortunately' the Italian constitution would not permit it being blocked, he was booed by members of his own coalition. Even his wife, Diana Vincenzi, disagreed with her husband, saying 'I'm on their side' (*Sydney Star Observer*, 1 June 2000).

World Pride was seen by many as a test of Italy's political will. The Council actions brought protests from the political left and Rome's Jewish community. Michael Mills, the IGLHRC's Rome conference co-ordinator, said: 'The city of Rome has already rescinded the money it had promised and now threatens to deny the fundamental freedoms of assembly, association, and expression. Either it will defend democratic freedoms, or it will follow Austria along the road of capitulating to the far right' (*Sydney Star Observer*, 1 June 2000).

In the event the parade on Saturday, 8 July was a huge success. Police estimated a turnout of 70,000, the media 200,000, and the organizers anything from 400,000 to 700,000. Whatever the exact figure, the televised parade passed by the Coliseum against the express wishes of the Vatican. Busloads of tourists arrived from Bologna, Milan and Florence. Katia Bellilo, Italy's Equal Opportunity Minister, was among marchers at the front of the parade which finished at Circus Maximus. The Pope condemned the parade the following day. The significance of World Pride lies in the way in which it has forced Italians to consider the presence of gays *in their midst* including the national government. The uproar moved Italy's Agricultural Minister, Alfonso Pecoraro, to declare his bisexuality. Sergio Lo Giudiuce, president of Arcigay, Italy's largest gay organization, said: 'in Italy invisibility has been the price of tolerance. But gays don't want to be invisible anymore' (*Washington Post*, 4 June 2000). He also stated that: 'rather than promoting a lifestyle, we are fighting for human rights, drawing attention to a sexual minority that has been denied its rights of expression for 2000 years' (*International Herald Tribune*, 4 June 2000). He was certainly correct. The range of people involved, the way it had an impact on the entire city and, most significantly, the way in which the issue of sexuality was broadened from being a matter for a sexual minority to becoming an issue around which the political commitment of the left was measured, shattered any assumption that it was simply the relationship between heterosexuals and homosexuals that was at issue. This is why I would class the effects of World Pride and the debate it provoked as a queer critique. The conflict also damaged the credibility of left-wing politicians in Rome and revealed some of the limitations of Vatican influence.

If the role of tourism in this social, cultural and, as it turned out, more than usually political event is not apparent, then perhaps a quote from a Dominican priest, the Reverend Stanislaw Heymo, will drive the point home. Heymo organizes the Polish pilgrimages and held a prayer meeting at the Coliseum on 7 July, the very same evening as the Leather World Pride Party was held in the city. The coincidence of the Christian Millennium celebrations and leather parties did not amuse him. He complained: 'This is a very bad thing. It would be better to spend money on the poor and immigrants, because homosexuals are rich, from rich families. They do nothing other than *travel throughout the world*, flaunting their sickness' (*New York Times*, 3 June 2000, emphasis added).

CONCLUSION

In what respects can the three broad types of tourism be said to pose a challenge to hetero-normative assumptions? As a form of flight or refuge, homosexual tourism has contributed to keeping the home country a relatively queer-free zone, at least with respect to public manifestations of same-sex eroticism. The main destinations of homosexual tourists have been countries in which homo-sexuality has been tolerated in private even if some forms of public display may be penalized. If it can be said to have a critical component, it lies in the opportunity it affords the homosexual tourist to access and imagine a world not so ruthlessly controlled by a hetero-normative regime. Gay and lesbian tourism is centred on the major urban enclaves, resorts and events of the gay and lesbian calendar. In terms of physical distance these are frequently not marginal sites but they may be marginalized socially, culturally and in political decision-making, even in a city like Amsterdam. None the less, gay and lesbian tourism is on occasion motivated by social, cultural and political concerns that are explicitly critical of hetero-normative regimes, even in the context of ludic celebrations. The articles in the Sydney gay press about the Olympics and the gossip of pub patrons share the same goal of making the gay presence known. But that knowledge is largely confined to the gay population itself. Drag-queens in the Olympic closing ceremony made gay men (but not lesbians) visible for the vast audience, but, as several commentators argued, it is a narrow form of visibility conforming to a homosexual stereotype. Moreover, even as the Olympic space admitted drag-queens, the organizers scrambled to deny and play down homosexual associations. Female impersonators were presented as first and foremost entertainers rather than sexual beings. As Victor Turner points out, the word 'entertainment' is derived from *tenir* and *entre* and means to 'hold in between' or 'held in between' (Turner 1982: 41, 114). Cordoned off from the everyday in what Turner refers to as liminal spaces, the entertainment's subversive potential may be blunted because it is separated from the everyday world. As the experience of the Sisters shows, female impersonators are acceptable for tourists in the liminal space of the stage or arena, but they are not welcome in Sydney's Opera House where they might alarm the sightseers.

The risk with this kind of visibility is that it can reinforce the notion that gays and lesbians comprise a minority qualitatively different from the putative heterosexual majority. The dangers of a minoritarian position have been extensively discussed in recent queer theory. In particular, the essentializing logic to which it is prone and the ease with which a 'mere' sexual minority can be ignored in the political process (see, for example, Seidman, 1997: 183–97, and more generally Warner, 1999). Queer tourism, as I have described it here, eschews any such clear distinction between heterosexuals and homosexuals by collapsing any neat division onto sexual types. It does so by revealing the queer co-presence in the history of places, contemporary institutions – like the Italian government – in national and international celebrations like the Olympics, and by reclaiming historical sites as areas for queer celebrations. When at its most effective, it also acts as a focal point for action in opposition to hetero-normative regimes that transcends a homosexual–heterosexual binary.

All three forms of tourism involve searching for clues and confirmation of how the world *really* is, appearances to the contrary. In all three cases there is the knowledge that same-sex desire exists elsewhere even if it may not be immediately apparent. The homosexual tourist of the eighteenth and nineteenth centuries picked through the classical texts and Greek ruins for evidence of the pederastic tradition, the gay gossipmongers strip away the heterosexual façade, and the queer tourist searches for the co-presence of a queer heritage.

According to MacCannell (1976), tourists are seekers after a meaningful whole in a modern world of fragmentation, discontinuity and flux in which things and people have been dislodged from traditional settings and thrown together in the confusion of modernity. 'The act of sightseeing', he writes 'is a kind of involvement with social appearances that helps the person to construct totalities from his [*sic*] disparate experiences' (MacCannell, 1976: 15). Tourism, he argues, is a modern form of religious seeking and tourists are modern pilgrims. However, their mission is doomed from the outset because tourism involves celebrating exotica and *differences* even as it tries to create a unity.

What evidence of this tourist behaviour have we seen? Homosexual tourism sought an aesthetic whole in the Mediterranean by searching for what was missing from the northern European homelands. Gay tourism likewise celebrates a unity of place, culture, identity and pleasure in the gay capitals. But when we look at queer tourism the picture becomes more problematic. Even with all of its internal contradictions the hetero-normative regime presents itself as a totality. Tourists search for the fragments of same-sex eroticism in order to build up a more coherent picture of a world that is not dictated by a hetero-normative imperative. The queer tourist sees the fragments as the progeny of homophobia and a hetero-normative regime, not as delightful exotica or a pleasing bricolage of differences. The queer critique attacks the dichotomy heterosexual–homosexual by positing a heterotopia of queer co-presence, rather than separate heterosexual and homosexual places. Its quest to 'dedifferentiate' (see Lash, 1990) marks it as postmodern in that it collapses a sexual difference that has been central to the modern West since the heterosexual and homosexual populations were labelled and differentiated by medical science over a century ago (Foucault, 1978). MacCannell's claim that tourists celebrate 'differentiation' needs qualifying.

Furthermore, MacCannell understands modernity to mean fragmentation. But, as Rojek (1995) points out in a discussion of leisure, modernity is not only chaos, it is also about order and discipline. The homosexual–heterosexual dichotomy is but one example of modernity's ordering of people into categories. Queer tourism does not seek to create order. Rather, it aims to dismantle the hetero-normative sexual order. This too is a form of sense-making but it differs from the kind MacCannell has in mind.

De-differentiation can also be understood as a device for making present or revealing dimensions of place that are not immediately apparent. Travel to a destination in order to experience the novel is one of the main goals of tourism. Queer tourism, because it deals with co-presence, is not necessarily reliant on travel. This absence of a need to travel any distance places a question mark over the automatic equation between travel and tourism that is so often made. For example, Urry's (1995) designation of tourism as involving movement to and from, and a stay in a destination for a limited time only, applies to homosexual tourism and gay tourism, but is not always true of queer tourism. The queer tourist can experience alternative dimensions of the place in which she finds herself. She 'travels' from the hetero-normative to the queer dimension and back again assuming that the queer signifiers that make this possible are accessible to her. But you can never fully return from what is a situation of co-presence. Queer by its nature is always present within the routine heterosexual world. Queer spaces revealed by queer tourism are counter-spaces (Lefebvre, 1991) not separate spaces. They are better understood as heterotopic spaces in which differences are co-present (Foucault, 1986). We are not, therefore, looking at two separate spaces but at the interpenetration of two competing versions of space. For this reason, we need to be careful about making hard and fast distinctions between centres and margins. In an influential work on spatial margins, Shields (1991) does just that. For Shields, margins exist at a distance from geographic, cultural, social, political and economic centres. He sees marginal places as sites for groups, or 'neo-tribes' (Maffessoli, 1996), engaged in transgressive behaviours and lifestyles. But he does not address margins as co-present aspects of the centre. This leads him to over-literalize the centre–periphery distinction, and his choice of case-studies – Brighton, Niagara Falls, northern England and the Canadian north – reinforces this.

The importance of vision for tourists, especially their ability to recognize a tourist sight when they see it, has received a great deal of attention. According to Urry: 'The tourist gaze is directed to features of the landscape and townscape which separate them off from everyday existence' (1995: 132). At first glance this seems to capture the relationship of the queer tourist to places. But recognizing the 'signs' and knowing the queer dimension of a site that is not immediately apparent is not so much seeing something that is novel as seeing the everyday in a novel way. These are not the signs that Urry describes (see also MacCannell, 1976). The plaques in New York (and similar plaques elsewhere) are interesting exceptions because they were not intended to be confined to known gay and lesbian places. They were to spill out into the space of the city more generally – a space coded as heterosexual by default. Therein lies their queer dimension. Signposts for tourists do not make places gay or queer in themselves; it matters where the signpost is located and for whom it is accessible.

How are we to understand the tourist gaze that 'sees' what is not there? An emphasis on the gaze inevitably favours that which is immediately visible. As Urry states, 'contemporary tourists are the collectors of gazes' (1995: 138), which are visual phenomena that can take a split second to consume. The emphasis on tourism's visual dimension presents tourists as collectors of cultural texts who, with the help of signs and prepackaged information, interpret, with varying degrees of sophistication, the sites and sights they see. But cultural texts are not only read; they are also produced. Those who can inscribe their version of the world into these texts enjoy an important advantage. Within anthropology the 'culture as text' metaphor is most closely associated with Geertz (1973). It has been criticized for privileging the dominant version of affairs because it sees culture as textual products rather than ongoing productions. On the whole, Urry and MacCannell place greater emphasis on how tourist sites as texts are products staged and framed for tourist consumption, rather than on the active interpretation and production of what they mean for those who see them. The kind of interpretation that queer tourism involves and which does not accept prepackaged meaning, receives little attention.

From a situation where heterosexual centres and homosexual margins existed as separate spaces, through the juxtaposition of gay places and heterosexual surroundings in centres to one in which queer signifiers can emerge virtually anywhere within ostensibly heterosexual centres, the gay tourist has steadily contributed to chipping away at the hetero-normative regime and its default construction of the world as heterosexual. I do not want to exaggerate the impact of tourism on hetero-normative regimes, but the impact is none the less real. The unpredictability and unexpectedness of queer re-significations that cannot be accommodated easily within a neat spatialized homosexual–heterosexual binary reveals how centres are inhabited by their margins. Indeed, the distinction between centres and margins begins to appear unstable. The criss-crossing of place by tourists, homosexual, gay and queer, who are out to make sense of the world (and to have fun in it) knits together previously separate places and trails after it signifiers of same-sex eroticism that leave their mark in even the most hetero-normative of sites. It helps to open up a space (a margin?) in which new ways, as yet difficult to specify, of seeing ourselves as sexual beings and as tourists can emerge.

NOTE

This chapter was written in 2000 while I was a Visiting Fellow at the School of Sociology, The University of New South Wales, Sydney. I would like to thank the Swedish Foundation for International Co-operation in Research and Higher Education (STINT) for the stipend that made my visit to Australia possible, and everyone at the School for their hospitality.

REFERENCES

Aldrich, R. (1993), *The Seduction of the Mediterranean: Writing, Art and Homosexual Fantasy*. London: Routledge.

Bailey, R. W. (1999), *Gay Politics, Urban Politics: Identity and Economics in the Urban Setting*. New York: Columbia University Press.

Beemyn, B. (ed.) (1997), *Creating a Place for Ourselves: Lesbian, Gay, and Bisexual Community Histories*. New York: Routledge.

Bell, D. and Valentine, G. (eds) (1995), *Mapping Desire: Geographies of Sexualities*. London: Routledge.

Butler, J. (1990), *Gender Trouble*. London: Routledge.

Carbery, G. (1995), *A History of the Sydney Gay and Lesbian Mardi Gras*. Parkville, Victoria: Australian Lesbian and Gay Archives.

Coombe, R. (1998), *The Cultural Life of Intellectual Properties: Authorship, Appropriation and the Law*. London: Duke University Press.

de Lauretis, T. (1991), 'Queer theory: lesbian and gay sexualities', *Differences*, 3: iii–xviii.

Duyves, M. (1995), 'Framing preferences, framing differences: inventing Amsterdam as a gay capital', in R. Parker and J. H. Gagnon (eds), *Conceiving Sexuality: Approaches to Sex Research in a Postmodern World*. New York: Routledge.

Eder, F. X., Hall, L. A. and Hekma, G. (eds) (1999), *Sexual Cultures in Europe: Natural Histories*. Manchester: Manchester University Press.

Foucault, M. (1978), *The History of Sexuality: An Introduction*. New York: Pantheon.

Foucault, M. (1986), 'Of other spaces', *Diacritics*, 16 (1): 22–7.

Friedman, J. (1994), *Cultural Identity and Global Process*. London: Sage.

Fuss, D. (1991), *Inside/Out*. New York: Routledge.

Geertz, C. (1973), *The Interpretation of Cultures*. New York: Basic Books.

Gluckman, M. (1963), 'Gossip and scandal', *Current Anthropology*, 4: 307–16.

Graham, M. (1998), 'Follow the yellow brick road. An anthropological outing in queer space', *Ethnos*, 63 (1): 102–32.

Hertz, B.-S., Eisenberg, E. and Knauer, L. M. (1997), 'Queer spaces in New York City: places of struggle/places of strength', in G. B. Ingram, A.-M. Bouthilette and Y. Retter (eds), *Queers in Space: Communities, Public Places, Sites of Resistance*. Seattle: Bay Press.

Ingram, G. B., Bouthilette, A.-M. and Retter, Y. (1997), *Queers in Space: Communities, Public Places, Sites of Resistance*. Seattle: Bay Press.

Lash, S. (1990), *The Sociology of Postmodernism*. London: Routledge.

Lefebvre, H. (1991), *The Production of Space*. Oxford: Blackwell.

MacCannell, D. (1976), *The Tourist: A New Theory of the Leisure Class*. New York: Schocken.

Maffesoli, M. (1996), *The Time of Tribes*. London: Sage.

Newton, E. (1993), *Cherry Grove, Fire Island: Sixty Years in America's First Gay and Lesbian Town*. Boston, MA: Beacon Press.

Paine, R. (1967), 'What is gossip about? An alternative hypothesis', *Man*, 3: 278–85.

Rojek, C. (1995), *Decentring Leisure: Rethinking Leisure Theory*. London: Sage.

Sedgwick, E. (1990), *Epistemology of the Closet*. Berkeley, CA: University of California Press.

Seidman, S. (1997), *Difference Troubles: Queering Social Theory and Sexual Politics*. Cambridge: Cambridge University Press.

Shields, R. (1991), *Places on the Margin*. London: Routledge.

Smith, V. (1978), *Hosts and Guests: The Anthropology of Tourism*. Philadelphia, OH: University of Pennsylvania Press.

Terry, J. (2000), '"Unnatural acts" in nature: the scientific fascination with queer animals', *GLQ*, 6 (2): 151–93.

Tomlinson, J. (1999), *Globalization and Culture*. Cambridge: Polity Press.

Turner, V. (1982), *From Ritual to Theatre*. New York: *Performing Arts Journal* Publications.

Urry, J. (1995), *Consuming Places*. London: Routledge.

Warner, M. (1994), *Fear of a Queer Planet*. Minneapolis, MN: University of Minnesota Press.

Warner, M. (1999), *The Trouble with Normal: Sex, Politics and the Ethics of Queer Life*. New York: The Free Press.

WEBSITES

The Sisters of Perpetual Indulgence (website giving information on the world network of Sisters): *www.thesisters.org*

World Pride Rome 2000 (website of the organizers): *www.mariomieli.it*

CHAPTER 2

Some Say Thailand
Is a Gay Paradise

DOUGLAS SANDERS

INTRODUCTION

Thailand has 62 million people. The capital, Bangkok, by far the largest centre, has a population of 5.6 million. Tourist destinations include the densely packed capital, beach resorts and northern hill areas. Since 1982 tourism has been the single largest source of foreign exchange and a great economic success story for the Kingdom (Richter, 1989). Facing a sluggish economy, Prime Minister Thaksin Shinawatra, in his first months in office in 2001, pressed officials to expand the tourism sector (Techawongtham, 2001). The Thai currency, the baht, has been a bargain for travellers since the 1997 Asian financial crisis. After a limited recovery, the currency again declined in value in 2000–1, giving more bargains to tourists:

> Thailand has been the most successful Southeast Asian country over the past few years in attracting tourists, partly because of the cheaper Thai baht since the economic crisis in 1997. In 2000, there were 9.5 million tourists, about 10 per cent more than the previous year, according to official figures (*Far Eastern Economic Review*, 2001).

> Tourist arrivals are estimated to reach about 10 million during 2001, generating income of about 303 billion baht, and 15.3 million tourists and 461.4 billion baht in 2010 (*Bangkok Post*, 2001c).

A significant part of Thailand's reputation as a tourist destination involves sex. An unnamed government official was quoted in 1988 as saying: 'Let's face it:

if there were no sex, there wouldn't be so much tourism' (*The Nation*, 1998). There is also a niche tourist market for sex-reassignment surgery and other forms of plastic surgery (Talbot, 2001). The country aims, as well, at retired people, including those who will use long-term care facilities.

The Kingdom has a domestic sex industry that is both highly visible and easily accessible to visitors. There are heterosexual host bars and massage parlours. And there are gay equivalents – host bars, discos, saunas, restaurants and gay-friendly hotels. The gay institutions function openly, with only occasional problems.

There are no laws against homosexual acts in Thailand. Thai Buddhism contains a prohibition against heterosexual adultery, and monks are forbidden any sexual activity. Otherwise, the religion is silent on issues of sex and sexual orientation. Thai Buddhism is not 'sex-positive', for the rejection of desire is a central teaching.

The first gay Thai magazine, *Mithuna*, was published in 1983. An English-language gay guidebook, *The Men of Thailand*, first appeared in 1987, written by an American expatriate Eric Allyn. He listed Dr John P. Collins, a sexologist, as the coauthor. Collins had played a role in introducing Allyn to the Thai gay scene, and asserted that Thailand was a 'sex-positive', non-homophobic society. Collins died in 1987 before the first edition was published. Allyn went on to write columns on gay Thailand for the Thai magazines, *Neon* and *Midway*, and for the San Francisco-based magazine *Passport*. The first edition of the guide-book described Thailand as 'a well-kept secret' and was self-conscious about the fact that a main feature of the book was its listing of gay host bars, which feature prostitution:

> Is this a sex guide? No. It is a guidebook on the Gay culture in Thailand. Guidebooks for Gays are sometimes charged with promoting sexual exploitation, especially if the guide is on a so-called third-world country. The Thai certainly don't apologize for having a sexuality. And we don't apologize for reporting on Thai Gay society (Allyn and Collins, 1987: i–3).

More recently, Jackson (1999b) cautions outsiders against criticizing the commercial gay scene, arguing that it 'provides a zone of relative autonomy for the expression of gender/sex difference within a generally unaccepting culture'.

Allyn has always been adamant in his goal to culturally sensitize visitors. In subsequent editions, he often changed format. The 1991 edition was in two volumes. The larger volume was a 290-page backgrounder entitled *Trees in the Same Forest*, accompanying a slimmer guide to bars and other venues: *Where to*

Sanook. The seventh edition was published in 1999, again as *The Men of Thailand*. It is in two volumes, plus a slim booklet of maps.

There are now at least five gay guides for Thailand, one in Cantonese, the others in English. *Midway*, the leading Thai gay magazine, published a guidebook in English in 1999. Also, in 1999 a free gay magazine, *Thai Guys* began publication with pictures, stories, maps and advertising (see listing of websites at end of chapter). Advertisements for gay host bars, massage parlours and escorts occur in *Look*, a regular give-away tourist magazine, along with more numerous advertisements for heterosexual venues and services. Some advertisements for female hosts indicate in words or pictures that men and ladyboys are also available. Two or three free gay tourist maps are published periodically, supported by advertisements. Some gay advertisements also appear in the classified sections of the Bangkok English language newspapers, the *Bangkok Post* and *The Nation*. *Metro Magazine*, a trendy English language monthly, has a gay column and gay listings, though it does not list gay venues that feature prostitution. A tourist would be hard pressed to miss the fact of an easily available commercial gay scene. The major international gay guide, *Spartacus*, calls Bangkok 'the gay capital of the South' (Bedford and Rauch, 2001).

Utopia Tours is a gay travel agency in Bangkok run by three *farang*, as foreigners are called. The Utopia-Asia website is a leading source of information for gay travellers to the region. Utopia publishes a gay map of Bangkok. There are many additional websites with information on travel to Thailand and the region, plus websites for individual bars, saunas and hotels (see listing in references below).

THE INSTITUTIONS

Organized prostitution is common in rural Thailand, with brothels and host bars. These Thai institutions have been replicated and expanded in Bangkok and other cities. It is commonly understood that the sex industry got a tremendous boost during the Vietnam War, when some American military were stationed in the country, and others came for 'rest and rehabilitation'. Military visits still occur and when American warships dock near the beach resort of Pattaya, prostitutes from other parts of the Kingdom travel to the area to join the local sex workers.

One of the central institutions of the sex industry is the host bar. It may be a unique Thai institution. Typically, it functions as follows. Young women work as service girls or hosts, each wearing a number. They are paid something for particular shows, or when a customer buys them a drink. The shows involve go-go dancing, and special sex shows for which Thailand is famous. One performance, in which a woman smokes a cigarette with her vagina, was shown in the famous erotic French film *Emmanuelle* (1973). If the customer wants to have sex with the host, he will pay an 'off fee' to the bar, in the range of 200–500 baht. That payment is not for the sexual activity. The amount of the payment for sex is up to the customer, and will not be paid until after the sexual activity has been completed. The general pattern of not negotiating the payment for sex in advance would certainly never occur in the West. Allyn has explained it as reflecting the status difference between the sex worker and the client. The status superior, in Thai society, would be expected to be generous. The customer will take the woman to his hotel or to a short-time hotel. Condoms are almost universally used. Sex workers, both female and male, have regular blood tests according to bar managers and the sex workers themselves. Sometimes the host has a card, which apparently verifies the fact of a recent negative blood test.

The young women who work in the bars come from the countryside, largely from Isan, the large poor northeastern region, bordering on Laos. There are also some women from Myanmar/Burma, who are mentioned occasionally in the *Bangkok Post*, usually in the context of raids on brothels. The Isan origins of the women give a clear class and ethnic character to the industry. Isan people are looked down upon by central Thai.

Many rural families sell their daughters into prostitution through recruiters who visit the villages and farms (for an early account see Phongpaichit, 1982). The young women send money home. In many cases, new houses are built and additional farming land can be purchased. The young women are seen as fulfilling a filial duty to their parents. Sons can bestow great merit on their parents by being ordained as monks. Most sons will be ordained for periods between one week and three months. Daughters cannot be ordained. They can gain merit by earning money for their parents. This explanation was recently repeated by Thongpao (2001), a human rights activist lawyer and elected senator, in the *Bangkok Post*. In a recent editorial, *The Nation* (2001c) commented on the established understanding of the patterns:

> . . . the leading 'star' of the drama [of prostitution] was the poor rural girl from the North, either sold by her parents to racketeers or who voluntarily left the family farm for the red-light district in a big city. Shy, introverted and unsophisticated, she was not doing it just for herself but for her people back home. The money went to relieve the debts of mum and dad, buy a younger

brother a motorcycle, or even help to rebuild a temple in her village. If lucky enough not to catch Aids after years in the sex service, the 'little bird' would fly home, set up a small beauty salon, or for the more fortunate ones, get married (*The Nation*, 2001a: 4A).

This editorial also highlights an apparently new pattern of urban female students taking up prostitution, on a part-time basis, to pay tuition fees or buy luxuries.

The extent and character of the sex industry is very embarrassing to the central Thai middle class. It is simply not true, as the *Spartacus* gay guide claims (Bedford and Rauch, 2001), that there is no stigma associated with prostitution. There was middle- and upper-class outrage a few years ago when an encyclopedia described Bangkok as famous for its temples and prostitutes. Because of this sensitivity, political elites and the English-language press commonly speak of young women as having been duped into the flesh trade. A recent report by Tumcharoen (2001) in the *Bangkok Post*, illustrates this:

An opposition member [of parliament] yesterday urged the government to combat a flesh trade preying on young, innocent women. Paveena Hongsakul . . . said firms posing as job-placement agencies were acting as a front for the flesh trade, actively recruiting teenage women moving from the provinces to Bangkok. Young women aged between 13 and 16 had been forced into prostitution after being lured by agents of a job-placement firm at Hua Lampong railway terminal, one of the busiest destinations for people coming from the provinces.

In June 2001 Interior Minister Purachai Piumsombun expressed embarrassment about the sex shows:

Purachai told Somvos [the chairman of the Venue Operators' Association] that he should strive to boost the service and image of entertainment places because countries such as China had already protested that their government officials had been taken to watch sex shows at night-entertainment places while on a visit to Thailand. 'It's very humiliating. We should allow no more sex shows to exist', Purachai said (*The Nation*, 2001b: 2A).

Pradech Phayakvichien, the Governor of the Tourist Authority of Thailand (TAT), expressed general opposition to sex tourism at a Regional Consultation on the Protection of Children from Exploitation in Tourism, held in Bangkok and co-sponsored by TAT and the World Tourism Organization:

Pradech said the TAT's strategies included the promotion of Thailand as a family destination, encouraging more female visitors, the development of cultural tourism and the launching of campaigns to deter tourists from visiting the country for sexual purposes of any kinds (Sakboon, 2001: 6A).

The gay host bars follow the general pattern of the heterosexual bars. There are perhaps a hundred gay host bars and other gay venues in Bangkok. The hosts are universally referred to as 'boys', though they will be at least eighteen. Jackson (1999a) comments that: 'use of the term "boy" for male sex workers is arguably problematic and suggestive of social inferiority, but it does reflect current Thai usage where both adolescent and adult males who work in any service capacity (sexual or otherwise) are widely called dek [boy].' In the discreet host bars the young men are dressed in street clothes and sit together facing the customers. Sometimes the 'captain' or manager will have a book of photographs of the boys to show to customers. In many bars there is go-go dancing and amusing shows. Some have cabaret performances, involving *kathoey* (transvestite) performers. At one or two bars the young men are fully nude when go-go dancing. A number of bars have sexy shows, big cock shows and fucking shows.

A large per centage of the male hosts come from Isan. The parents of the male hosts do not know that their sons are prostitutes. In many cases, the secret is kept from the young man's peers and even from room-mates. The recruiting patterns that exist for female hosts have no parallel for the young men. When asked how they connected with the bar, the most common answer is to identify some friend from up country who worked in the bar already. The young men, like the young women, send money home. They probably tell their parents that they work in a restaurant. Parents don't ask intrusive questions – a general Thai pattern within family units, particularly in relation to sons. Allyn and Chiayani (1999: 126) suggest that 'sexual matters are not typically discussed by the Thai among themselves' and Miller (1992: 110) refers to 'conventions of privacy within the Thai family'. Carlisle (2001), states: 'In many Thai families, there is a tacit don't-ask-don't-tell policy, especially for boys, especially about sex. And if a strange secret emerges, one that doesn't fit the picture the parents want to see, sometimes it's easiest not to see it.' Jackson (1999a: 12) comments:

The general dominance of a cultural norm of avoiding talking about unpleasant or disturbing things means that most g/l/t men and women have probably never talked about their sexuality with family members, except perhaps a close brother or sister. This avoidance can at times take extreme forms in the eyes of Western observers, such as families tolerating an adult gay son's boyfriend staying with him almost every night of the week 'as a good friend', but never mentioning the sexual nature of the 'friendship'.

One result of this discreet avoidance is that there is less pressure to marry.

Some of the boys do fairly well financially and work in the bars for a number of years. Most do not last very long, however, and the turnover in the host bars is very high. In some bars there seem to be new boys almost every night. Surprisingly, given the visual images presented to tourists, the Thai boys are self-conscious about the nudity involved in bar performances.

There are now gay host bars in most cities of any size. Allyn and Chaiyana (1999: 169–70) give an account of the beginnings of the gay host bars:

In the late 1950s or early 1960s a Thai named Tiwa, one of the owners of the Rome Club Disco opened the first bar for homosexual men. It was a place to dance and meet like-minded friends. Then, soon after, came the famous 'Sea Hag', which provided drinks, dancing and a decade of gay romances. Inspired by 'Sea Hag', a twenty-year-old tailor, named Nuwat, from southern Thailand, opened Tulip Bar in 1968. His bar was the longest running in Thailand, but after moving to a new location in 1991, closed a year later. The original, simple bar only had a jukebox for dancing, yet for the next twenty-four years the business flourished.

In 1965 or 1966 Twilight was opened by a drag-queen Kun Yosawadee, who had previously opened a house with boys in the early 1960s. It opened where Dream Boys Barbier is now, and was modeled on the female go-go bars in nearby Patpong. The bar employed go-go boys, was the first bar to have off-boys, and even had sex shows, although this was, and still is, illegal.

Two factors crushed the cruise-style gay bar as a meeting place for homo-sexuals: First, a 1978 law that forbade dancing in entertainment facilities without a license, which was nearly impossible to obtain. This forced Tulip and other bars to switch to go-go boys and the off system. Second, customers like the off system. Khun Nuwat, now in his fifties, explained, 'The guys at the off-bars didn't reject you.'

The bars are not just for foreigners:

In Thailand, Gay bars do not survive on tourism – and tourists always seem to over-rate their importance here. Tourism is seasonal, and though it is lucrative, it is not enough to operate yearly. Even bars with heavy tourist clientele report that Thais make up 80 to 90 per cent of their customers annually (Allyn, 1988: 12).

This pattern of gay host bars continues, but in the last decade it has been supplemented by a number of other gay venues – saunas, discos, massage parlours, restaurants, cruise bars, hotels.

> . . . by 1992 there was a subtle transformation in the Kingdom's gay scene. It had 18 gay pubs and restaurants without offboys; three of its seven saunas, and two of its four gay discos, had no offboys. . . . Since the mid 1980s there had been an average of five Thai gay magazines, now [1997] there are some 15 . . . There was also an astonishing surge in the number of gay venues without male sex workers – gay shops, saunas, pubs, restaurants, and discotheques. . . . The number of host bars remains steady and appear to have reached a plateau (Allyn, 1997: 6–9).

A leading cruise bar, Telephone, was established in 1987 by *farang*, celebrating its 14th birthday with a party in June 2001. The Babylon Sauna, founded in 1987, is elegant and famous. It has been so successful that it recently doubled in size and added Babylon Barracks, a hotel with 40 rooms (see listing of websites below). In addition to the saunas are massage parlours with young male masseurs. These too have been quite successful. One of them, V Club, opened a Moroccan-style sauna, Chakran, across the street in 2001.

It is widely known that police receive payments from heterosexual and homosexual bars, saunas, massage parlours and other businesses, as part of a general pattern of police demands. Some bar managers have willingly disclosed to the author the amount of the payments and the branches of the police who received the payments. Occasional police raids of gay bars occur. In these raids, customers are never questioned or arrested. Some bar boys or managers may be detained briefly. The raids are understood to relate to some lapse in the pattern of payments to the police, or result from a new zealous police chief in the district asserting his authority. Police do not harass gay tourists in other situations either. When a taxi with a *farang* and a young Thai man is stopped in a routine police check for drunk driving, the taxi is always waived through as soon as the police see the *farang* tourist. Thai police do not look to foreign tourists for bribes.

When Allyn published the first edition of *The Men of Thailand* in 1987, he gave the age of consent as sixteen. It was common at that time, to see boys who appeared to be fourteen or fifteen looking for customers outside Robinsons department store on the corner of Silom and Rama IV. At least one out-of-the-way bar had boys as young as thirteen or fourteen in the late 1980s. The owner commented to the writer that in the past, there was no problem in having a thirteen-year-old in a bar, but now it was very risky. Later Prime Minister Chuan Leekpai, while at a regional meeting in Singapore, was highly embarrassed by accounts of underage prostitution in Thailand. This led to a fairly strict enforcement of eighteen as the minimum age for hosts. This is the legal age of consent when prostitution is involved (Allyn and Chaiyana, 1999: 187). At present, young boys are no longer to be found in front of Robinsons or in the host bars.

THAI ATTITUDES TOWARDS HOMOSEXUALITY

Time Magazine published survey results in March 2001, rating Thai people as the most 'gay-friendly' people in Asia – a story prominently featured in the *Bangkok Post* (2001a). However, the question of the extent of real acceptance is now often posed. The *Bangkok Post* ran a major article on homosexuality in June 2001, which began with this overview:

> Bangkok, at least on the surface, is a place where there is tolerance for homosexuals. 'Tomboys' and 'ladyboys' walk along busy streets with no fear of being harassed, as might happen in many cities. And beauty pageants with transvestite contestants draw almost as much attention as those with genuine Thai beauties. But what about real acceptance in society? (Meksujit, 2001: 6).

With these four sentences, this sympathetic investigative report, in a major liberal newspaper, began by identifying homosexuals by the obvious stereotypes – masculine lesbian 'tomboys' and the effeminate male 'ladyboys'. These continue to be the dominant images of 'homosexuals' in Thai society. There are no prominent openly 'gay' figures in the country. The term 'gay' itself, is still relatively new in Thailand, and is not used in the same way as in the West. Thai people do not copy the Western polarization of straight and gay. Sinnott (1999: 105) states: 'Western concepts of two mutually exclusive categories of sexual beings, homosexual and heterosexual, are not widely held by Thais, especially concerning women.' Sinnot also claims that toms see their feminine 'dee' partners as bisexuals who will likely marry men.

Other researchers have commented, with Western surprise, that a high percentage of bar boys in the host bars do not identify as 'gay' (van Wijngaarden, 1999: 193; Storer, 1999: 142–3). Some bar boys are married to women. The lack of gay identity leads to a standard joke: *Question*: 'Are you gay?' *Answer*: 'I'm gay when you pay.' If a tourist customer asks a bar boy if he likes ladies or men, a standard answer is 'fifty-fifty'. The manager in Tomahawk Bar in 2000 assured customers that the boys were all '100 per cent gay', apparently seeing this as an assurance customers would appreciate. One host confirmed this new guarantee, saying he was '100 per cent gay', but added that when he finished working in the bar he would settle down and marry a woman. Another interesting pattern is the willingness of some young men in the army or navy to supplement their low salaries with part-time prostitution, freelancing or in host bars. They convey a strong image of masculinity. They are real men, not gay, though they may have had sexual experience with ladyboys, who are available and less expensive than female prostitutes.

Some young men who work in the bars are not able to sustain erections and successfully play an active role in sex with men. Others will only play an active role, associating a passive role with ladyboys. Sometimes a manager will assure a customer that a certain boy 'can do everything', confirming that not all the bar boys are equally 'versatile'.

While Thailand is seen as an exceptionally tolerant society on sexual issues, it is clear that the departure from normative heterosexuality is viewed negatively. Lesbians, gay men and transgendered people are stigmatized. There is in Thailand 'little concern with what people do privately, although there is low public acceptance of homosexual identities' (Brummelhuis, 1999: 127). As Sinnott (1999: 103) suggests: 'public revelations of what are perceived to be private and personal affairs are not considered proper'. The silence around sexual behaviour means that it is 'hard to find explicit prohibitions in cultural discourse on homosexuality for men, and the same is true for female homosexuality' (ibid.: 103). Anjana Suvarnananda of the lesbian group Anjaree comments:

> Although Thai people aren't violent or hostile towards homosexuals in a way that some countries' societies are, there is another kind of control mechanism at work here that's just as traumatic for those on the receiving end. . . . [Thai] society doesn't see lesbian relationships as legitimate or meaningful (quoted in Otaganonta, 1995: 31).

Ladyboys and tomboys are publicly very visible in Thailand, but the tomboys in particular seem hidden from view even when in plain sight. Sinnott (1999: 102) comments on perceptions of the gendered patterns of 'toms' (for tomboys) and 'dees' (for ladies):

Thailand is reputed to be a tolerant society in terms of personal behavior, including homosexual, as long as one does not 'flaunt' or make such behavior apparent (see Jackson, 1995). 'Coming-out', the verbal declaration of one's homosexuality, is not common in Thailand, even among women who are easily recognized as *toms*, and therefore lesbians. Almost all the *toms* interviewed said that their families knew that they were *toms*/lesbians, but very few *toms*, or *dees*, had actually had open discussions with their families about their lesbianism. Even in relatively supportive families, where a *tom* brought home her girl friend to meet her family or live together, *toms* usually communicated their identity in non-verbal ways such as through their dress and behavior. As Jackson (1995) points out, there is very little open and frank discussion about the realities of sex, especially homosexual sex, in Thailand, as public revelations of what are perceived to be private and personal affairs are not considered proper.

Jackson and Sullivan (1999: 11) note the view that the Thai middle and upper classes, especially those of Chinese ancestry, are less tolerant of homosexuality than others in Thai society. This is a possible explanation for the homophobic nature of much of the academic writings on homosexuality in Thailand: 'Thai academic writings commonly problematize male homosexuality as a "perversion" (*khwam-wiparit*) that needs to be "corrected" (*kae-khai*), or a "disease" or "illness" (*rok*) that needs to be "treated" or "cured" (*raksa*)' (Jackson, 1999b: 227).

Allyn and Chaiyana (1999: 115) argue that Thailand is a 'sex-positive' society, and a society that lacks homophobia:

> When we say that Thailand is not a homophobic society, this doesn't mean it *accepts* homosexuality. It simply means that it neither culturally fears nor loathes homosexual behavior or homosexual men. There are, in fact, some Thai who espouse Western homophobic ideas, but they haven't had much impact on social attitudes. Chinese-Thai and Islamic-Thai gay men are very much victim to their subculture's homophobic attitudes.

And what of the transvestites and transsexuals identified as *kathoeys*? Jackson (1999b) writes that Thai society traditionally thought in terms of three sexes, with the term *kathoey* used to refer either to effeminate men or masculine women. Over time, *kathoey* has come to refer exclusively to effeminate men. It is supplemented by the term 'lady boy'. *Kathoey* and 'gay' are constantly equated in discussions in Thailand. Allyn and Chaiyana (1999: 119–20) write:

Westerners are astonished by how ubiquitous are Thai transvestites. There's no debate about what to call them: *ga'tuhy* is the most widely used term for them, though there are perhaps a dozen terms. The feminine male who sometimes cross-dresses and has sex with men is a clear socially articulated model in Thailand. For this reason, if a young Thai male is at all effeminate, he might slip into the role model of *ga'tuhy*, a character regarded with good-hearted mirth in some upcountry areas, and growing derision in others, particularly in large cities. It seems that even the smallest village has at least one, and family and neighbors do not shun him. He may be teased and even flirted with, but he's still part of the clan, the family, the village.

As in Malaysia and Indonesia transgendered males are a well-known and visible group who are involved in entertainment and sometimes sex work. In each of the three countries, ladyboys and transgendered people are common characters in television programmes, to the occasional concern of elites. In Thailand, *kathoeys* feature in major tourist shows in Pattaya, Bangkok and Phuket. Busloads of families from Hong Kong and Singapore stream into the famous Alcazar and Tiffany theatres in Pattaya. A Thai documentary (*Ladyboys*) followed two ladyboys from their participation in upcountry beauty pageants to auditions for Alcazar and Simon Show (a bar with a transvestite cabaret) in Pattaya (Herman-Wurmfeld, 1995). The annual 'Miss Tiffany' contest has been broadcast nationally beginning in 2000. In 2001 there were fifty competitors and a first prize of 100,000 baht and the chance to compete for the title of 'Miss Gay Universe' in Los Angeles (Alsdorf, 2001a). The second highest grossing Thai film is *Satree Lek* (Iron Ladies) (Thonghonkum, 2000), a comedy about the *kathoey* volleyball team from Lampang that won the national championships in 1996.

My impression is that *kathoeys* have a better social and economic niche in Thailand than in other parts of South East Asia. This may reflect less stigmatization, somewhat more tolerance. It can also reflect the economic niche that certain *kathoeys* have in the entertainment, bar and tourist scenes. In April 2001 the Thai government announced that transsexuals would be able to get special passports that showed both 'before' and 'after' photographs, to facilitate travel. This was the first legal recognition of transsexuals, and came about due to German concerns with the number of Thai transsexuals who were travelling there on forged passports (Alsdorf, 2001b; Tansubhapol, 2001). It was not a positive recognition.

If the state does or says anything, it will involve either anti-homosexual rhetoric or official acts of discrimination. In 1997 the Rajabhat Institute, the national system of 36 teacher-training colleges, announced that it would ban homosexuals from entry into its programmes (Jackson and Sullivan, 1999). Homosexuals, it was claimed, set a bad example for students; moreover they had short tempers. The *Bangkok Post*, a liberal paper, covered the story. It followed up with a special feature quoting comments solicited from a range of people around the world. Initially the Thai authorities said they would not bow to protests. After a few months, a retreat was announced, but in an ambiguous, face-saving way (Bunnag, 1997):

> The Rajabhat Institute has lifted its ban on admission of homosexuals to its teacher training campuses, apparently under pressure from foreign bodies such as NGOs. But the institute has simultaneously proposed a new rule to keep out what it describes as 'sexually abnormal' people, according to Sawat Udompot, deputy secretary-general of the Rajabhat Council. There are seven types of 'sexual abnormalities', according to Wanlop Piyamanotham, director of the psychological counseling centre of Srinakharinwirote University's Prasanmit campus. Mr Wanlop, a member of the council, said that among these were: copulating with inanimate objects; exposing oneself in public; deriving pleasure from sado-masochistic acts; and harassing others orally. He said the old ban had been imposed out of a misunderstanding of the nature of sexual deviance. 'The institute misunderstood and used the wrong word. That's why it seems to violate human rights. The best way is to single out sexually abnormal people', he said ... 'Sexual deviants are not always sexually abnormal. Sexual abnormality is worse. They can't be good teachers – they're emotionally abnormal.'

On 27 April 1999, the Public Relations Department ordered that people with sexual abnormalities be banned from appearing on television programmes (Assavanonda, 1999):

> The ban was imposed after a viewer e-mailed the prime minister to assert that homosexuals and transvestites set a bad example for youngsters. Leading the alliance [protesting against the ban] are Anjaree Group for Lesbian Rights, and the Friends for Women Foundation. Other supporters include the Anti-Aids Gay Group, the Women and Constitution Network, Empower, the YMCA, the Hot-Line Centre Foundation and Mahidol University's Human Rights and Social Development Office. Anchana Suwannanont, of Anjaree, said the international consensus among psychiatrists was that there was nothing abnormal about the target groups and that to describe them as such could foster prejudice. . . . Pakorn Pimthon, organiser of the Bangkok Gay Festival, said many of his gay

friends had been forced out of jobs by programme producers. 'Many supporting actors who are gay and transvestites are crying now since they do not know where to go', said Mr Pakorn, a dancer. 'Some have no other career, they need entertainment work for their survival.' About 90 per cent of dancers and 70 per cent of actors are gays and transvestites, he said.

As before, the *Bangkok Post* did an extensive response in its Saturday 'Outlook' section, under a banner headline 'GET REAL!' (*Bangkok Post*, 1999). Opinions from ten different people were prefaced by these comments:

Fearing youngsters may imitate 'unfavourable examples' the Public Relations Department recently issued a directive asking TV stations to limit the number of shows featuring transvestites and transsexuals. But when 'Outlook' asked a number of television producers, academics and TV watchers for their opinions most thought the directive was misguided and missed the point. The general agreement was that kids do not suddenly decide to be gay after watching 'kathoeys' on TV, that the government should lay off such censorial and discriminatory comments and that programme makers should act more responsibly in their portrayal of gay people.

As of writing, the ban has not been officially repealed, but will probably never be implemented.

Jackson (1999a: 11), commenting on legal and political aspects of the situation of homosexuals in Thailand, concludes:

In legal terms, the greatest hurdle that Thai gay/lesbian/transgendered people face is to be taken seriously by policy formulators and law makers as forming a genuine constituency with rights that need to be acknowledged and protected. The absence of anti-gay/lesbian/transgendered statutes on Thai law books does not reflect any form of institutional or formal support, but rather a pervasive attitude that gay/lesbian/transgendered people are not 'worth' giving consideration to.

GAY ORGANIZATIONS

While Thailand has had a flourishing gay bar scene for 30 years, and apparently relaxed social attitudes, the lack of Western-style gay organizations has been striking. As Allyn and Chaiyana (1999: 128) note: 'Despite exposure to Western gay culture, a Thai gay community barely exists, except as a commercial entity in certain cities.'

The first modern visible organization in Thailand was the Fraternity for Aids Cessation (FACT), founded in 1989 by Natee Teerarojjanapongs. Natee, who had studied in the United States, was Thailand's 'first Western-style gay activist' (Miller, 1992: 125). He created an educational dance group called the White Line Dancers. The name was taken from his favourite musical, *A Chorus Line*. The group became famous for their AIDS education shows in gay bars. The pioneering role that FACT played in HIV/AIDS education was eclipsed by government programmes when Dr Mechai Viravaidya, head of the national family-planning organization and famous for promoting condom use, became the cabinet minister responsible for tourism and AIDS prevention (D'Agnes, 2001; Pravattiyagul, 2001). Media stories on AIDS generally do not mention homosexuality, giving statistics that focus on intravenous drug use and heterosexual transmission (*Bangkok Post*, 2000a; 2001b). While FACT is now inactive, Natee has worked to keep the name alive.

The Third Asian Lesbian and Gay Conference met in Bangkok in August 1990. It was instigated by the Japan International Lesbian and Gay Association, which hosted the previous two meetings in Japan, part of a failed attempt to create an active Asian regional grouping within the International Lesbian and Gay Association. JILGA's contact in Bangkok was Nukul Benchamant, editor of *Neon Magazine*, a Thai gay magazine. Nukul had been hosted in Japan, and, for a while, was a slightly visible gay spokesperson in Bangkok. But he had no organization, and before the conference lost his job as editor. The job of organizing the conference fell to Natee and Eric Allyn. Only about fifteen people were involved on the first day: nine Asians (Thailand, Japan, Malaysia) and six *farang*. On Sunday afternoon there were 21 people. Letters came from Australia, Taiwan, Hong Kong and South Korea. The Thai lesbian group Anjaree was formed, but was not yet public. Anjana Suvarnananda and three others came to the Sunday morning session. Anjana spoke on condition that her name and that of the organization would not be used. She refused interviews with *The Nation* newspaper, which had a reporter at the conference, and with the American writer Neil Miller, who included an account of the meeting in his book *Out in the World* (Miller, 1992).

Anjaree had funding from The Netherlands for a lesbian conference in December 1990. It went on to become the most serious and most public lesbian or gay-identified organization in Thailand. It published a small, good-quality magazine. It became publicly involved in the fight against the Rajabhat Institute's ban on homosexuals. In that campaign, Anjaree brought together prominent academics and medical professionals to speak on behalf of lesbians at a public forum (Rattachumpoth, 1999: xvi): 'Feminist-inspired lesbians have been politically active in Bangkok, and they played an impressive role during the Rajabhat controversy in publicly countering the discriminatory ban against homosexual students and appearing before a parliamentary committee which inquired into the ban.' Each year Anjaree holds a public reception or party, an event that makes the social page of the *Bangkok Post* (Mahitthirook, 2000). Anjana Suvarnananda is now the spokesperson media representatives will turn to for an informed viewpoint on gay and lesbian life (Otaganonta, 2000). But there are still no lesbian bars or coffee shops in Bangkok.

A branch of the London based Long Yang club started in Bangkok in 1996, involving expatriates and their Thai friends and partners. It has a branch in Chiang Mai in the north. In May 2001 the Utopia website listed two additional organizations: Lesla for women and Peuan See Muang (Purple Friend) for men.

THE BANGKOK GAY FESTIVAL

In 1999 a new group formed to hold the first Bangkok Gay Festival, culminating with a parade on Halloween Sunday. The parade was preceded by a series of parties and fund-raising events. The Gay Festival idea defied conventional wisdom, for it involved a Western style 'pride parade', a dramatic shift from Thai patterns of discretion, privacy and polite silence. The new strategy arose out of a convergence in interests between successful Bangkok *kathoey* entertainers (an already visible grouping) and foreign-owned gay-oriented businesses (for whom visibility was important). The key couple was Pakorn Pimthon, a Thai entertainer, and his Swiss partner Lukas, one of the owners of the Tarntawan Hotel, which advertises itself as 'gay-owned and managed'.

The idea for the festival came from the famous Sydney Lesbian and Gay Mardi Gras. Business sponsors have included the Tarntawan Hotel, Dick's Café, Telephone Bar, The Balcony Bar, DJ Station (disco), Sphinx Restaurant, Freeman Dance Arena, Ambience Hotel, Aqua Spa Club, Dreaded Neds (see website listing below), Icon Club, Rock Records and Utopia Tours. Most of these businesses are owned by *farang*. None of the businesses is a host bar, meaning that none have a direct link to prostitution. The lead role of *kathoey* performers meant that there would be splendid shows.

The major problem faced by the Gay Festival in 1999 was with the police (Sanders, 2000). The organizers understood that they had the required police approvals for the street parade that would follow a circular route involving Silom and Suriwong roads. But there were a couple of surprises. Far more spectators turned up than had been expected. Quite a number of people had come to Bangkok directly from the regional AIDS conference in Kuala Lumpur. The corner of Silom and Rama IV was jammed, and the police said they had no knowledge of the parade. But the event could not be stopped. A jubilant group of *khatoeys* and bar boys danced on floats representing a set of local gay businesses, including host bars. Once the parade had circled over from Silom to Suriwong, and was out of the sight of the media and the crowds, the police halted the parade and seized floats and a bevy of costumes and wigs. Both local English-language newspapers, the *Bangkok Post* and *The Nation*, had positive coverage of the parade on their front pages the next morning, neither realizing that the parade had been stopped by the police. In 2000 the organizers publicized the fact that they were having problems with the city administration over the parade permit, but in the end the parade went ahead with some police support (Ngamkhan, 2000).

The Bangkok Gay Festival marked a significant change. Whatever organizational problems existed, Bangkok was now being held out internationally as a gay centre with a major gay event. It was claiming its place alongside Amsterdam, Sydney and San Francisco. In 2000 the Bangkok festival was followed by a Phuket Gay Festival. In 2001 festivals are planned in Bangkok, Phuket and Pattaya. The first Pattaya Gay Festival is planned for 29 November to 2 December 2001.

The festival organizers increasingly function as a gay rights organization. In May 2000 Pakorn publicly called for a gay-friendly governor (mayor) for Bangkok, attempting to appeal to a gay vote (Antaseeda, 2000a; 2000b). In March 2001 Pakorn and others performed a safe-sex play in the Bangkok Remand Prison (Assavandonda, 2001). In June 2001 Pakorn, and others, were featured in the *Bangkok Post* investigative report on homosexuality, 'Free to Choose' (*Bangkok Post*, 2001d).

In 2001, 23 of the gay-oriented businesses in Bangkok, Pattaya and Phuket established the Thailand Alternative Travel Association (TATA). TATA will enable some co-ordinated publicity identifying Thailand as a gay destination. Organizers hope for a link to the government's Tourism Authority of Thailand (TAT). Douglas Thompson of Utopia Tours in Bangkok has actively promoted the link with TAT:

TAT officials have incorporated niche marketing into their master plan. We hope they will soon officially recognize the potential for gay and lesbian visitors to contribute billions of baht to the Thai economy by including us in their promotional plans. With a little cooperation our Bangkok, Pattaya and Phuket parades can quickly compete with Sydney and San Francisco (*Thai Guys*, 2001).

After all, at least a dozen countries, cities, states or provinces in the West actively promote gay tourism. The Sydney Mardi Gras is the single biggest tourist draw for Australia. The possibility or hope of a link to TAT means that TATA must distance itself from 'sex tourism' and prostitution: 'Membership is open to businesses in Thailand that are committed to promoting a positive image for gay and lesbian visitors and publicly subscribe to TATA's code of ethics regarding child prostitution. Membership is not available to any person or business that is involved in prostitution' (*Thai Guys*, 2001).

CONCLUSION

Jackson, and others, in their writings emphasize Thai difference. The differences are real. A Western 'gay' identity is not traditional for Thais, and is as yet uncommon. Thai society is more tolerant than Western society, but less publicly accepting of lesbians and gays than current patterns in the urban centres of Europe and North America. Individuals have a remarkable degree of privacy within the family setting, allowing homosexual relationships and activities to be overlooked. This avoids what otherwise could be strong patterns of discrimination and rejection. There is an extensive commercial gay scene in much of which caucasian *farang* are privileged. It operates quite differently than in other parts of the world. The young men involved are surprisingly polite, friendly, cheerful, deferential and unjaded (or so, at least, they successfully portray themselves to tourists).

Other writers (e.g. Altman, 2000), see an internationalization of 'gay' identities occurring in various regions of the world, including South East Asia. With the expansion of gay venues beyond host bars, with the Mardi Gras-style gay festivals, with the appeal to TAT to recognize the commercial value of gay tourism, with lesbian and gay advocacy work, certain elements in Thailand are making a Western-style appeal to gay tourists and working for increased visibility within Thai society. With an expansion of fitness clubs and gyms, a Western-style gay gym culture has emerged in a segment of the middle-class Thai gay scene. The Internet is now giving some middle-class Thai men access to potential male sexual partners in all parts of the country, bypassing the public commercial scene (a recent development in the West as well). Both the Bangkok Gay Festival organizers and Anjaree are, to a significant extent, the same kind of gay and lesbian rights organizations that exist in the West. Whether these developments result from the diffusion of Western models, or parallel development reflecting local conditions seems not very important. The changes can be seen.

While the gay festivals may increase gay tourism, the other aspects of the gay scene in Thailand do not need to change or Westernize in order to appeal to gay tourists. Thai difference is the major attraction, including, of course, the existing easy access to sexual services. Enhanced Western trappings, in terms of the newer gay friendly hotels and restaurants (and the shopping bargains), serve simply as additional perks for the gay tourist.

REFERENCES

Allyn, E. (1988), 'Bangkok diary', *Passport*, 12 May.
Allyn, E. (1997) (6th edn), *The Men of Thailand*. San Francisco, CA: Bua Luang.
Allyn, E. and Chaiyana, S. (1999) (7th edn), *The Men of Thailand: Thailand's Culture and Gay Subculture*. San Francisco, CA: Floating Lotus.
Allyn, E. and Collins, J. P. (1987), *The Men of Thailand: Noom Thai*. San Francisco, CA: Bua Luang.
Alsdorf, M. (2001a), 'Thailand crowns trans beauty queen', *PlanetOut.com*, 3 April.
Alsdorf, M. (2001b), 'Trans Thais to get special passports', *PlanetOut.com*, 16 April.
Altman, D. (2000), 'The emergence of gay identities in Southeast Asia', in P. Drucker, (ed.), *Different Rainbows*. London: Gay Men's Press.
Antaseeda, P. (2000a), 'Candidates need our vote, say gays', *Bangkok Post*, 13 May.
Antaseeda, P. (2000b), 'Samak tops the pink poll on past results', *Bangkok Post*, 30 May.
Assavanonda, A. (1999), 'Activists demand lifting of gay ban', *Bangkok Post*, June.
Assavanonda, A. (2001), 'Safe sex play staged in jail', *Bangkok Post*, 30 March.
Bangkok Post (1999), 'GET REAL', 'Outlook', 29 May.
Bangkok Post (2000), 'A long road ahead', 30 November.
Bangkok Post (2001a), 'Thai people Asia's most gay-friendly', 12 March.
Bangkok Post (2001b), 'More patients progress to full-blown disease', 22 March.
Bangkok Post (2001c), 'Chiang Mai forum to find ways to lure foreigners', 18 April.
Bangkok Post (2001d), 'Free to choose', 3 June.
Bedford, B. and Rauch, R. (eds) (2001) (30th edn), *Spartacus International Gay Guide: 2001–2002*. Berlin: Bruno Gmünder Verlag.
Brummelhuis, H. ten (1999), 'Transformations of transgender: the case of the Thai Kathoey', in P. Jackson and G. Sullivan (eds), *Lady Boys, Tom Boys, Rent Boys: Male and Female Homosexualities in Contemporary Thailand*. New York: Harrington Park.
Bunnag, S. (1997), 'College lifts its ban on gay entrants', *Bangkok Post*, 11 September.
Carlisle, S. (2001), 'Business as usual', *Fridae Magazine*, 12 April.
D'Agnes, T. (2001), *From Condoms to Cabbages*. Bangkok: Silkworm.
Far Eastern Economic Review (2001), 'Thai tourism touts car rental', 29 March.

Jackson, P. (1999a), *Homosexual and Transgender Rights in Thailand*, unpublished.

Jackson, P. (1999b), 'Tolerant but unaccepting: the myth of a Thai "gay paradise"', in P. A. Jackson and N. M. Cook (eds), *Genders and Sexualities in Modern Thailand*. Bangkok: Silkworm.

Jackson, P. and Sullivan, G. (1999) (eds), *Lady Boys, Tom Boys, Rent Boys: Male and Female Homosexualities in Contemporary Thailand*. New York: Harrington Park.

Mahitthirook, A. (2001), 'Lesbian group plans campaign in schools', *Bangkok Post*, 7 November.

Meksujit, S. (2001), 'Free to choose', *Bangkok Post*, 3 June.

Miller, N. (1992), *Out in the World*. New York: Random House.

Ngamkham, W. (2000), 'Pink parade plans disrupted by route ban', *Bangkok Post*, 20 October.

Otaganonta, W. (1995), 'Women who love women', *Bangkok Post*, 'Outlook', 21 July.

Otaganonta, W. (2000), 'Twenty-first century love', *Bangkok Post*, 'Outlook', 3 January.

Phongpaichit, P. (1982), *From Peasant Girls to Bangkok Masseuses*. Geneva: International Labour Office.

Pravattiyagul, O. (2001), 'Contraceptive incentive', *Bangkok Post*, 12 May.

Rattachumpoth, R. (1999), 'Foreword', in P. Jackson and G. Sullivan (eds), *Lady Boys, Tom Boys, Rent Boys: Male and Female Homosexualities in Contemporary Thailand*. New York: Harrington Park.

Richter, L. K. (1989), *The Politics of Tourism in Asia*. Honolulu, HA: University of Hawaii. (See Chapter 4, 'Thailand: where tourism and politics make strange bedfellows'.)

Sakboon, M. (2001), 'In-flight warnings proposed', *The Nation*, 2 July.

Sanders, D. (2000), 'Sex and the foreign correspondent', *Thai Guys*, August–October.

Sinnott, M. (1999), 'Masculinity and tom identity in Thailand', in P. Jackson and G. Sullivan (eds), *Lady Boys, Tom Boys, Rent Boys: Male and Female Homosexualities in Contemporary Thailand*. New York: Harrington Park.

Storer, G. (1999), 'Rehearsing gender and sexuality in modern Thailand: masculinity and male–male sex patterns', in P. Jackson and G. Sullivan (eds), *Lady Boys, Tom Boys, Rent Boys: Male and Female Homosexualities in Contemporary Thailand*. New York: Harrington Park.

Talbot, M. (2001), 'Nip, tuck and frequent-flier miles', *New York Times Magazine*, 6 May.

Tansubhapol, B. (2001), 'Sex change Thais flock to Germany', *Bangkok Post*, 12 April.

Techawongtham, W. (2001), 'Thaksin in danger of laying an egg', *Bangkok Post*, 4 May.

Thai Guys (2001), 'Full speed ahead', May.

The Nation (1998), 'Ing, Of foreign bodies, false shame and becoming a NIC', 23 July.

The Nation (2001a), 'Editorial', 15 June.

The Nation (2001b), 'Clean up the nightspots', 22 June.

Thongpao, T. (2001), 'Time to let women be monks too', *Bangkok Post*, 6 May.

Tumcharoen, S. (2001), 'Job agencies recruit girl sex workers', *Bangkok Post*, 4 May.

van Wijngaarden, J. W. de L. (1999), 'Between money, morality and masculinity: bar-based male sex work in Chiang Mai', in P. Jackson and G. Sullivan (eds), *Lady Boys, Tom Boys, Rent Boys: Male and Female Homosexualities in Contemporary Thailand*. New York: Harrington Park.

FILMS

Ladyboys (1995) (Thailand), director: Charles Herman-Wurmfeld.
Satree Lek (2000) (Thailand), director: Yongyuth Thongkhonkum.

WEBSITES

Babylon and Babylon Barracks, Bangkok: *www.babylonbkk.com*
Bangkok Post newspaper: *www.bangkokpost.net*
Dreaded Ned, information on gay issues in South East Asia: *www.dreadedned.com*
Fridae: Asia's Gay and Lesbian Network: *www.fridae.com/magazine/*
Men of Thailand (books by Eric Allyn): *www.floatinglotus.com*
Thaiguys magazine: *www.Thaiguys.com*
Utopia Asia tour company: *www.utopia-asia.com*

CHAPTER 3

A Case-study in Contradictions: Hawaii and Gay Tourism

MATTHEW LINK

INTRODUCTION

The aim of this chapter is to delve into the fascinating case-study of a large tourist destination and its relationship with gay tourism. Unique in the world in many ways, the specific example of Hawaii cannot be easily equated with other gay-friendly destinations. The story of its very homosexual past, its colourful society with distinct mores, its radical politics and its sharp perception among gay travellers makes it a compelling real-life drama of a staid society coming to grips with, and attempting to avoid, modern realities. Perhaps the most isolated island group on the planet, Hawaii has been one of the most mass-marketed tourist destinations the world has ever known. Nearly inventing the concept of American package tourism, the islands had never known economic hardship until their tourist market crashed in the early 1990s, when Hawaii finally learned the weaknesses of a one-market economy based on tourism. Entrenched with political corruption and lack of will, the state has barely been able to move forward on any economic front in recent years. So when it comes to the story of gay tourism, it is no surprise that the road has been a long, hard and frustrating one. This is despite the fact that Hawaii consistently ranks as one of the top gay travel destinations worldwide (Link, 1999).

The first Europeans to the islands gave in-depth (albeit disgusted) reports on the tradition of *aikane*, or homosexual friendships among the island royalty. These relationships were viewed as normal and even functional for certain members to achieve a higher rank. The Hawaiians, like their Polynesian cousins in other island groups, also have the role of *mahu*. A *mahu* is a man who chooses, usually from an early age, to dress and act as a female, and he is accepted as such without fuss. This tradition of open cross-dressing carries on today, particularly on the rural island of Molokai, where the *mahu* are quite prevalent in the local *hula* scene. Personal accounts and quotes will illustrate this phenomenon.

Hawaii became the focal point of international gay politics in the early 1990s when it looked as though it would become the first state in the United States to legalize same-sex marriages. This chapter also briefly overviews the rise and subsequent defeat of the same-sex marriage issue, and how the media coverage affected gay tourism and local attitudes. The out-of-character ugliness that the marriage vote brought about was unheard of previously in Hawaii.

Hawaii's racially mixed society is another important factor in its perceptions of gay people, both within the state and outside of it. Quotes from a number of gay residents on the local culture on the islands and its attitudes towards them will be included, illustrating the contradictory nature of the island society. The actual attitude towards gays and lesbians is mixed, especially from island to island. Hawaii has a strong family-based society with Asian influences, and for many local gays and lesbians, the policy is: 'don't ask, don't tell' with respect to being out, publicly or privately.

Hawaii's gay infrastructure has experienced significant change in the past decade due to the state's economic situation, and the chapter will discuss the direct effects of this on gay tourism. The realities of gay life in Hawaii contrast with its perception from outside as a gay Mecca. Ironically, the perceived social ideals of Hawaii work to its advantage in attracting visitors, and the truth does not seem to challenge the perception.

This chapter will discuss recent attempts to implement a gay marketing programme in Hawaii. A group of gay businessmen and travel-marketing professionals met with the Hawaii Visitors' and Convention Bureau more than once, but despite their efforts and lobbying, the Bureau did not consider gay tourism important enough for funds. This was despite the overwhelming popularity of Hawaii as a gay tourist destination, and the need to attract more tourists to the islands, given the dire economic situation.

HISTORICAL PERSPECTIVE ON HOMOSEXUALITY AND GAY LIFE IN HAWAII

To understand the state of gay life in Hawaii and its modern developments it is important to take into consideration Hawaii's unique history of incorporating homosexual behaviour into its cultural structure. This sheds much light on current social attitudes towards gay and lesbian residents and tourists in Hawaii. Hawaiians have an extremely strong connection to their past, and this needs to be appreciated when studying contemporary views towards homosexuality, in order to understand the cultural atmosphere of the islands.

Anthropologists agree that Polynesians are descendants from a South East Asian race of peoples who emigrated from Indonesia into the Pacific and what is now Melanesia. Carbon-dating places the first humans in Fiji (the cradle of Polynesian culture) as early as 3500 BC. Pushed onward by subsequent darker-skinned immigrants, the Polynesians fanned out eastward into the Pacific and eventually occupied the 'Polynesian Triangle', which occupies roughly the area between New Zealand in the southern Pacific, Easter Island to the east, and Hawaii in the northern Pacific. Hawaii was the last part of Polynesia to be inhabited, around AD 500–600, and was occupied in two major migrations from the Marquesas and Tahiti island groups in the south, the second wave occurring around AD 1200 (Joesting, 1972).

Hawaii has always been a unique corner of the world, both physically and culturally. All recorded information about pre-contact Hawaii was written after European contact, however, and reflects the bias of foreign observers. Hawaiians have a strong heritage of *mele* or chants that explain pre-contact Hawaii. European historians tend to treat oral history as unreliable, but not so the Polynesians. Chants were sacred, and the passing down of words and *hula* movements and their meanings was a strict discipline requiring years of tutelage by knowledgeable elders. One foot out of place or the transposing of a word was grounds for beatings and, in some cases, death (Malo, 1976). *Hula* and its chants are popularly called the 'lifeblood of the Hawaiian people', and the transferring of culture and information in this manner was of utmost importance to the early Hawaiians.

The Hawaiian culture's straightforward views on sexuality are reflected in the ancient *mele ma'i*, or genital songs, usually in honour of an *ali'i*, or royalty. The Hawaiians respected and revered the procreative function of sex. The following Polynesian *mele* (a name chant for *Kaualiliko'i*) is performed as a *hula o'helo*, or reclining dance, in which the suggested motions are most vital to the meaning (Cunningham, 1995):

> *Tu 'Oe* (You are Erect)
> *Ae, Tu 'oe, tau 'oe, tu'i tele la*
> *Tu 'oe, tau 'oe, tu'i tele la!*
> *'Awe, 'awe, 'awe, 'awe, 'awe, 'awe la!*
> *'no ta mea, ta mea nui la!*

Ti'o lele, ti'o lele, ti'o lele la!
Kaualiliko'i, liliko'i, tu'i tele la!
Ho'i iluna la!
Ha'a ilalo la!
Ho'i iluna la!
Ha'a ilalo la!

Indeed, You are erect, you place it, hit liquid
You are erect, you place it, hit liquid!
Tentacle, tentacle, tentacle, tentacle, tentacle, tentacle!
The thing is mean, the big thing!
Thrust out, thrust out, thrust out!
Kaualiliko'i, liliko'i, hit liquid!
Return up!
Go down below!
Return up!
Down below!

This example illustrates attitudes towards sex in Hawaii. In this *mele*, genitals are treated with honour and no shame attached to their existence. According to Hawaiian scholars, sexuality in old Hawaiian culture was treated as a loving, fluid part of everyday life. It had both vitality and poetic characteristics. These *mele ma'i*, or songs in honour of genitals, were performed at events such as the birth of a great chief. In fact, Hawaiians often named their genitals as a matter of course: King Kalakaua's penis had the impressive name of *halala* (literally translated as 'to bend low'), and Queen Lili'uokalani's vagina was called *'anapau* (which means 'frisky') (Westervelt, 1977).

Common throughout Polynesia, Hawaiian family structures were collective and extended, unlike the Western practice of the 'nuclear' family. Many related and unrelated aunts, uncles, cousins and *hanai* (adopted) family members together form an *'ohana* (extended family), which also included friends and non-relatives as well. According to tradition, first-born children were often given to their grandparents or other relatives to bring up. Long-term mates were given the poetic label of *noho ai*, or 'one to lay with' (Pukui and Elbert, 1995). Since private property was not a concept to the collective-thinking Hawaiian tribes, marriage and its underlying concept of ownership was unheard of. Mates lived together for as long or as little as they pleased, sexual monogamy was not seen as vital to the relationship (Handy and Pukui, 1972). Although family lines were blurred in this way, genealogy was of utmost importance to the Hawaiians. Most of the old chants provide information on lineage.

Old Hawaiian society had an established class system, and the *ali'i* or royalty were believed to be directly descended from the gods. Thus, they had great *mana* or spiritual power. The bones of the *ali'i* were always hidden after death to preserve this *mana*. The commoners, or *maka'ainana*, were the farmers and fisherman and everyday workers, while the *kauwa* or slave class were marked by specific facial tattoos. The *kauwa* class was only allowed to live in certain designated areas and were routinely used for human sacrifices at the temples of the war god, Kuka'ilimoku (but never thrown into live volcanoes as the popular myth goes) (Malo, 1976).

Hawaiian scholars say that old Hawaii was neither purely a heterosexual nor homosexual, but a bisexual culture. Same-sex relationships were frequent, and many men and women had *aikane* or *punahele*: close friends or 'favourites' with whom they were at times involved sexually. No particular shame was associated with same-gender sex at all, and sodomy was not considered wrong. The words *ho'okamaka* and *moe aikane* were common terms used to denote same-sex relations. The more explicit way to put it was *upi laho*, which translates to something like testicle-pressing, or literally 'scrotum-squirting' (Pukui and Elbert, 1995). The word *aikane* itself relates to a particular sexual relationship in old Hawaii. It is a combination of *ai*, meaning to have sex with, and *kane*, meaning man. *Aikane* nowadays is used in Hawaii to mean 'good friends', and most Hawaiians don't realize what the word actually once pertained to (Pukui and Elbert, 1995).

Aikane relationships between men in old Hawaii are only recorded among the *ali'i* and high chiefs, but probably occurred between commoners as well. Royal *aikane* were a whole rank of men and some women who were granted special social and political status because of a sexual role with the royalty. Since the high *ali'i* had an obligation to mate with other specific royals, *aikane* were chosen voluntarily out of desire rather than duty. They were kept as exclusive concubines to the chiefs. Most *aikane* rose up from the lower ranks of royalty, and their sexual friendships with higher *ali'i* increased their *mana* and power (Morris, 1990). Although *aikane* were usually young male sexual companions to the *ali'i*, they often had their own wives and children, and were not seen as less masculine in any way. *Aikane* relationships didn't seem to be regulated by any 'top or bottom' order, and they were regardless of age or ranking. There were also female *aikane* (the word often occurs in the Pele goddess legends), but since women were subjugated in many aspects of society, the caste of royal *aikane* was male-dominated (Morris, 1990). The *aikane* role seems to have been honourable and noble, and was not hidden at all. In fact, it was even boasted about to shocked European sailors. *Aikane* relations were talked about freely and often in Hawaiian culture, since they were an important part of the royal hierarchy and had social value (Morris, 1990).

Traditionally, it is documented that the first Europeans to set eyes on the Hawaiian Islands were aboard Captain James Cook's vessel in 1779 (despite the historical evidence that Spaniards described coming across strikingly similar islands in 1627). When he first appeared, Cook was mistaken for the Hawaiian god Lono, since he was white, appeared during the Lono harvest festival, and his sails resembled the banners used to represent Lono (Joesting, 1972).

The ship journals during this voyage described a culture that was ambiguously bisexual to Western eyes. Cook's men wrote horrified accounts of close, brotherly *aikane* relationships within the *ali'i* – 'a shocking inversion of the laws of nature, they bestow all those affections upon them that were intended for the other sex', as one of the sailors put it. They recorded the kings of Maui, Kauai and the Big Island all having their own *aikane*. There is even one account of Chief Kalanikoa of Kauai asking if a certain young handsome European sailor would become his personal *aikane* for a little while, and he offered six valuable hogs for him (Morris, 1990).

Certain passages of the Cook expedition journals have long been overlooked by heterosexual scholars. In the early 1990s, Robert J. Morris made a concerted study of the logs from the ships *Discovery* and *Resolution*, which revealed some vital records of old Hawaiian culture (Morris, 1990):

From the log of David Samwell, ship's surgeon, 29th of January, 1779:
'Of this Class [*aikane*] are Parea [Palea] and Cani-Coah [Kanekoa] and their business is to commit the Sin of Onan upon the old King. This, however strange it may appear, is fact, as we learnt from the frequent Enquiries about this curious Custom, and it is an office that is esteemed honourable among them & they have frequently asked us on seeing a handsome young fellow if he was not an Ikany [*aikane*] to some of us.'

From the log of Charles Clerke, second in command, March, 1779:
'. . . every Aree [*ali'i*] according to his rank keeps so many women and so many young men (I'car'nies [*aikane*] as they call them) for the amusement of his leisure hours; they talk of this infernal practice with all the indifference in the world, nor do I suppose they imagine any degree of infamy in it.'

From Samwell's log of the 10th of February, 1779:
'He [Kamehameha] with many of his attendants took up quarters on board the ship for the Night: among them is a Young Man of whom he seems very fond, which does not in the least surprise us, as we have had opportunities before of being acquainted with a detestable part of his Character which he is not in the least anxious to conceal.'

Besides the tradition of *aikane*, another notable queer aspect of the Hawaiian culture is the *mahu*. Transvestism was, and still is, frequent in parts of Polynesia, where a man may choose to don women's apparel, grow up as a girl and even become a wife of another man, perhaps one of several, sometimes even cutting his/her thighs to 'menstruate'. Some traditions tell of a male, usually a younger brother, being compelled to take on the feminine role of family caretaker and keeper of traditions when a suitable daughter is lacking. *Mahu* in old Hawaii referred either to an effeminate male or a masculine female – someone who took on the opposite gender's role. Whether or not that meant homosexuality was not important. They held a necessary role in the *'ohana* and were not outcasts. Some Hawaiians profess that *mahus* were sometimes encouraged to follow the warriors into battle, not to fight but to provide a female role while the men were away from their homes for so long (Malo, 1976).

Nowadays the word *mahu* usually refers to a local male transvestite or an effeminate man, who is primarily gay and non-white. At times it is also used simply to mean any gay man, even a 'butch muffy,' or a 'fag' from the Mainland, in local slang terms. *Mahu* is now seldom used for women, and there is really no Hawaiian word for lesbian (Pukui and Elbert, 1995). Molokai in particular is known for its resident *mahus* who live and work within the local society with few problems.

Despite aspects of an inclusive, *'ohana* society, pre-contact Hawaii was still a vigorous and potent culture. Society was strictly regimented by the *ali'i* in the form of *kapu* (taboo) laws. For instance, stepping on the king's shadow was grounds for execution, as was failing to kneel or prostrate oneself in his presence. *Kapu* laws, however arbitrary, kept everyone in check and the chiefs' often-warring societies running somewhat smoothly (Joesting, 1972).

There are also accounts of women sometimes taking on the traditional male role of warrior and accompanying their men in battle. These Hawaiian Amazons were called *wahine kaua*, or battle women. They asked to be warriors, and the men obligingly trained them in this traditionally masculine occupation. They were seen as nothing especialy out of the ordinary, and they would return to their family life after war.

Between men and women, there were many *kapu* laws and social mores. Women could not fish nor even touch men's fishing equipment. Women could not eat certain kinds of fish, pork, coconuts or bananas. Despite these traditions, older women were looked upon very highly. They could become honorary *kupuna* or elders, setting down the laws of a region. In some instances, women were given the male role of priest from birth and could become a *na kaula wahine*, or woman-prophet (Joesting, 1972).

Some specific *kapu* may have worked to coincidentally encourage homosexual behaviour. One edict stated that after seven or eight years of age, men could only sleep in the men's house while women slept in the women's house. King Kamehameha himself practised this law. Men and women could not eat together, only with members of the same sex. However, there are accounts of *mahu* men being allowed to eat and sleep with the women as one of them (Tregaskis, 1973).

With the fall of the *kapu* system and the coincidental arrival of the first European missionaries shortly after, in 1820, many old Hawaiian customs slowly became extinct. Although it is easy to condemn the oppressive missionaries for the obvious destruction they inflicted upon Hawaiian culture (not to mention the custom of wearing lots of clothes!), the good ones did set up hospitals and schools for the islanders. They also helped to create the first Hawaiian alphabet and written language. Their adversaries, the whalers, made prostitutes out of the women and displayed less concern for the native-born. There are similarities between Hawaiian and Christian beliefs. The Hawaiian creation myth closely mirrors the one in Genesis. The Hawaiians also believed in a great god Lono who would return to Earth, and in the loving and forgiving high god Kane, to whom all life was sacred.

During this time of cultural upheaval, many *mahus* were involved in carrying on the outlawed *hula* dance and chants clandestinely. Even today, many gay men are *kumu hula* (mentors of *hula*) and *hula* dancers, and are respected for their talents and creative abilities.

A good personal illustration of how homosexuality was viewed in recent Hawaiian history is the case of writer and poet Charles Warren Stoddard. A one-time secretary to Mark Twain and friend of queer poet Walt Whitman, this 'Boy Poet of San Francisco', as he was known, set off to Hawaii in 1864 at the age of twenty-one in search of adventure. Corresponding with his friend Mr Whitman, he explained that among the islands he could act out his 'nature' in a way that he could not, 'even in California, where men are tolerably bold'. Stoddard had not only fallen in love with Hawaii's beauty and culture, but with many 'coffee-coloured' teenaged boys. His descriptions of rapturous evenings spent with island youths fills his stories with blatant homoeroticism, like passages from this story about a visit to Molokai in 1869: 'I was taken in, fed, and petted in every possible way, and finally put to bed, where Kana-ana monopolized me, growling in true savage fashion if anyone came near. I didn't sleep much, after all. I must have been excited.' And, 'Again and again, he would come with a delicious banana to the bed where I was lying, and insist upon my gorging myself . . . He would mesmerize me into a most refreshing sleep with a prolonged and pleasing manipulation' (Stoddard, 1869/1987). In the autobiographical story 'Chumming with a Savage,' which took place in one of Molokai's lush north-shore valleys, Stoddard slips out in the middle of the night by canoe, only to have his 'little sea-god' Kana-ana rushing madly after him, completely naked in the waves, calling out his name.

Although blatantly homoerotic, in the late nineteenth century homosexual escapades were not considered a valid reality, and many critics at the time brushed Stoddard's work off as colourful, and even silly. Stoddard travelled a number of times to Hawaii and Tahiti, each time falling in love with 'untrammelled youths', calling them by the intimate phrase 'aikane – bosom friend'. Stoddard's tropical affairs were passionate and earnest, but ill-fated. Usually his accounts ended with an agonizing departure, unable to fulfill this 'impossible love'. In spite of this, his personal accounts shed a revealing light on homosexuality in Hawaii in the late nineteenth century.

MODERN GAY RIGHTS AND POLITICS

Although Hawaii is seen as one of the most liberal and leftist-leaning states in the United States. (earning it the nickname 'The People's Republic of Hawaii'), the current political reality of the islands is complex. Politics and culture are two constantly intertwined entities, and nowhere else is this more true than in Hawaii.

The possibility in the 1990s that Hawaii would be the first state in the United States to grant same-sex marriages shone a political spotlight on Hawaii that it had never experienced before. Gay and lesbian tourists in general tend to be concerned about the general political climate of the places they travel to, and whether they will be accepted there, and in the interests of safety and comfort will tend to support gay-friendly destinations. Given this attitude, political developments in Hawaii are pivotal in our discussion of the development of gay tourism.

Since Hawaii was the first US state to legalize abortion and ratify the Equal Rights Amendment, Hawaii seems like a natural environment for the legalization of same-sex civil marriages. The irony is that Hawaii has a rural and traditionalist electorate state-wide, an island culture that discourages forwardness and 'boat-rocking', and a somewhat politically indifferent gay community. Given also the tremendous national backlash against same-sex marriage, both in the media and in other states' legislatures, it is understandable that the road has been a long and bumpy one, filled with enormous blocks.

First, it is important to highlight the history of gay rights in Hawaii up to the 1990s. Media is a good place to begin to gauge the attitudes of the times, and articles from the 1960s seem to illustrate growing acceptance of homosexuality. In 1963 for example, the *Honolulu Advertiser* ran a three-part article entitled 'The Deviate', about the growing problem of homosexuality in the Honolulu community. In 1964 there was an article about transvestites and the people who liked to watch them. Reference was made to a law passed that same year that required all men dressed as women to wear a card that said 'I'm a boy' or 'I'm a male.' In 1967 there was another article about 'The Strange World of Oahu's Different People', and in 1968, a piece about Hawaii's so-called loneliest citizens: 'Mahus are People, too'. It wasn't until 1969 that the paper finally relented and ran a more positive article that suggested homosexuality was actually natural for some people.

Homosexual acts in private were decriminalized in Hawaii in the early 1970s. In 1975, Hawaii's first homosexual protection bill was introduced in the state legislature. It was passed by the House but rejected by the Senate. In 1977 it was reintroduced but died in committee, and in 1978 a gay rights amendment to the state constitution was also killed off. It wasn't until 1992 that a law prohibiting job discrimination based on sexual orientation was finally passed by the state legislature.

The same-sex marriage issue began in December of 1990, when three homo-sexual couples (two lesbian and one male) applied for marriage licences at the Honolulu City Hall. They were denied a couple of months later. Attorney Dan Foley filed a suit on their behalf, which became known as the *Baehr vs. Miike* case. The case was ultimately appealed to the State Supreme Court, which ruled in favour of the gay couples in 1993. In the Court's opinion, the state was refusing to grant marriage licences (and thus marriage rights) due to the sex of couples applying. Technically, the sexual orientation of the couples had nothing to do with it. The Hawaii State Constitution is probably the most human rights-oriented state constitution in the United States, and strongly prohibits discrimi-nation based on sex/gender. Although this amazing ruling was handed back down to a lower court, and did not become law, it made headline news around the globe. Thus began the backlash against 'Hawaii's gay marriages'. State

legislatures across the United States scrambled to pass laws and change consti-
tutions limiting marriage to one man and one woman. Hawaii's ruling ultimately
led to President Clinton reluctantly signing the Defense of Marriage Act to make
sure no other state would have to recognize what Hawaii had done (or, what
everybody perceived it had done).

In retaliation to the Supreme Court's 1993 ruling, the Hawaii legislature
abruptly passed Act 217 in the spring of 1994. The Act asserted that procreation
was the basis for marriage. This was despite the fact that procreation had been
taken *out* of the statute in 1984 as discriminatory against the elderly and
disabled. The act was widely understood as ineffective and unconstitutional.
Two other attempts to amend the state constitution were killed in legislative
committees. One interesting thing that Act 217 did was to create a Commission
on Sexual Orientation and the Law. The Commission looked at marriage rights
and privileges, heard public testimony and examined many witnesses. In late
1995, after studying the overwhelming evidence, the Commission recommended
full marriage benefits for same-sex couples. In late 1996, when the issue was
relayed into a lower court, Judge Kevin Chang finally ruled that there was no
compelling state interest in *not* issuing marriage licences to same-sex couples.
That monumental decision technically allowed same-sex marriage in Hawaii. But
the Department of Health refused to issue licences. Judge Chang granted a stay,
which meant it went back to the State Supreme Court.

In the meantime, a very watered-down form of same-sex marriage was passed
on 1 July 1997, called the Reciprocal Beneficiaries Act. It gave only 60 out of the
400 benefits that married people enjoy. The licence is technically a legal
document between two unmarried people (a mother and son could get one). It
covers important areas of insurance, worker's compensation, hospital visits,
survivorship rights and survivorship benefits. And it must be said, it is better
than most domestic partnership laws in effect locally and regionally around the
United States. However, in actual usage, the Reciprocal Beneficiaries Act has
proved to be quite weak, with many challenging its very function. Many say the
licence is not worth the paper it is written on. One thing that appeals to mainland
gays is the fact that one does not need to be a resident to obtain an 'RB' licence.
It could also prove beneficial for insurance policies and estate planning in other
states.

The State Supreme Court was expected to rule on Judge Chang's verdict in
favour of gays in early 1998. This would have been the final ruling and, whatever
the outcome, it would be legally binding. The Hawaii Supreme Court, which had
already ruled in favour once, would have no choice but to abide and allow same-
sex couples the right to marry. However, the Supreme Court held off on its ruling.

It was decided that this sensitive civil rights issue should go to unprecedented popular statewide vote in November instead. The results were disastrous. Mainland money on both sides of the issue began pouring into Hawaii. The conservative political group Save Traditional Marriage began distasteful television and print ads, including one with actors portraying tourists explaining why they wouldn't visit Hawaii if the ruling was passed, and another with a child reading a same-sex marriage book and asking disturbing questions. The group Protect Our Constitution, funded in part by the gay political entity Human Rights Campaign, was on the other end, itself criticized for linking the issue to abortion and sweeping the homosexual aspects of the issue under the rug. Political sign-waving along Hawaii's streets, a quaint island tradition during election time, at times turned into ugly shouting matches. The 'land of Aloha' appeared to be losing its inclusive spirit. Over 70 per cent of the vote was against same-sex marriage. Many island gays and lesbians who had long felt safe and accepted in Hawaii began to question their presence on the islands. Conservative groups announced a victory of common sense and denounced those who labelled them 'homophobic'.

Why didn't same-sex marriage pass? It could have been the strong presence of the Mormon and Catholic churches on the islands that resulted in funding for this campaign, but the 'gay' side had almost the same level of funding. It could also have been the fact that Hawaii's voters tended to be elderly, or that Hawaii had wrestled with the issue for so long that even liberal voters had become sick of it. Tourist-fuelled Hawaii is also very sensitive about its image on the mainland, and did not want to be labelled as a land of extremists. Or simply, it could have been that same-sex marriage was just too radical and far-reaching for modest Hawaii to tackle.

A few days after the vote, in late 1998, Governor Ben Cayetano dedicated himself to passing a strong Domestic Partnership Bill in place of gay marriage. In December of 1999, over a year after the vote, the State Supreme Court announced a reversal of the lower court order and ruled in favour of Miike against the gay and lesbian plaintiffs.

In 2000, two state representatives (one from Oahu and one from the Big Island) brought forth Hawaii House Bill (HB) 1468 that introduced a Civil Union Bill (similar to Vermont's). The Bill would have allowed for almost everything but the 'marriage' word. It was not heard in committee by the deadline necessary to keep it alive, and died in March of 2001. There wasn't enough support in the House Committee on Judiciary and Hawaiian Affairs, the only committee to which the Bill was assigned, to pass it out for further consideration.

HB 1468 was open to any two adults regardless of sex, over the age of eighteen, who were otherwise competent to enter into a legal contract. The Bill did not mandate religious solemnization, rather leaving that question up to the individual churches, as the issuance of a civil union licence would come from the Director of the Department of Health. The Bill also would have allowed for state recognition of substantially similar legal arrangements from other jurisdictions. Activists say they will endeavour to get the Bill introduced in the next Legislative Session, to begin in January 2002.

As far as local gay Hawaii activism during this whole battle is concerned, in the early 1990s the Hawaii Equal Rights Marriage Project (HERMP) was established in Honolulu to help raise funds for the legal costs of *Baehr vs. Miike*. In 1997 HERMP became Marriage Project Hawaii, which now informs the public, media and legislature about the court cases and civil rights issues involved in same-sex marriage and equal rights. A group called the Civil Unions–Civil Rights Movement announced its birth in December of 2000, and is undertaking non-violent protests such as sit-ins and walks to draw attention to the remaining needs of Hawaii's gay citizens, as well as community and religious outreach. Their hope is that someday Hawaii will grant civil unions to same-sex couples.

In the summer of 2000 Vermont instead of Hawaii became the first US state to issue same-sex 'civil unions'. Vermont has experienced much exposure from both the gay and straight press for its decision, and gay tourism to Vermont has boomed as a result of the ability of out-of-state residents to get married. Hawaii, in nearly a decade-long economic slump (due to government corruption, the lack of economic diversity and inability to initiate new economic projects) did not end up enjoying these tourism benefits of becoming the first ground-breaking state to legalize same-sex marriage. But just the exposure during the 1990s about 'Hawaii same-sex marriages' was enough to bring many gays and lesbians visiting as well as moving to the warm islands as permanent residents, invigorating local politics and gay life.

MODERN HAWAIIAN VIEWS AND ATTITUDES TOWARDS HOMOSEXUALITY

Aloha is a word that is in common usage in Hawaii's tourism industry to mean hello and goodbye. The word literally translates as: 'the breath of life' (Pukui and Elbert, 1995), and is used by island residents to denote an attitude of love, forgiveness and friendship. Hawaiians are known the world over to be naturally warm, generous and kind people. To live *aloha* simply means to live in the light, to do unto others as you would have them do unto you. *Aloha* is the keystone to understanding the (theoretical) spirit of inclusiveness in Hawaii. Geographically limited and forced to rely on one another to survive, Hawaiians have always emphasized harmony and acceptance of individual differences. Everyone has a place in society, as previously mentioned in respect to *mahu*. The Hawaiian culture has always been traditionally tolerant with its famous 'hang loose' attitude. Subsequent immigrant groups for the most part have embraced this, making for a society where unique distinctions are celebrated and seen as beneficial. This sense of *'ohana,* or a circle of close friends and family, includes gays and lesbians too. This is after all a culture where men regularly wear flowers on their head and sing in falsetto. The small handful of male street hustlers in Waikiki is usually allowed to carry on business, and many straights will visit gay restaurants or gay bars without a hint of embarrassment. In fact, nearly all gay businesses around the state cater to both straights and queers (Link, 1999).

Gays in Hawaii still face the same challenges as they do elsewhere. In some island neighbourhoods, towns and beaches, gay or lesbian couples may not feel welcome. Public displays of affection do not happen too often between gays, even in Honolulu. Gay-bashing is not unheard of, job and housing discrimination happens, and undercover stings on cruise spots, with televising of the offender's face as a shame tactic, have also occurred. The strong influence of Catholic and Mormon congregations in local politics and attitudes is also felt, especially in the political arena.

Hawaii still has a strong family-based society with Asian influences. Some ethnic groups view coming out as bringing shame upon the whole family. Coming out on an island where everyone has known you since you were a child may not even be necessary in the Western sense. For others, the family and the *'ohana,* is more important than one member's sexual orientation, and queers are integrated with *aloha* (Aki, 1995). As Tania Jo Ingrahm, the former editor of the gay and lesbian publication *Island Lifestyle*, says:

> Hawaii is not a large place, only one million people statewide, and our communities are spread across five major islands. Overall, the local people are accepting. Hawaii is laid back . . . people don't get upset as easily about things as Mainlanders do, and that is also seen in relationship to gays and lesbians. For many people in the non-gay community it's just not a big deal. The aloha spirit is here (Link, 1999: 105).

For many Hawaiians no outing is necessary. You just are who you are, no explanation or specific details are warranted, since blatant forwardness has always been frowned upon in the Hawaiian culture. Many local gays and lesbians do not identify themselves with the mainstream gay world at all. Their race or heritage is a much more important issue than their sexual orientation. This leads to a situation where many island residents never bother coming out at all. There are many stories of local men who enjoy having sex with gay men, only to remain in a heterosexual posture, never admitting to or fully living out this side of themselves. It is common for these 'closeted' men to remain living with their families, all the while pursuing guys on the side. Since they are not 'muffy' (effeminate) types, they are not 'gay' (Aki, 1995).

On the American mainland, the culture allows 'straight-acting' gay men to be more easily accepted into the cultural framework, while effeminate men are more ridiculed and seen as a threat to the masculine society. In Hawaii, the opposite holds true. Effeminate men are historically accepted within the Poly-nesian culture, and one finds many 'muffies' happily integrated in Samoa, Tahiti and other parts of the Pacific (Aki, 1995). Kawika Trask, who is the former owner of Punani's, a mixed gay and straight bar in Honolulu, states: 'Being gay is part of the Polynesian heritage. There are *mahus* all over the South Pacific and honey, everyone's got a muffy in their family! They're the ones who take care of the family, look after the kids. Maybe no one talks about it, but they're accepted' (Link, 1999).

A case in point of the tendency about straight-acting gays not being out is Ryan Best, who lived and surfed on Oahu and wrote software in his spare time. He was originally from the mainland, surfed in Hawaiian waters for years, and found that even though he was out, many other masculine surfers were not:

> I've told people in gay bars that I'm a surfer, and their eyes kind of glaze over, like *Wow*! There have been other times I recognize other surfers in gay bars. It's frustrating for me because there are all these good looking guys out there on the waves, but for the most part they won't risk it [coming out] . . . the surfers know that there's cruising at some of the beaches, but they usually won't venture in. As far as local resident surfers being out, at least in a Mainland sense, it doesn't happen too often. I have one other gay surf buddy and he's pretty closeted (Link, 1999: 80).

Ryan describes Hawaii as a very tolerant place, but ironically, due to its size many people don't feel free to come out since everyone knows them: 'A lot of the time it's an understood thing, and people don't need to tell everyone they're gay. But the surf world can be homophobic, even paranoid about it at times. I tried to start a group of gay dedicated surfers and I barely received any calls' (Link, 1999: 80).

The story is different from island to island and ethnic group to ethnic group. Hawaii is famous for its racial diversity where it seems no one race is dominant throughout the islands; although European-Americans do make up the largest ethnic group. A common island saying is 'Everyone's a minority in Hawaii.' Most people born on the islands are of mixed Asian, Pacific Islander and/or European descent. Sadly, pure-blood Hawaiians are few and far between (the majority are located on the private island of Niihau), although there are a lot of people that are part-Hawaiian. Most non-white people get lumped into the category of 'locals'. However, these locals may still be proud of their Filipino, Samoan or Japanese roots and practices. A minority's distinct attitude towards gays can override the general consensus (Aki, 1995).

In my research and interviews, the tendency was for Hawaiians to be the most accepting of homosexuals as long as explicit sexual acts were not spoken of (Link, 1999). The Hawaiians have an 'implicit' culture where things are hinted at, but it is seen as rude and aggressive to bring them up directly. Japanese and Chinese residents appear to be the most closeted, lying to their own families about their sexuality and not forming long-term romantic relationships with other gays. The European-Americans tend towards a liberal live-and-let-live attitude towards gays, but that group also makes up the main driving force behind fundamental religious politics in Hawaii as well.

Many residents, especially on the outer islands, broadly describe Hawaii as two societies: one that is locally born and raised (hence 'local'), and one that has immigrated to the islands (hence 'mainland'). The locals tend to be of mixed race and brown-skinned, while the mainlanders are usually white. The racial tensions between the two groups can at times be tangible. Many white people don't feel comfortable visiting remote parts of islands where they are eyed suspiciously by the locals and treated as outsiders, even though they may have lived in the islands for years. Many locals feel that their culture has been subverted by American influences and lifestyles, and that sensitivity to their culture by white people is distinctly lacking. Also, Hawaiians and part-Hawaiians are the most economically disadvantaged ethnic group in the state, while many white people who move to the islands are retirees with financial resources. For locals, their ancestors died from foreign diseases, their language was nearly lost, and they have been treated as the lowest group on the islands.

Another gap between the two societies is pidgin English. Technically called 'Hawaii Creole English', pidgin has its roots in Hawaii's plantation days when different nationalities needed to communicate with the white landowners and with each other. It is not a language but an abbreviated form of English peppered with local phrases and slang with a distinct and heavy island accent. Proper Hawaiian and the informal pidgin often overlap. Pidgin is colourful and usually difficult for the uninitiated to understand (Simonson, 1981). Since many *haoles* (whites) cannot speak pidgin, they are not able to blend into 'local' society. The ones who can speak pidgin have better relationships with locals, but even these relationships can be strained for lack of cultural understanding between the two societies. Honolulu, with its modern metropolitan atmosphere, is perhaps the main exception to this scenario.

Unlike native American Indians who are specifically protected by the American Constitution, Hawaiians have no rights to ancestral lands, economic autonomy and college tuition funds. Most importantly, they have no right to organize their own nation (as do native American nations on the mainland). In 1993 President Bill Clinton signed an official apology on behalf of the American businessmen who overthrew and deposed the Hawaiian Queen Lili'uokalani in 1893. It acknowledged the deprivation of the rights of native Hawaiians to self-determination. This was because the Hawaiian people never officially and voluntarily relinquished their claim to sovereignty. The United Nations also recognizes this fact. This has helped fuel the Hawaiian islands' sovereignty movement, which is now focused on retribution and compensation for ceded lands. Most residents of Hawaii favour a 'nation-within-a-nation' framework for the Hawaiian people. Most sovereignty activist groups seek only to have a council of native Hawaiians consulted to approve all land transactions in the state. A handful of groups advocate complete secession from the United States, causing much controversy within the *haole* community. The movement has grown in the last ten years, and is a potentially divisive issue in the future.

Ku'umeaaloha Gomes is a professor at the University of Hawaii at Manoa, where she teaches a class on gays and lesbians in Hawaii. She is also the founder of Na Mamo O Hawaii (Hawaiian Lesbian and Gay Activists). She regularly holds anti-oppression workshops on interrupting oppressive behaviours. Although a big part of her work is about the sovereignty issue for native Hawaiians, Gomes explains her group is multi-issue (Link, 1999: 36): 'We wanted to show that the same-sex marriage issue is not just about middle-class, white transplants to the islands, but also about people that are born here, in our family.' The issue of heterosexism is also a factor for Hawaiians as well: 'We as native Hawaiians who are gay do not want our Hawaiian community to become our colonizers, and prevent us from our equality in society ... Na Mamo O Hawaii is trying to be the bridge between the Hawaiian and the gay communities.' Gomes' view is that heterosexism, sexism, racism and classism are all interrelated, and must be tackled as a whole:

> The gay communities and the Hawaiian movement need to interact. The native people are the most oppressed here, with no right to self-government, and the gay community cannot isolate the issues. . . . For a lot of residents, they have come here as gay people into this place, and they have to realize that the native Hawaiians are their hosts. They should know the history and understand it, and celebrate the culture (Link, 1999: 36).

HAWAII'S GAY INFRASTRUCTURE: OVERVIEW AND RECENT CHANGES

Some visitors expect Hawaii to be a homosexual holiday party heaven like Palm Springs, Provincetown, Key West, or other American warm-weather gay resorts. That is not the case. The rural aspects of the islands, and the limited general infrastructure, make for a rather tame gay holiday, even in the city of Honolulu. Hawaii is actually more for the eco-adventure or honeymooning type of vacationers. Many travellers with high expectations of a large and uniform gay scene in Hawaii are usually disappointed. Despite the attention Hawaii gets for its liberal politics and lifestyle, there are no major gay parts of town, no all-gay resort areas, and relatively few gay island establishments to patronize. And as with a lot of small businesses in Hawaii, many gay-oriented ones have a hard time surviving. The reasons could be isolation, island culture and lack of community support. Ironically, it is probably also due to the fact, that gays *are* more integrated into the general society here than in other places.

Mainland homosexuals have been moving to the islands for decades, including a large influx in the 1970s. Some are attracted to the warm culture and climate; others come for reasons of health or simply to escape the typical American lifestyle. Many find that residing in the islands, with its high cost of living and limited job opportunities, is a very different experience to *vacationing* on the islands, and it is common for many of these mainlanders to move back after a short stint as residents. Other mainlanders stay, and migrating from large gay cities, these transplants have invigorated and organized the island's overall queer community, though whitewashing it in the process. Separated from their own mainland families for one reason or another, these *haoles* (whites) and other mainlanders are more involved with politics and setting up an alternative gay society. The local born and raised don't feel the need to be as defiant in their gayness. Their focus is more on the *'ohana* and their own extended community.

Nearly all established gay nightlife in Hawaii happens in Waikiki. The traditional gay centre was up until recently a unique stretch along Kuhio Avenue between Kalaimoku Street and Lewers Street. The block was given relatively inexpensive rent for decades by the benevolent gay landowner Bob McGoon, who also owns the gay-friendly Eaton Square mall. Market pressures finally won out in 1997, and this funky block of old shops and buildings was sold to make way for a modern shopping centre – a common occurrence in Honolulu. The loss of this 'gay block' was devastating to Hawaii's gay and lesbian community, since nearly all of the queer establishments in Honolulu resided here. The majority of them never reopened, due to Waikiki's high rents and the fickleness of local gay consumers. In addition, the state's main gay newsmagazine for almost a decade, *Island Lifestyle*, printed its last issue in August of 1998.

The original home of the famous Hula's Bar and Lei Stand stood on the west end of the Kuhio block. Nestled under a majestic banyan tree for nearly a quarter of a century, it was a Honolulu icon, along with adjoining bars Trixx and Treats. Hula's was one of the few businesses that did reopen, and its current home is across the street from the Honolulu Zoo on Kapahulu. It is on the second floor of the Grand Waikiki Hotel, with large windows overlooking the tranquil park. Since Hula's has always been the epicenter of Hawaii's gay universe, it was expected that other gay businesses would follow in that area. (To date, none have.) The new Hula's business has dropped dramatically since its move, and there has been speculation that it too will close.

The only gay accommodation in Waikiki for years, the Hotel Honolulu, standing on the east end of the Kuhio block, closed in 2000. Luckily, The Cabana at Waikiki, a gay-owned hotel, opened its doors in 1999, and is now the only gay accommodation. Through staunch marketing and word of mouth, it has been one of the only bright spots in Hawaii's gay business community.

Eaton Square, an enclosed courtyard-style group of buildings located in a section of northwestern Waikiki, also acts as a small gay enclave. Eaton Square has a couple of private sex clubs for men and a bar. The existence of these businesses is a direct result of this complex being owned by Bob McGoon, owner of the old Kuhio gay block.

Within the islands, gay lifestyles can vary radically. Being gay on Oahu, with its openly homosexual beaches and bars, is completely different to being gay on rural Molokai, where wearing full-time drag is an acceptable way to be 'gay'. Gay communities between the islands don't interact much, except maybe through Honolulu, leading to a situation where gay visitors may know much more about gay Hawaii than gay residents do. This geographical isolation makes for a distinct mood on each neighbour island. A local saying states that the Hawaiian islands are like sisters, each with their own personality and character; this is mirrored in the gay communities.

The following is an overview of Hawaii's gay business infrastructure, taken from the *Rainbow Handbook Hawaii* (Link, 1999). The numbers reflect only gay-owned or gay-marketed establishments:

Accommodations: 57 (nearly all bed and breakfast variety)
Tour companies: 17
Restaurants: 11
Bars/Pubs/Clubs: 10
Publications/Newsletters: 8
Stores: 4
AIDS Bike-a-thons: 1
Gay TV shows: 1

These statistics reflect the lack of nightlife and emphasis on bed and breakfasts run by people out of their homes. Many of these businesses listed also serve heterosexuals as well.

ATTEMPTS AT GAY TOURISM IN HAWAII

Tourist marketing, aimed directly at gay and lesbian travellers, has experienced a boom in recent years. London, Paris, Amsterdam, Berlin, Key West, Palm Springs, Montreal and other places have produced brochures and marketing campaigns aimed at this lucrative market. With Hawaii's reputation as a gay-friendly destination with progressive politics, an open culture and a tolerant populace, gays have Hawaii high on their list of vacation destinations. In 1999 a poll conducted by Community Marketing, Inc. & Travel Alternatives Group (a gay travel market research group based in San Francisco) rated Hawaii as the second most popular travel destination in the United States among gay American travellers (see Roth and Luongo, this volume, for more recent results).

With all these factors working for Hawaii, it would seem to follow that the state was ripe for a gay marketing campaign. The only product available for marketing to gay tourists was *The Pocket Guide to Hawaii* (Kay, 1998), a small advertising-funded booklet produced by Pacific Ocean Holidays, a gay tour agency (with supporting material on their website). Most tourists obtained the pocket guide once in Hawaii. There were only a couple of privately funded Hawaii-based websites that included gay listings or information.

When I decided to publish the *Rainbow Handbook Hawaii* (Link, 1999), there was nothing other than this pocket guide for gay tourists. In fact, the divisive geography of the islands made for little cohesion and interaction between gay businesses on the other islands. My book was the first attempt at gathering all the gay and lesbian information for the whole state in one place, including gay tour operators, bed and breakfasts (many of which were illegal due to Hawaii's strict zoning laws and did not advertise), bars (again, some of which were very discreet) and other resources such as gay groups and AIDS agencies. The *Rainbow Handbook Hawaii* broke new ground, introducing gay business people to each other who lived within a few miles of one another, but never knew of each other's existence (see Figure 3.1).

During my media campaign, I sent copies of my book to each visitor's bureau on the four major Hawaiian islands, since each acted separately at that time from the others. I received a letter back from the visitor's bureau on Kauai that informed me that I was promoting illegal behaviour by encouraging nude sunbathing on the beaches listed in the *Rainbow Handbook Hawaii*. Nude sunbathing *is* technically illegal in Hawaii, although *de facto* nude beaches have existed on the islands since the 1930s, and are popular with locals and tourists alike, both gay and heterosexual. The tone of the letter was cold, and copies of the letter had been concurrently sent to the mayor's office and chief of police. I used this rebuff to my advantage, sending out news releases to local media that the Kauai Visitor's Bureau had rejected my efforts and my book. I was interviewed on statewide television news about the rejection, and the lack of support from the state visitor's bureau for gay tourism. The story was also covered in local newspapers.

After this media exposure, the Visitor's Bureau was apparently ready to talk about gay tourism with gay business people. Together with Jack Law, a gay activist and owner of Hula's, we decided to bring in a gay marketing expert from San Francisco and for all of us to meet with the Hawaii Visitor's and Convention Bureau to discuss the possibility of gay marketing for Hawaii. We met with the highest marketing people in the organization, showing them similar programmes put out by other bureaus, and explaining how a little investment could work in attracting gay and lesbian tourists to the islands, since so many social factors and positive perceptions about Hawaii for gays were already in place. Our plan

Figure 3.1. *Rainbow Handbook Hawaii.* *Source*: Matthew Link, Link Publications.

was that after we secured partial funding through the Visitor's Bureau, it would be much easier to collect additional funds through individual businesses for a co-op advertising campaign for gay Hawaii.

After the course of two meetings with the Bureau, we were given the cold shoulder and basically told that they did not have the budget for such an undertaking, even though we were asking for a mere $10,000 for our co-operative campaign, and that we would raise the rest of the money through other gay business people. They alluded to how difficult it was for them to obtain budgets for any undertaking, and especially hard for a 'controversial' one such as gay marketing. They also told us they had no means in place for specialized campaigns, and that they 'target no one group in particular'. I left the state in order to work for a gay travel publication and website in California, and to date no one else has attempted to launch a gay-marketed campaign for Hawaii.

CONCLUSION

Hawaii remains an enigma: tolerant yet closeted; progressive yet traditional; liberal but wary; gay-friendly but not gay-positive. Hawaii is and always has been her own woman – unique and defiant in her uniqueness to a fault. The irony is that despite the overwhelming vote by Hawaii's residents against civil marriage rights for gays, the closing down of much of Honolulu's gay infrastructure, and the refusal of its Visitor's Bureau to support gay tourism, Hawaii remains popular with gay tourists. Despite the lack of gay marriage laws, same-sex couples still flock to Hawaii to get 'married'. Despite the lack of gay nightlife, single gay men still flock to Honolulu. And despite lack of initiative on the government's part, most gay men and lesbians feel it is a gay-positive state. This is largely because most visitors' (gay or straight) perceptions of Hawaii are based on tourist mythology, and do not encompass the island's underlying history, events and dynamics.

Hawaii is famous for perpetuating a perfect illusion of herself. In fact, in its golden age from the 1940s through to the 1970s, Hawaii was perhaps the first hugely successful tropical mass-marketed destination, a case-study in its own exploitation. Through images on pineapple cans and sugar boxes, through glamorous TV shows and movies, and most of all through slick brochures and travel agents, Hawaii still prides itself on being 'Paradise', and most tourists who stay only a few days heartily agree. Yet, despite the throngs of tourists and plastic atmosphere of some of the state, Hawaii's natural wonders, friendly people and mellow atmosphere still reign. But scratch beneath the surface, and economic troubles, racial tensions and a schizophrenic attitude towards gay people remains.

So, what steps could be implemented to make Hawaii a truly 'gay' destination? I believe they would be two-fold. One would happen on the political front. If the state government was serious about civil rights for minorities it would pass a civil union law, or at least a stronger version of the Reciprocal Beneficiary License. This would not only allow Hawaii's gay and lesbian tax-paying citizens to enjoy the rights offered to the majority, but it would also attract gay men and lesbians from other parts of America to come to Hawaii to get 'married' (Vermont allows out-of-state residents to marry there, for example). Given that the Reciprocal Beneficiary License already exists, it would be easier to develop that rather than go through another messy legal battle and vote, to pass 'gay marriage', which won't happen again anyway.

The second would be for the Hawaii Visitors and Convention Bureau to act like business people instead of government bureaucrats and support a wider range and diversity of tourism. Instead of merely thinking of Hawaii in terms of mass hotel-packaged tour groups (which is a kind of tourist dinosaur), why not implement bolder campaigns, to attract ecotourism, young travellers, racial minorities and gays and lesbians to its shores? Recent surveys suggest that gays spend more money on vacations, travel more frequently and are more loyal to destinations and companies that go out of their way to prove their gay-friendliness (see also Stuber, this volume). There are many other destinations actively courting the gay vacation dollar, and if Hawaii does not get into the twenty-first century, it will be losing an important future market. Gay press trips, sponsoring of gay events and funding of gay-marketing programmes are some easy first steps to take.

Hawaii needs to think differently in order to survive the coming decades. It will take more than mere beauty and warmth to compete with the wide range of international modern destinations now available to the traveller. The islands' marketing efforts have paid off handsomely in the past, but they need radically rethinking in order to keep pace with developments elsewhere. The Hawaiian economic downturn of the 1990s shows that the time to do this is now. Let's hope Hawaii can rise to the challenge.

REFERENCES

Aki, S. L. (1995), 'Attitudes Toward Homosexuality in Hawaii. Hilo, Big Island', unpublished PhD Thesis, University of Hawaii.

Cunningham, S. (1995), *Hawaiian Religion and Magic*. St Paul, MN: Llewellyn Publications.

Handy, E. S. C. and Pukui, M. K. (1972), *The Polynesian Family System in Ka'u, Hawaii*. Rutland, VT: Charles S. Tuttle.

Ingrahm, T. J. (ed.) (1998), *Island Lifestyle*. Honolulu, HI: Island Lifestyle.

Joesting, E. (1972), *Hawaii: An Uncommon History*. New York: Norton.

Kay, J. (ed.) (1998), *Pocket Guide to Hawaii*. Honolulu, HI: Pacific Ocean Holidays.

Link, M. (1999) (2nd edn), *Rainbow Handbook Hawaii*. Kona, HI Missing Link Productions.

Malo, D. (1976), *Mo'olelo Hawai'i* (Hawaiian Antiquities), (trans. Nathaniel B. Emerson, first published 1898). Honolulu, HW: Bishop Museum Press.

Morris, R. J. (1990), 'Aikane: accounts of same-sex relationships in the journals of Captain Cook's third voyage.' *Journal of Homosexuality*, 19 (4): 231–58.

Pukui, M. K. and Elbert, S. H. (1995), *New Pocket Hawaiian Dictionary*. Honolulu, HI: University of Hawaii Press.

Simonson, D. (1981), *Pidgin To Da Max*. Honolulu, HI: Bess Press.

Stoddard, C. W. (ed. Winston Leyland) (1869/1987), *Cruising the South Seas*. San Francisco, CA: Gay Sunshine Press.

Tregaskis, R. (1973), *The Warrior King: Hawaii's Kamehameha the Great*. Honolulu, HI: Falmouth Press.

Westervelt, W. D. (1977), *Hawaiian Historical Legends*. Rutland, VT: Charles S. Tuttle.

WEBSITES

Rainbow Handbook Hawaii: *www.rainbowhandbook.com*

Gay-friendly Hawaii websites

Kalani eco-resort: *www.kalani.com*
The Cabana at Waikiki: *www.cabana-waikiki.com*
Royal Hawaiian Weddings: *www.hawaiigayweddings.com*

CHAPTER 4

Tourism Marketing Aimed at Gay Men and Lesbians: A Business Perspective

MICHAEL STUBER

INTRODUCTION

The grand historic gay milestones such as Magnus Hirschfeld's work in the 1890s or the Stonewall Riots in 1969 had societal, cultural and political content. It was not until the 1980s that economic aspects of gay life in the workplace or marketplace were discovered as relevant themes for scientists, gay activists, media or companies (see Susser, 1986; Zillich, 1988; Escoffier, 1995; Stuber, 1998a, b; Kates, 1998; Wardlow, 1996). Obviously, gay tourism has economic dimensions, and this chapter offers a systematic overview of marketing to gays and lesbians in the travel industry.

In 1994 I was one of the first practitioners in Europe to develop professional frameworks around gay/lesbian workplace and marketplace issues, interacting with the media, the business world and academic research. This work became one building block for the foundation, in 1997, of a European consulting company for 'diversity management and marketing'. Many statements in this chapter are a reflection of experiences during those years – especially with regard to co-operation with companies – and draw on previously unpublished reports or reflect personal views that require scientific validation (Stuber, 1999; 2000; 2001a, b).

WHY CONSIDER MARKETING TO GAYS AND LESBIANS?

Over the years, we have talked to many professionals in different business fields who had never previously considered marketing to gay men and lesbians. During the first discussions, the most commonly posed question was: 'Why do we need to do something special for homosexuals?' Such a question points to various underlying feelings or assumptions, which may not be conscious. Here are some we have identified several times:

- some people don't feel comfortable with 'the issue' and therefore prefer to avoid it;
- some people are not aware of the fact that usual mainstream communication actively excludes homosexuals by only talking about and/or showing hetero-sexuals (couples or straight male/female stereotypes);
- some people do not ask themselves: 'Why not?';
- some people are not aware of the societal situation of gay men and lesbians.

Actually, if these and similar factors drive people to question the necessity to consider homosexual market segments, they point directly to some possible answers, and they stress the relevance of our considerations.

In the United States, 'diversity' and 'managing diversity' have become big issues since the mid 1980s (an early press coverage can be found in Copeland, 1988a; 1988b). Companies, Non-Governmental Organizations and the public sector were looking for new tools to handle differences in the workforce, in the marketplace and in society. But which kind of diversity should be taken into consideration: all the ways in which we may differ, or just 'race and gender'? In order to get to grips with the new approach, diversity specialists developed a framework to structure differences in the early 1990s (Gardenswartz and Row, 1994). They described 'core dimensions' for diversity, which included those factors that people are given 'by nature', things that nobody can change (see Figure 4.1).

The key principle is that any characteristic over which people have no control should have top priority when it comes to 'protection against discrimination'. Sexual orientation, no matter whether to the opposite sex, the same sex or to both sexes, is one of those factors about which no one makes a choice. Homosexuality is just as natural (or normal) as heterosexuality. It is no coinci-dence that the new Article 13 of the Treaty of the European Union (EU), the draft Charter for Human Rights in the EU, and the non-discrimination directive

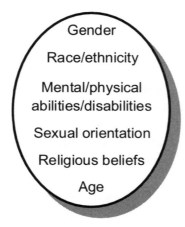

Gender

Race/ethnicity

Mental/physical
abilities/disabilities

Sexual orientation

Religious beliefs

Age

Figure 4.1 Core dimensions of diversity. *Source*: based on Gardenswartz and Rowe (1994).

of the EU, all mention the same six dimensions as being of equal, fundamental relevance.

Unfortunately, marketing has not yet picked up many of the themes that are suggested by the above framework. Few efforts are being made to attract not-so-mainstream segments of the overall market: senior citizens, ethnic minorities, religious communities, people with disabilities, young people – and even a majority of society is all too often overlooked: women. Overall, it seems that most Western societies still need to come to terms with the fact that significant diversity exists, and that most differences are just matter-of-fact and not something to define in terms of superiority or inferiority.

As for homosexuality, we have observed that a lot of people say that they 'don't have a problem with it – but . . .' Further discussion often leads to the impression that almost everybody, except the person we are talking to, will most probably be less favourable about the issue. It could be argued that this shows some kind of projection – our counterpart does not want to reveal his or her negative attitude and therefore quotes third-party opposition. Such examples certainly provide evidence for the fact that homophobia still prevails in some parts of the business world.

At the same time, it should be remembered that it is not 'sexuality' that creates tension, since heterosexuality has been a well-accepted theme in marketing and communication. As briefly mentioned earlier on, heterosexuality is already a common issue in marketing: family special offers or pictures of happy (straight) couples in tourism catalogues are but two examples. In commercials, it is also quite common that the products are advertised as making a person (more) attractive for members of the opposite sex. Another usual mechanism is that consumer communication stereotypes gender roles, showing 'real men' or 'good women', while gay characters are missing in these contexts. If marketers looked at the world through the eyes of gay people more often, they would immediately understand that such communication does not reach homosexual consumers at all – it is simply irrelevant for them, as it does not show any part of their personal reality. However, gay men and lesbians have become used to the fact that mainstream society does not actively acknowledge their existence (Gross, 1996). Therefore, homosexual consumers are sometimes not even expecting 'targeted communication'.

Overall, it can be said that most current marketing and communication in the tourism industry does not reach gay men and lesbians as consumers. This presents a strong business case to enhance existing strategies in this respect.

For marketing, it is important that homosexuals have obtained a new position in society – both in terms of self-understanding and in terms of acceptance. For the United States, Adams (1993) provides an overview. For Europe, evidence can be found in three figures:

- the increasing number of Gay Pride events that are taking place;
- the increasing number of gay men and lesbians attending these events;
- the increasing number of heterosexual visitors coming to these events.

A growing number of events prove that gay men and lesbians are everywhere, not only in the big metropolitan cities. The increasing total number of partici-pants shows that homosexuals are no longer willing to hide themselves or be assimilated into the mainstream. A growing number of straight visitors prove that the acceptance and integration of gay men and lesbians in 'normal' society is not just a myth but has become tangible reality. Actually, the figures speak for themselves: the European Pride Organizers' Association (EPOA) has gathered data since 1993 about events taking place, and, since 1995, about the number of participants and visitors. Between 1993 and 2000, the number of European countries where Gay Pride events were being organized more than doubled (from ten to twenty-two), while the overall number of events has more than tripled over the same period (from nineteen to sixty-eight) (see Figure 4.2). The total number of participants and visitors increased from approximately 700,000 in 1995 to more than 3.5 million people in 2000 (see Figure 4.3).

Products and services in the travel industry have become increasingly alike and interchangeable. Therefore, companies are striving to create clear-cut

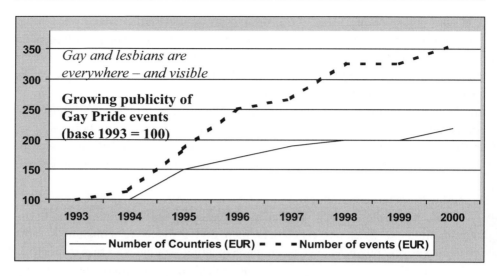

Figure 4.2 Gay Pride events in Europe. *Sources*: EPOA, mi.st [Consulting

market profiles and brands that distinguish themselves from others. One of the corporate strategies is leadership and innovation, to be ahead of competitors. Including gay men and lesbians in marketing is still one of the business models not many companies have adopted. At the same time, its relevance is likely to

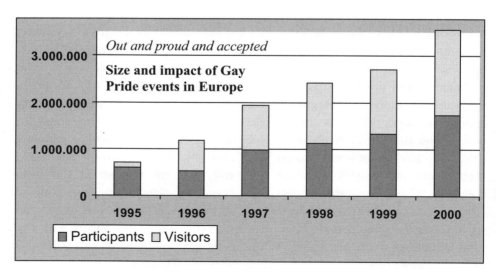

Figure 4.3 Gay Pride participants and visitors (Europe). *Sources*: EPOA, mi.st [Consulting

grow (see Dwek, 1999, for a discussion of 'marketers' reluctant flirtation with gays'). Combining the two aspects, we argue that gay marketing may serve as one strategic differentiator and as an investment in the future. Added value is provided by the fact that brands that enter a segment first may well remain the leaders in that niche. Companies whose competitors are moving in an inclusive diversity direction will feel significant pressure to follow. Otherwise, the market(s) will regard it as a deficit not to acknowledge the existing diversity of consumers.

The gay community began to rate tourism companies with regard to their gay-friendliness some years ago. A variety of travel guides, on-line and off-line, provide information on the conditions under which gay men and lesbians can take vacations around the world. A large on-line survey by *Advocate* magazine, for example, revealed that 54 per cent of respondents had experienced some form of homophobia on vacation (see, Kirby, 1999; Savage, 1999; Flippen, 1999). More specifically, the well-respected travel specialists *Out & About* analyse airlines, hotel chains and car-rental companies on a regular basis with regard to sexual orientation issues. This 'travel industry rating' looks not only at gay marketing issues but also at the level of service, value-added features and internal policies regarding gay men and lesbians (see *www.outandabout.com*).

At this point we may conclude that a number of strong business reasons speak for gay marketing. At least this option should be thoroughly considered, while the relatively small potential of backlash should be investigated on a case-by-case basis.

DO GAY MEN AND LESBIANS QUALIFY AS A TARGET GROUP?

Before any marketing concept can be developed for a specific segment, marketers are advised to assess whether the potential target group fulfils the criteria to serve as a segment of its own (see Fugate, 1993, and Penaloza, 1996, for an alternative view). Criteria often used to decide on target groups include (Mucha, 1999):

- accessibility
- measurability
- profitability
- stability
- (homogeneous) consumer behaviour

In addition to looking at all these criteria, it is important to add strategic considerations to this list, especially in the light of the sociopolitical aspects touched above.

Accessiblity

Whether or not a target group can be accessed is crucial when considering a market segment. If it cannot be reached (directly or in a focused way), there is obviously little sense in defining it as a target group. In the case of gay men and lesbians, the fact that they were excluded from society or discriminated against for many years has made them form their own communities, using specific symbols and coded language. It has also lead to the development of specific infrastructure, including bars, restaurants, clubs, shops, media and events. Today, most of this can be used to communicate with gay and lesbian consumers (see Wilke, 1996). For example, we have calculated that in Germany one-quarter of the total homosexual population can be reached directly through such community platforms. This is a higher penetration than most other segments offer. In addition, gay men and lesbians outside the community may be reached by using specific codes (e.g. the pink triangle, the rainbow flag) or phrases that have double meanings or specific relevance (e.g. 'family', 'lifestyle', 'diversity', 'a friend of Dorothy').

Measurability

This criterion raises one of the historic questions about homosexuals: how many people of each population are gay, lesbian or bisexual? Even at the beginning of the twenty-first century, it seems that there are as many answers to this question as researchers. Some major examples of research are: Fay et al. (1989); Billy et al. (1993); Michael et al. (1994); Binson et al. (1995); Sell et al. (1995); and Bagley and Tremblay (1996), and overviews can be found in Diamond (1993) and Singer and Deschamps (1994). Without scientific ambition, but through the marketing lens, we analysed (internally) 28 studies that enquired about sexual identities or sexual behaviour using large samples. Taken together, the results suggest that the percentage of men who are 'gay' is between 7 and 9 per cent while the percentage of women who are 'lesbian' is about half that figure, between 3 and 5 per cent.

Furthermore, it must be noted that social scientists claim that only half of all homosexuals are open about their sexual orientation (to themselves and/or to others) (see e.g. Schneider et al., 1998). Those 50 per cent who are not open about their homosexuality, at least to a certain degree or towards themselves, are almost irrelevant for marketing purposes, although a certain sub-segment might be accessible through specific messages. Those 50 per cent who live openly as gay men or lesbians might do so as part of the 'community'. Considering that only one quarter of all homosexuals can be reached directly through gay communication platforms (see above), we conclude that the 'remaining quarter' lives openly as gay or lesbian, but assimilated in mainstream society. This sub-segment is probably more difficult to reach, but it is accessible through mainstream media.

In order to evaluate marketing activities, another facet of measurability must be considered, i.e. whether representative samples or relevant panels are available to carry out market research. Although many institutes have tried, we are not aware of a single representative survey of the homosexual target group (Fett, 1998; Mucha, 1999). In fact, practically every sampling method through which gay men and lesbians are contacted contains inherent biases (interviews in the scene/at events, questionnaires online/in printed media, etc.). Nevertheless, all companies that have wanted specific information have found ways to generate relevant research results – mostly through focus groups or panels (see e.g. Adams, 1993). It appears that the lack of representative samples has never had a negative impact on the decision to define a homosexual target group.

Profitability

The costs of a gay marketing campaign determine one part of the potential profit the segment may offer. Actually, many gay and lesbian communication platforms charge less money per thousand contacts than 'normal media' (Adams, 1993). Nevertheless, homosexual communication platforms offer excellent quality contacts, as very few non-gay readers buy gay magazines or attend lesbian events.

Profitability will also be influenced by the demographic profile of the target group in question. In the case of gay men and lesbians, numerous surveys have shown that on average, homosexuals are young and well-educated, have no children but high (disposable) income. Simmons Research for example, conducted the first gay reader survey in the United States (in 1990 for *Advocate* (Miller, 1990; 1992a, b), which was expanded in 1998 on a larger scale (for eight gay newspapers). The report by Overlooked Opinions in 1992 received much public attention as well (Schwartz, 1992; Johnson, 1993a, b). More recent surveys for the travel industry include Community Marketing (2001) and Our World (1996). The first large survey in the UK was for *Gay Times* (cited in Wharton, 1995) and in Germany by Remy (1995). However (all) these data are based on samples from the gay community, and are therefore highly biased. In addition, the results contrast with workplace surveys that suggest that gay men and lesbians are still discriminated against and therefore remain in disadvantaged situations (see Badgett, 1997).

Although no strong evidence can be given, we want to argue none the less that an attractive demographic profile may be taken for granted for out gay men. The higher-than-average education suggested by research cited above can be explained by the fact that 'coming out' is probably more difficult (i.e. less likely) in a traditional 'workers' environment'. Thus, few openly gay people are found in that (large) societal group, while a relatively high percentage is well-educated. Good education often correlates with higher income, which may explain the figures cited by many reader/user surveys. Finally, gay men and lesbians are less likely to have children than their straight peers, giving them more financial flexibility, and they might be more inclined to live in the present rather than in the future.

Stability

As sexual orientation is one of the 'natural dimensions' (see above), gay men and lesbians have always existed, and most probably always will exist, in any human society. What does vary quite significantly is their position in different societal or cultural systems. But our considerations are focused on the Western world where the acceptance of homosexuals has been increasing, and probably will continue to do so in the future. In addition, the self-confidence of gay men and lesbians is growing steadily. Overall, it can be said that the segment offers enough stability over time for marketing purposes.

Homogeneous consumer behaviour

Following common stereotypes, gay men and lesbians form a homogeneous target group of 'early adopters', 'hedonists' and 'aesthetes' (Remy, 1995; Luken-bill, 1995). But as we have shown earlier in this chapter, the total population of homosexuals is almost as diverse as society as a whole, and in some respects maybe even more diverse (Friedheim, 1998). Therefore, we argue that there is no such thing as 'gay consumer behaviour'. Instead, we have developed a framework to explain different, seemingly conflicting, consumer patterns, which we, and some of our clients, have identified through (internal) market research in the gay market.

The fundamental question arises as to whether or not there are things that all gay men and lesbians have in common. We want to argue that three factors are relevant in a marketing context:

- coming-out experience – whether smooth and easy or difficult and painful;
- awareness of existing exclusion – no matter whether the person has experienced such himself/herself;
- awareness of existing discrimination – no matter whether the person has experienced such himself/herself.

Psychologists and social scientists have long agreed that such experiences or awareness certainly has some impact on a person – ranging from minor personality changes to the sad examples of higher-than-average suicide rates found among gay youth in Western societies (see Bowes, 1996, for a discussion of the effects of discrimination and exclusion). We want to discuss the possible consumer-related impact that these three factors may have.

Coming-out experience

It is widely acknowledged that coming out is a turning point in a homosexual's life. Some feel they want to redefine themselves, using all the freedom their new situation offers. They are glad to be different and they might well be ready to show this to some extent. Others feel a great emptiness after having lost (some of) the values and/or points of reference that have helped them navigate their lives until then. They might well try to compensate this deficit by striving for as much 'normality' as possible. Depending on the effects of the coming-out process, a person might become either an unconventional, trend-setting, or a conservative, classical type of consumer. Both types are spread widely in the gay market segment.

Exclusion

Although the situation of homosexuals in Western societies has improved in terms of acceptance and integration, gender-stereotypes still prevail and being heterosexual is still seen to be the norm. This atmosphere tends to send messages to gay men and lesbians that they are less welcome or less valued than straight people. Homosexuals know about this mechanism of exclusion, whether or not they have had such experience themselves. We assume that there are two major strategies for gay men and lesbians to deal with this situation: 'obeying' or 'uproar'.

The 'obeying type' will strive to create their own 'pockets of comfort' where they can live their lives, not bothering about the mainstream, and not being bothered by it. This type of consumer pays attention to issues such as 'home and gardening', cooking, health and frequent travelling to remote parts of the world – maybe in a discreetly gay context (Bosanko, 1995).

The 'uproar type' ignores mainstream attitudes and overcompensates for the negative feeling exclusion may cause by extensively enjoying 'queer' life to the affordable maximum. They go out and show the world that they are happy, beautiful and successfully participating in societal life – as gay men or lesbians. This type of consumer loves to dine out, to go shopping, to look for up-to-date fashion, to care about fitness and sports, and to travel to gay-friendly desti-nations or to gay events. Obviously, the two types present different product affinities and different communication patterns to be taken into account by marketers.

Discrimination

Similar to the awareness of existing exclusion, practically all gay men and lesbians know about discrimination against homosexuals. Again, this aware-ness exists whether or not a person is directly affected by any juridical, economic or social disadvantage. Social scientists describe group dynamics such as 'solidarity' caused by discrimination. The same applies for homosex-uals. As mentioned above, they have created their own 'gay community' with (a) diversified infrastructure catering for some of their specific needs; (b) sym-bols helping to identify members of the community; and (c) coded language to enable internal communication that is protected against insight from the exter-nal world.

With regard to consumer behaviour, the impact of discrimination-related communities on marketing is manifested in various ways:

- The segment shows stronger-than-average affinities for ethical marketing concepts such as charity marketing (Wagner, 1997; Fett, 1998).
- Overall, political correctness tends to be an important issue, i.e. no bad-taste joking about minorities, inclusive language, etc.
- Gay and lesbian consumers pay attention to charitable donations that a company may give back to gay/lesbian organizations so as to honour the business that is generated in the community (Mulryan, 1995).

- The reverse applies for companies that support anti-gay activities of any kind. Such policies have caused boycotts from the gay community in the past.
- It is not unusual for homosexual consumers to ask about the internal policies a company has installed with regard to providing equal protection, rights and benefits to their gay and lesbian employees.

Overall, no reliable information about the importance of the 'community' or 'discrimination' factor can be given. Some research suggests that the vast majority of gay and lesbian consumers prefer to buy from companies that openly show they care about homosexual issues or support gay/lesbian activities (Community Marketing, 1999). Other results show that product features and price as well as place and people are the overriding criteria on which homosexuals base their buying decisions, while gay-friendliness of any kind will come second or as a value-added factor. No matter where the truth lies, any marketer dealing with the gay/lesbian market will have to make sure he or she has insider information and contacts for his/her project available – in order to avoid 'political' mistakes.

Strategic considerations

It has been shown that the gay and lesbian segment fulfils commonly used criteria for identifying target groups. Large, high-profile companies, especially, will want to consider the strategic impact of gay marketing. A stakeholder-oriented 'check for negatives' helps to pinpoint pros and cons. In our consultancy work we use the following framework to present relevant factors:

- the market/consumer perspective: gay community and homosexual individuals;
- the internal perspective: employees and corporate policy;
- the business environment: society, political landscape and business partners;
- the shareholder perspective: financial markets and/or public authorities.

Market and consumer perspectives

In previous sections, we showed that gay men and lesbians have become a more 'out and proud' and economically self-confident group that can be accessed by marketing. However, marketers should keep in mind that practically no societal group outside the mainstream will be specifically keen to be a market segment, and that there will always be homosexuals that regard marketing to gays and lesbians as inappropriate (Bowes, 1996). In addition, as mentioned above, the gay community has emerged as the major communication platform for gay marketing, and today offers many professional tools for this purpose. However, many parts of the community have their (historic) roots in the civil rights movement (gay and lesbian liberation), and this may still cause occasional tension with regard to the pure, hard business nature of marketing (see contributions in Gluckman and Reed, 1997, on this issue).

Marketers will always want to consider whether gay marketing moves might cause a backlash in established market segments, for instance from more traditional customers. A number of episodes are known in which special interest groups have attempted to make companies stop their marketing campaigns targeted at gays and lesbians. For example: religious groups attacked Levi's, American Airlines and Disney for their various gay-friendly activities, and Walt Disney Co. also faced resistance regarding their plan to produce a lesbian-themed series 'Ellen' (Morgenthau, 1997). However, the respective companies stood firm in the face of criticism, which may be seen as a form of loyalty (Adams, 1993). Nevertheless, companies, and especially high-profile companies, are advised to consider potential backlash and plan appropriate reaction prior to launching gay campaigns (see Baker, 1997, for an example of a balanced approach).

Another strategic market consideration is the question whether the gay/lesbian market segment can be used to initiate trends. The industry seems to agree on the fact that at least many homosexuals are so-called early adopters (Dwek, 1999; Caggiano, 1996). Finally, the gay/lesbian market may serve as a strategic niche for smaller brands that could not compete with their large competitors in the mainstream market. In the homosexual segment, not-so-common products or services can be positioned more easily as high-profile companies often overlook or exclude what they consider niches.

Internal perspective

Due to globalization and societal, cultural and political changes, the past fifteen years have seen a significant shift from widespread corporate monocultures to open, multicultural work environments. 'Diversity' has become more than a flavour of the month, and continues to shape large companies as well as small, innovative ones. In this context, gay men and lesbians became more accepted and integrated in the workplace, and their straight peers became more used to dealing with sexual orientation among other dimensions (Day and Schoenrade, 1997; Simons and Zuckerman, 1995; Caudron, 1995; Stuber, 1998a, b, c). In this light, internal stakeholders are much less likely to be a source of backlash than they might have been twenty years ago. Nevertheless, this issue requires attention when concrete marketing activities are planned.

Business environment

Over the past ten years, most Western societies have adopted a more open attitude towards gay men and lesbians. This can be seen in the results of large-scale polls that have been taken on current gay or lesbian issues (such as registered partnerships, etc.) (Schmalz, 1993, presents one of the earlier polls). In addition, the results usually showed that the younger generation feels more positive about diverse sexual orientation issues than senior citizens. Assuming relative stability of a person's core values, this means in turn that the society of the future will on average be more open than today's. We assume that there is also an interplay between general societal attitudes and the mass media, which are increasingly including homosexual issues in a non-sensational way. A significant number of series and films with gay characters are but examples of this development (e.g. 'Ellen', 'Queer as Folk', 'Lindenstrasse'). This rather new kind of content might be seen either as meeting the preferences of a 'modern' audience or as a reason for changing attitudes in mainstream society.

As political systems change according to societal developments, the legal situation of gay men and lesbians has improved in many Western countries. Moreover, some political systems even actively support equal rights for homosexuals in corporate environments. Such is the case in some states in the United States, where public contractors are required to prove that they are actively pursuing equal opportunity work, often including sexual orientation issues. In this context, companies might have to provide the same domestic partner benefits for their gay/lesbian employees as they do for heterosexuals regarding legally married spouses.

In the light of the above-stated developments, we see little risk that business partners of a company might perceive gay marketing as something negative. After all, there are no reports of cases where backlash has damaged a company's business or even made companies pull back from the market.

Shareholder perspective

In the case of private investors, the overriding criteria to support or criticize business activities are stock price and profit or 'return on investment'. If both perform well, no negative reaction may be expected from this side. We have already indicated that gay marketing is likely to be a profitable activity. Thus, private shareholders will probably favour such projects (Baker, *et al.*, 1995). Moreover, some stock indexes in the United States show that 'managing diversity' pays back. One example is the *Domini 400 Index*, which outperformed the *S&P 500 Reference Index* over many years (see *www.domini.com*).

In the travel industry, however, many companies or organizations are publicly owned (e.g. some airlines or railway companies, many tourist boards) or part of public authorities (e.g. some tourist boards). In this case, the shareholder perspective can slightly change and shift to a more political perspective. It might happen that gay marketing activities fit the political profile of one administration but not the preference of another one. Looking at the activities of large tourist boards, most of which are closely linked to the respective government/administration, it is clear that those destinations which approached the gay market first were mainly those countries or regions with a very open/liberal reputation: The Netherlands, Australia, Miami Beach and Key West (Elliot, 1992). Other destinations followed, and it may or may not be a coincidence that the British Tourist Authority did not launch gay marketing activities until the Labour government had installed itself in Downing Street.

Another example which might touch different strategic considerations is of Swiss Air, which runs gay and lesbian ads in the United States but didn't want to support the EuroGames that took place in Zurich, in their 'home country' Switzerland – the Dutch airline KLM then became proud sponsor of the event in 2000.

MARKETING TO GAY MEN AND LESBIANS

Before developing a marketing concept and a related campaign, fundamental questions need to be addressed. In the case of gay marketing, some specific considerations should be made which include (Fett, 1998):

- *Strategic positioning*: Are homosexual market segments fully integrated into the overall marketing strategy, or defined as one specific, separate target group?
- *Strategic approach*: Are homosexual issues addressed explicitly, implicitly, in a coded way, or not at all?

If gay men and lesbians were a fully integrated facet of a company's marketing, they would appear 'every now and then' in the market communication, and gay/lesbian media or other communication platforms would be regularly used –

among other media. This strategy seems to be applied by some of the big fashion or food brands that have never launched specific gay campaigns (e.g. Prada in the United States, Silk Cut in the UK, Sony in The Netherlands). The problem with this strategy is that gays and lesbians might not realize that they are in fact appreciated as customers – they might even see themselves limited to be 'cash-cows'. Integration might also happen in 'invisible' ways so that it is again not perceived.

In the travel industry, most activities targeted at gay men and lesbians are explicitly set up for gay and lesbian customers. It is necessary to show clearly that a tourism product is aimed at the homosexual market – a necessity that brands in other sectors might not face.

On the market side, our own internal market research has identified two big themes for strategic gay marketing in this respect. Many gay or lesbian consumers would like to see companies acknowledge homosexuals as one 'normal' part of reality – something natural and casual, integrated in day-to-day marketing and business. At the same time, gay men and lesbians demand open, clear and credible moves from companies trying to woo the gay community, meaning clear-cut gay/lesbian profiles, messages and activities.

We feel that in most cases, specific activities will be needed in the beginning of any gay marketing work while the ultimate objectives might be that gay men and lesbians become an integral yet visible part of most if not all marketing activities.

Gay and lesbian issues can be addressed along a continuum from open or explicit to invisible or neutral. Some of the common explicit approaches are the use of pictures with same-sex couples or simply using expressions like 'gay destination' or 'gay-friendly hotel'. Successful coded approaches often include the use of the rainbow (flag or colours) as the most important symbol of gay/lesbian solidarity or word-plays that have different meanings in a gay context than in the mainstream. The approach may also be neutral by avoiding any reference to lifestyle or sexual orientation. In such cases, the context (e.g. advertisement in a gay newspaper) will have to make sure the audience understands the implicit message that the offer is actually meant to appeal to homosexuals as well.

Integrated or specific positioning and explicit, coded or neutral approaches may be combined to different strategic gay marketing settings (see Figure 4.4).

Having described the strategic range for basic gay/lesbian marketing approaches, we may now proceed to present concrete building-blocks for gay marketing campaigns in order to describe relevant marketing contexts. These strategic directions will set the scene in which a marketing concept can be

Figure 4.4 Examples for implementing six possible strategies of gay marketing.

Positioning	Approach		
	Explicit	**Coded (symbols, phrases)**	**Implicit (neutral, invisible)**
Specific	Gay brochure, ad, website, special offers for gay organizations	Postcards with wordplays or rainbow colours	Handing out mainstream material on a gay event
Integrated	Gay pages in main(stream) catalogue	A clickable rainbow banner on a mainstream website	Mainstream, lifestyle and gender-neutral ad in gay magazine

developed. Specialists have used models of three, four or five 'Ps' for many years (see Kotler and Bliemel, 1995; Chrétien, 2000). Applied to gay marketing in the travel industry, the framework describes a wide field of possible options and alternative approaches:

- *product strategy*: using standard products or designing specific products for gay/lesbian consumers;
- *price strategy*: fixing low, standard or high prices;
- *promotion* (market communication): advertising or 'below-the-line' communication (i.e. all forms of communication other than traditional advertising), in homosexual or in mixed (mainstream) contexts;
- *place* (sales): using established (mainstream) or gay/lesbian-specific sales channels;
- *people* (mainly for the service industry): using gay/lesbian or mixed staff.

Product strategy

This part of a marketing strategy describes the features a product uses to attract customers from a market segment. We want to discuss three possibilities with regard to the gay market:

- standard products
- special products for gay/lesbian consumers
- variations of standard products.

Standard products, i.e. identical products for mainstream and gay and lesbian markets, are used when the product itself is highly complex. Air transportation or car rentals as well as hotel rooms are such products that can hardly be changed to meet the specific needs of a target group (pricing is not included in this consideration).

On the other hand, tour operators have created a large variety of special products for gay men and lesbians (Mackovich, 1998). Travel packages to Sydney Mardi Gras or lesbian cruises are but two examples from the field. Special products will only be profitable if their creation is not too expensive and enough profit can be generated. In the case of gay or lesbian cruises, tour operators have sometimes faced difficulties with destinations they integrated in their tour. Gay cruise ships were booed and harassed when docking at the Bahamas, and passengers not allowed to disembark at Cayman Islands in 1997 (Newman, 1998) and in Turkey in 2000. Special homosexual tourism products are certainly not an obvious option for everyone.

Some products can be changed in order to respond to some specific needs of gay men and lesbians. Examples of such variations can be found at tourist boards: the British Tourist Authority installed a toll-free gay/lesbian visitors' line through which travellers will reach the 'normal' call centre, but where the agent answering will be aware of the nature of the enquiry. Some tourist boards provide gay/lesbian welcome packages, which contain some specific information about homosexual infrastructure or events in addition to general information (see Figure 4.5 for examples).

A German hotel chain is planning to launch special rooms for female guests – in co-operation with a women's magazine. Beyond stereotypes, standard rooms will be complemented with selected features that women travelling alone might prefer over the standard features usually targeted at male guests.

Price strategy

This part of a marketing concept describes the price level for the products offered. The range for possible pricing covers not only 'normal or standard' prices but also lower or higher ones. A special model is the 'charity-related' pricing. Standard prices are probably the most common strategy if the product or the promotion already relates to a target group, or if price changes are

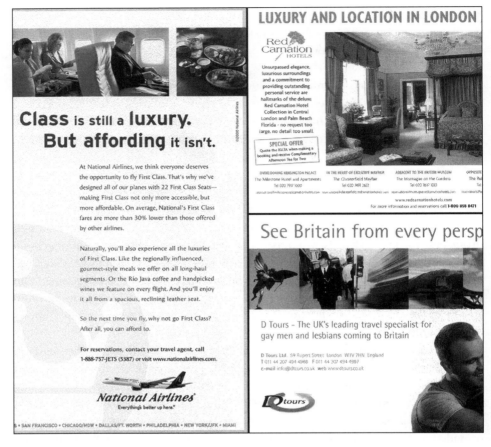

Figure 4.5 Product strategies: (a) National Airlines advertises for a standard transportation product (with no gay/lesbian aspect); (b) Red Carnation Hotels offer a complementary afternoon tea for IGLTA members (variation); (c) D Tours advertises as a specialized gay/lesbian incoming operator (specific product). *Sources*: (a) Dik Shimizu, Director Corporate Communications, National Airlines; (b) David Eck, Red Carnation Hotels; (c) Daryl Bennett, D Tours Ltd.

difficult to make. Lower prices will be used in highly competitive contexts, where many products are interchangeable (car rental, some transportation, some accommodation). Such may include promotional offers on special occasions. For example, Lufthansa USA offered discounts on standard airfares for participants of the gay and lesbian soccer world championship (Cologne, October 2000). Higher prices are often hidden behind variations of standard products through which companies try to increase their margin.

A common mechanism in the gay/lesbian market is the charity-related price model. The idea of this is that part of the revenue generated in the community (usually a fixed sum or a fixed percentage) is given back to some non-profit-making organization. Most famous is probably the Rainbow Card, a credit card by VISA targeted mainly at gay men and lesbians in the United States or the similar Red Ribbon International VISA card in the UK.

Promotion strategy (communication)

As described above, the gay and lesbian market provides different sub-segments with regard to self-identification and lifestyle, resulting in differing possibilities to access the respective group.

The vast majority of gay media, gay events and other gay-specific communication platforms provide access to those homosexuals who choose to live as part of the 'gay community'. Many other gay or lesbian consumers do not read specific publications or make any use of gay infrastructure. This part of the market can mainly be reached through mainstream communication. In both contexts, the different strategic approaches as described above may be applied. In addition, the range of possible communication tools is just as broad in gay and lesbian as it is in non-gay or mixed areas (see Figure 4.6). Obviously, one-to-one marketing such as direct mail won't make much sense to a mixed group if the offer is targeted at gay men and lesbians.

Advertising

Advertising to gay men and lesbians leads to similar results as in the mainstream: awareness for a brand or product rises. However, the context in which an ad is placed may change the impact it has. Many advertisements in gay media do not show gay-specific pictures, nor do they use explicit gay language. Obviously, the fact that a 'normal' ad appears in a homosexual magazine sends an implicitly pro-gay message (Levin, 1993). On the other hand, advertisement to gay men or lesbians in non-gay or mixed media needs to be explicit about some gay message or at least coded for a gay clientele in order to be meaningful to the target group. Some brands placed gay advertisements in the *New York Times* and similar media in order to reach gay men and lesbians beyond the community. Such advertisements might be too explicit for the mainstream audience, though, as was the case for a Virgin Vodka television advertisement showing a gay couple kissing (Snowdon, 1996) (see Figure 4.7 for a gay advertisement produced by the British Tourist Authority).

✔ effective	platform/context	
# sometimes effective	Gay	Mixed
Advertising	✔	✔
Public relations	✔	✔
Sponsoring	✔	#
Event marketing	✔	#
Promotion	✔	#
Direct mail	✔	
Co-operation marketing	✔	#
Online-marketing	✔	✔

Below-the-line (rows: Public relations through Online-marketing)

Figure 4.6 Communication strategies.

In the United States there are even specialized media for travel-related issues, such as *Our World* or *Gay Travel News*. These provide specific advertisement opportunities in the field of gay tourism.

Printed material

In order to communicate on below-the-line platforms, some kind of promotional material is needed. Naturally, most companies opt for brochures or posters highlighting their selling points (see Figure 4.7 for examples). Destinations and tour operators use brochures to disseminate the complex information about their products and services. Airlines, hotel chains and car rental companies focus more on brand marketing, involving less information but more emotional messages (flyers, stickers, badges). The pioneers from the field – Amsterdam, Miami, Australia, American Airlines – focused strongly on marketing to a travel industry audience (journalists, travel agents, tour operators, see Drummond, 1995). The objective must have been to reach multipliers and to generate sales.

The past three years saw the development of a new dimension in gay tourism marketing (mainly in the United States), led by the British Tourist Authority campaign, followed by Quebec/Montréal, Palm Springs and later France. It wasn't until these campaigns were initiated that full-colour brochures for end-consumers were produced. While the gay-specific perspective dominated earlier marketing efforts, often supported by gay/lesbian business guilds, the new style focused on all the major attractions a destination had to offer, presented in a gay context.

Public relations

In the light of past discrimination, gay men and lesbians tend to be reserved about, if not critical towards, external partners. They are, just as many other 'target groups', reluctant to see themselves as 'cash-cows' for big companies who might not care about the specifics of gay lives. At the same time, gay men and lesbians seem to trust other homosexuals more than 'externals'. Therefore, it is important for any gay marketing campaign that one intense communication stream is targeted at gay and lesbian multipliers, especially the media. In some cases the value of an eight-line article might be greater than that of a full-page advertisement. The first international invitation for journalists to Miami Beach was even reported in *Newsweek* magazine (Drummond, 1995).

Sponsoring

Traditional sponsoring may be the most effective way to show a company cares about issues that are important to gay men and lesbians. One important 'side effect' is that consumers usually don't perceive this as a (direct) marketing activity. The most important opportunities for sponsoring are gay/lesbian non-profit-making organizations or big events. Main sponsors usually receive special exposure and exclusive access to members or participants in defined contexts. One of the biggest sponsorships in recent years was KLM's support for the Gay Games in Amsterdam, 1998 (see Figure 4.8). All the large Gay Pride events in the United States, Great Britain and Germany offer sponsoring co-operation for companies.

Event marketing

Closely linked to event sponsoring are other forms of event marketing that may be applied in a gay context. One of the common tools is presence at events with some form of stand, booth or tabletop display. More promotional are flags or the active distribution of information (flyers, postcards) or give-aways. In the United

Figure 4.7 Printed material and advertising: (a) Promotion brochure 'The gay desti-nation' (Key West); (b) Gay/lesbian co-op advertising 'A rainbow of choices' (British Tourist Authority, London Tourist Board and British Airways Holidays); (c) Gay/Lesbian promotion leaflet 'Welcome in Hamburg'. *Sources*: (a) Albert Jennings, Florida Keys and Key West; (b) Bib Titley, British Tourism Authority; (c) Kummer von Börries, Hamburg Tourism.

States, specific events (Expos) for gay and lesbian tourism take place each year. Many companies exhibit at these events, reaching consumers who are specifi-cally interested in travel-related information. In Germany, most Gay Pride events offer companies a stand on the festival ground where information or give-aways can be spread, raffles or contests can be organized or recruiting contacts can be made. For the travel industry, events also serve as tourism products – for

transportation companies, tour operators, agents and suppliers (hotel, car rental companies) alike. But also the city or region where the event takes place might be extremely interested in attracting such events: the fourth Gay Games in 1994 were said to have brought $100 million into New York's economy (Tilsner, 1994). In 2001 Montreal is one of the very active bidding cities for the Gay Games 2006 (see Figure 4.9).

Promotion (sampling)

Active distribution may take place not only on events but also on 'the scene', where give-aways or information can be spread (contests, raffles). In the case of spirits or cigarettes, free samples are frequently offered. Give-aways often carry the logo of the respective brand or the URL of a related Internet site.

Figure 4.8 Sponsorship: (a) Sponsoring the Gay Games 1998 (Amsterdam), KLM coded postcard and sponsorship/co-op advertisement; (b) American Airlines platinum sponsorship of Human Rights Campaign HRC (banner on HRC website). *Sources*: (a) Sandra Mass, KLM; (b) Michael Fricke, American Airlines.

Direct mail

Another form of one-to-one marketing is direct mailing, which features mainly in the United States, where relevant databases are available, as well as a range of services through which direct marketing can be rolled out. These mechanisms would be regarded as highly unusual in most parts of Europe, where the use of a private address in a gay context would cause irritation on the consumer's side. Even in the United States, it seems to be effective, if not appropriate, to use community-based services to access gay men and lesbians directly. One professional service is Our Tribe promotion packs where almost any company can insert one of their special offers. Most of the cards provide direct-response

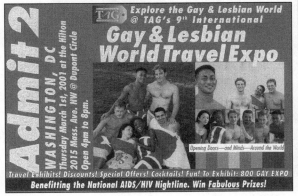

Figure 4.9 Event marketing: (a) Co-op promotion road show 'Gay and Away' at four German Gay Pride events; (b) Invitation to Gay & Lesbian Travel Expo; (c) Logo for Gay Games 2006, bid of Montreal. *Sources*; (a) Michael Stuber; (b) Tom Roth, Travel Alternatives Group; (c) Jean-François Perrier, Tourisme-Montreal.

opportunity. In Germany, direct mail can be organized in co-operation with mail-order companies that will piggyback promotional information in selected contexts (see Figure 4.10).

Co-op marketing

In the context of gay marketing campaigns, co-operating with 'internal' community organizations or companies should always be considered. The external partner benefits from the credibility and contacts of the insider, while the community partner benefits from the power and reputation the mainstream

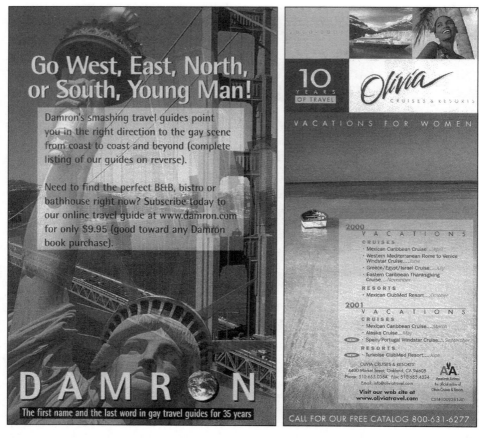

Figure 4.10 Direct mail and co-op marketing: (a) Damron advertisement; (b) Olivia Cruises advertisement; (c) Gay Guide to Palm Springs. *Sources*: (a) Gina Gatta, Damron Company; (b) Judy Werk, Olivia Cruises and Resorts; (c) Matthew Robinson, INN Advertising.

brand brings to the party (see Figure 4.10). Preferred co-op partners are tour operators, as their business is moving beyond image-building to generating revenue. (See Cogswell, 1996, for an example of co-operation between a large wholesaler and a gay tour company.)

A not-so-usual co-operation took place in the late 1990s in Germany, where the Stena Line, offering transportation between the European mainland and Great Britain and Scandinavia respectively, offered same-day return tickets at a discount rate. All of the revenue was donated to an AIDS-prevention organization, while profit was made from the money the travellers spent on board the

ferries. The project received a lot of publicity at almost no cost. A similar initiative is the special flights the German airline LTU offers on World AIDS Day. Tickets are 100 Euro. Passengers are given a two-hour flight from and to Düsseldorf with entertainment on board. Another form of co-operation may be organized with associations. Special membership rates can be offered, as a hotel chain and a car rental company does for members of the Völklinger Kreis (German gay managers' association).

Internet marketing

Some research results suggest that gay men and lesbians have a high affinity for the Internet (Community Marketing, 1999). Even the famous Gay Days at Disneyland have their roots in the Worldwide Web. Currently, a lot of information

Figure 4.11 Internet marketing and mainstream marketing: (a) Online travel resource QTmagazine.com; (b) One of two gay/lesbian pages in German (general) main guide of British Tourist Authority. *Sources*: (a) Serge Gojkovich, publisher, *QT Magazine*; (b) BTA.

is spread and collected via the Internet and a number of marketing opportunities can be found for the travel industry in particular. Quite a few portals, e-zines or other websites specialize in tourism issues, and an increasing number of companies install special sections or specific websites for their gay marketing activities. The latest and most innovative venture is *www.gayjet.com* where information and booking are actually linked (see Figure 4.11).

Place strategy (sales)

In the context of gay marketing, two major sales strategies can be applied. One is focusing on the gay community and its tour operators, travel agents and direct marketing opportunities. The second option is to use established mainstream structures in order to reach gay and lesbian consumers who do not use community-based services.

116

Considering the overall structure of the target group as described above, both sales strategies must be used in order to cover the larger part of the market. But most current activities focus on internal community places to sell their products, which is consistent with the fact that most communication is targeted at the community part of the market segment. Again, it has been the British Tourist Authority, who piloted a new style: in their mainstream catalogue for Germany, two pages on gay and lesbian Britain were included in 2000 and 2001. This way, homosexual clients who did not read the gay press were made aware of BTA's diversified customer focus and mainstream travellers were pointed to the fact that Britain is a destination that welcomes different kinds of visitors. This has increased the credibility of gay marketing activities significantly and has added integrated aspects to a specific campaign (see Figure 4.11).

People strategy

For almost any company, the 'face to the customer' is of vital importance. But the gay tourism arena seems to be somehow special, as the global network of experts and multipliers is tightly knit, for example in special interest associations such as the International Gay and Lesbian Travel Association. Naturally, the people involved in a marketing project will have to be part of the roll-out plan. In contrast to the more comprehensive diversity scene, gay marketing in the US travel industry is almost exclusively dominated by gay men and lesbians (Roth, 1995). This results in many excellent personal links that can easily be set up between gay representatives from 'mainstream companies' and their community partners. The downside can be that companies are accused of tokenism, and there are risks that gay men or lesbians in charge bias their work according to their own experience or preferences.

In Europe, the professionals working on gay marketing tend to come from various backgrounds. This might be due in part to the fact that the operations in different European countries are not as big in terms of staff numbers as they are in the United States, so that gay men or lesbians are often not 'available' to deal with gay issues. We want to argue that from a diversity standpoint, mixed teams should in general be preferred over homogeneous ones. Moreover, the message of inclusiveness and integration will be stronger and clearer if gay *and* straight representatives from a company welcome gay customers on board a plane, in a hotel or to a destination. Our work with travel industry companies included workshops with front-end employees (directly serving customers) from call centres and tourist information. This way, the respective companies ensure that their employees are aware of various differences between customers and this is not limited to sexual-orientation issues, but includes different lifestyles, gender-specific questions, ethnicity, religion and other dimensions of diversity.

LEARNING AND BENCHMARKING

Considering the overall framework for gay marketing as a whole, it is surprising how these opportunities have been overlooked for a long time. A small piece of research in Germany (Fett, 1998) tried to investigate the reasons behind this, and one of them was incredibly simple: lack of information. The survey asked for the criteria companies were using to select market segments. Later, marketers were asked about the information deficits they perceived regarding the gay/lesbian target group, which they said they were not considering. The four information deficits that came out strongest were at the same time among the five most important selection criteria for market segments (in general). These results show that one reason why many companies are still reluctant to include gay men and lesbians in their marketing plans is that they lack key information they need to make a positive (or negative) decision.

Apart from being herewith reminded of the necessity to collect in-depth information and do the related 'homework', there are more lessons, which companies and experts have already learned. And some cases have already made it into 'the history' of gay marketing in the travel industry.

The most common mistakes that companies and operators make can be summarized as follows:

- *isolating*: handling gay/lesbian issues as a separate project disconnected from (general) marketing activities;
- *simplifying*: reducing gay marketing to gay-specific issues (the scene, gay events, sexual issues) and over-emphasizing gay aspects of a product;
- *stereotyping*: getting stuck in clichés about gay men and lesbians, their lifestyles and preferences;
- *miracle agenda*: expecting quick wins with low budgets;
- *minimizing*: starting with no long-term, strategic plan and no inside community expertise;
- *all commercial*: focusing on advertisement and sales, ignoring below-the-line, the Internet and image-related factors.

Conversely, the most important success factors include:

- *strategic approach*: identifying the linkage of brands, products and strategic marketing with gay/lesbian values and realities;
- *inclusive approach*: dealing with diverse sexual orientation as one natural facet among many;
- *comprehensive approach*: thinking also about gay/lesbian employees, business partners and other stakeholders;
- *openness and loyalty*: making sure gay marketing is as public as any other marketing issue, standing firm in the face of criticism;
- *credibility*: getting involved in the community – associations, networks, even politics;
- *co-operation*: teaming with other companies or non-profits from within or outside the community – join forces (and budgets).

CONCLUSION

Today, there are no reasons not to consider marketing to gay men and lesbians as one of several options to attract customers. While heterosexuality has already become a widely accepted if not appreciated marketing theme, attraction to the same sex is an often overlooked or actively excluded variation of 'sexuality'. But gay men and lesbians have become increasingly visible, accepted and proud over the past decades, so that they can no longer be ignored. As major companies from almost all relevant sectors have started to woo homosexual market segments, other players see a competitive need to follow.

Analysing current segmentation criteria leads to the conclusion that gay men and lesbians qualify as a target group. Moreover, the homosexual market segment can be reached directly and cost-effectively, thus offering significant potential for profit and growth. Marketing to gays and lesbian also provides extra value as it creates public attention, and will be rewarded by loyal members of the community. A strategic, stakeholder-oriented check for negatives may help companies identify potential sources for backlash from markets, employees, business partners or shareholders. Such scenario-building is an important part of the professional development of a gay marketing campaign. It has to be highlighted, however, that the rewards from such activities have always out-weighed the limited negative reactions generated.

Marketing to gay men and lesbians requires consideration of a large variety of strategic and operative options, some of which are specific to the homosexual market. Gay/lesbian segments can be either integrated in the overall (mainstream) marketing or positioned as a separate target group. The approach to this market can be explicit, implicit or coded with symbolic language or signs. Companies planning to court the gay and lesbian segment will have to find out which combination of strategic options provides the best fit with their brand positioning and with their corporate policies. There are no general 'best ways' to set up a gay marketing strategy.

All the 'traditional elements' of the marketing mix (product, price, promotion, place, people) can be used to shape a gay campaign. Deciding on special products or variations of standard products, 'normal' prices or charity elements, mainstream or gay community sales partners are some of the options in this field. The design of the communication plan (promotion) is key to the success of a gay campaign. In addition to all marketing rules, the specific historical and societal background of gay men and lesbians must be taken into account. Stereotypes, politically incorrect statements, commercial overselling and controversial community issues must be avoided. Instead, a sophisticated combination of promotional and charitable mechanisms has proved to be the most promising approach.

Obviously, gay men and lesbians are not the easiest of all market segments to choose. But probably no other part of society has undergone such enormous developments during the past twenty years – and the business world has not yet responded to this.

Companies seem to follow societal trends only after a significant time-lag. This has already been the case for the integration of women and ethnic minorities in the workplace and the marketplace. Today, the corporate world struggles with yet another dimension of diversity, 'sexual orientation', which was a significant taboo throughout most of the twentieth century.

All business relies on the effective co-operation of different internal and external stakeholders. These stakeholders are becoming more diverse in many respects. Such developments present a strong business case for companies, driving them to anticipate these trends, acknowledge the value of individuality and realign their strategies accordingly.

In addition to shareholder values, however, personal values and interests drive businesses everywhere in the world. The spirit of diversity has not yet captured corporate cultures, so that traditional monocultures still prevail. These organizations cannot be expected to take the lead towards individuality. Nevertheless, business culture has already embarked on the diversity journey and will gradually discover the benefits of leveraging differences – all differences.

REFERENCES

Adams, M. (1993), 'The gay nineties', *Incentive*, September: 58–62.

Adams, M. (1996), 'Selling out', *Sales & Marketing Management*, 10: 78–88.

Badgett, M. V. L. (1997), 'Beyond biased samples: challenging the myths on the economic status of lesbians and gay men', in A. Gluckman and B. Reed (eds), *Homo Economics: Capitalism, Community and Lesbian and Gay Life*. London: Routledge.

Bagley, C. and Tremblay, P. (1996), 'On the prevalence of homosexuality and bisexuality in a random community survey of 750 men aged 18 to 27', *Journal of Homosexuality*, 36 (2): 1–18.

Baker, D. (1997) 'A history in ads', in A. Gluckman and B. Reed (eds), *Homo Economics: Capitalism, Community and Lesbian and Gay Life*. London: Routledge.

Baker, D. B., O'Brian Strub, S. and Henning, W. (1995), *Cracking the Corporate Closet: The 200 Best (and Worst) Companies to Work for, Buy from, and Invest in, If You're Gay or Lesbian – Even if You Aren't*. New York: HarperCollins.

Billy, J., Tanfer, K., Grady, W. and Klepinger, D. (1993), 'The sexual behaviour of men in the United States', *Family Planning Perspective*, 25: 52–60.

Binson, D., Michaels, S., Stall, R., Coates, T. J., Gagnon, J. H. and Catania, J. A. (1995), 'Prevalance and social distribution of men who have sex with men: United States and its urban centers', *Journal of Sex Research*, 32 (2): 345–54.

Bosanko, D. (1995), 'Stress and gay life', *American Demographics*, 1 March.

Bowes, J. E. (1996), 'Out of the closet and into the marketplace: meeting basic needs in the gay community', in D. L. Wardlow (ed.), *Gays, Lesbians, and Consumer Behaviour: Theory, Practice and Research Issues in Marketing*. New York: Haworth, pp. 219–43.

British Tourist Authority (BTA) (2000), *Media Coverage Gay Campaign (Germany)*. Frankfurt (internal).

Caggiano, C. (1996), 'A brew apart', *Inc.* 3: 62–9.

Caudron, S. (1995), 'Open the corporate closet to sexual orientation issues', *Personnel Journal*, August: 42–55.

Chrétien, J. B. (2000) 'Allocution', Presentation at the First International Conference on Gay Tourism, 7 April, New York.

Cogswell, D. (1996), 'A new marketing match', *Travel Agent*, 6 May: 58, 68.

Community Marketing (1999), *5th Annual Gay & Lesbian Travel Survey*. San Francisco, CA.

Community Marketing (2001), *6th Annual Gay & Lesbian Travel Survey*. San Francisco, CA.

Copeland, L. (1988a), 'Making the most of cultural differences at work (valuing diversity, part 1)', *Personnel*, 6: 52–60.

Copeland, L. (1988b), 'Pioneers and champions of change (valuing diversity, part 2)', *Personnel*, 7: 44–9.

Day, N. E. and Schoenrade, P. (1997), 'Staying in the closet versus coming out', *Personnel Psychology*, 1: 147–63.

Diamond, M. (1993), 'Homosexuality and bisexuality in different populations', *Archives of Sexual Behavior*, 22 (4): 291–310.

Drummond, T. (1995), 'Vamping for new visitors', *Time*, 25 September: 42–3.

Dwek, R. (1999), 'Pursuing the pink pound', *Marketing Business*, May: 12–15.

Elliot, S. (1992), 'Dutch promotion for gay travelers', *New York Times*, 10 June.

Elliot, S. (1994), 'A sharper view of gay consumers', *New York Times*, 9 June.

Escoffier, J. (1995), 'The material world', in L. Witt, T. Sherry and E. Marcus (eds), *Out in All Directions*. New York: Warner Books, pp. 569–78.

Fay, R. E., Turner, C. F., Klassen, A. D. and Gagnon, J. H. (1989), 'Prevalence and patterns of same-gender sexual contact among men', *Science*, 243: 338–48.

Fett, D. (1998), Zielgruppenmarketing für Homosexuelle in der Nahrungs- und Genussmittelindustrie – eine strategische Analyse, diploma thesis, Giessen University.

Flippen, A. (1999), 'Hot spots still sizzle', *Advocate*, 20 July: 39–44.

Friedheim, E. (1998), 'Bias hurts business', *Travel Agent*, 24 August: 21.

Fugate, D. L. (1993), 'Evaluating the US male homosexual and lesbian population as a viable target market segment', *Journal of Consumer Marketing*, 10 (4): 46–57.

Gardenswartz, L. and Rowe, A. (1994), *Diverse Teams at Work: Capitalizing on the Power of Diversity*. Chicago, IL: Irwin.

Gluckman, A. and Reed, B. (1997), 'The gay marketing moment', in A. Gluckman and B. Reed (eds), *Homo Economics: Capitalism, Community and Lesbian and Gay Life*. London: Routledge, pp. 3–9.

Gross, L. (1996) 'Out of the mainstream: sexual minorities and the mass media', in D. L. Wardlow (ed.), *Gays, Lesbians, and Consumer Behaviour: Theory, practice, and research issues in marketing*. New York: Haworth, pp. 19–46.

Harry, J. (1986), 'Sampling gay men', *Journal of Sex Research*, 1: 21–34.

Johnson, B. (1993a), 'The gay quandary', *Advertising Age*, 18 January: 29, 35.

Johnson, B. (1993b), 'Advocate's audit challenge', *Advertising Age*, 18 January: 3, 33, 37.

Kates, S. M. (1998), *Twenty Million New Customers: Understanding Gay Men's Consumer Behavior*. New York: Haworth.

Kirby, D. (1999), 'Trouble in paradise', *Advocate*, 20 July: 24–33.

Kotler, P. and Bliemel, F. (1995), *Marketing Management: Analyse, Planung und Steuerung* (8th edn). Stuttgart: Schaeffer-Poeschel.

Levin, G. (1993), 'Mainstream's domino effect: liquor, fragrance, clothing advertisers ease into gay magazines', *Advertising Age*, 64: 30, 32.

Lukenbill, G. (1995), *Untold Millions: Positioning your Business for the Gay and Lesbian Consumer Revolution*. New York: Harper.

Mackovich, R. (1998), 'The big gay boat ride beckons', *Icon*, April: 13–15.

Michael, R., Gagnon, J., Laumann, E. and Kolata, G. (1994), *Sex in America: a Definitive Study*. New York: Little, Brown & Co.

Miller, C. (1990), 'Gays are affluent but often overlooked market', *Marketing News*, 24 December: 2.

Miller, C. (1992a), 'Mainstream marketers decide time is right to target gays'. *Marketing News*, 20 July: 8, 15.

Miller, C. (1992b) 'Two new firms market exclusively to gays', *Marketing Weekly*, 20 July: 8.

Morgenthau, T. (1997), 'Baptists vs. Mickey–why the boycott against Disney faces steep odds', *Newsweek*, 30 June: 51.

Mucha, M. (1999), Rosa Zielgruppe: Konsequenzen des gesellschaftlichen Einstellungswandels gegenüber Homosexuellen für Käuferverhalten und Marketing-Aktivitäten, diploma thesis, Cologne University.

Mulryan, D. (1995), 'Reaching the gay market', *American Demographics*, May: 46–7.

Newman, J. L. (1998), 'Controversy in the Caymans', *Condé Nast Traveler*, 38: 4.

Our World Magazine (1996), 'Survey results' (advertising information). Daytona Beach, FL: *Our World* Publishing Corp.

Pela, R. L. (1997), 'Disney steps out', *Advocate*, 29 April: 37–40.

Penaloza, L. (1996), 'We're here, we're queer, and we're going shopping! A critical perspective on the accommodation of gays and lesbians in the US marketplace', in D. L. Wardlow (ed.), *Gays, Lesbians, and Consumer Behaviour: Theory, Practice, and Research Issues in Marketing*. New York: Haworth.

Remy, V. (1995), *Schwule Männer in Deutschland – die neuentdeckte Zielgruppe der neunziger Jahre*. Koblenz: R&M, internal report.

Roth, T. E. (1995), 'A tale of two airlines', *Next News*, April: 26–7.

Rothman, C. (1999), 'Big companies are openly courting gay consumers', *Los Angeles Times*, 18 May: C1.

Savage, T. (1999), 'Open-door policy', *Advocate*, 20 July: 33–5.

Schmalz, J. (1993), 'Poll finds an even split on homosexuality's cause', *New York Times*, 5 March: A14.

Schneider, N. F., Rosenkranz, D. and Limmer, R. (1998), *Nichtkonventionelle Lebensformen*. Opladen: Leske & Butrich.

Schwartz, J. (1992), 'Gay consumers come out spending', *American Demographics*, April: 10–11.

Sell, R. L. and Petrulio, C. (1996), 'Sampling homosexuals, bisexuals, gays, and lesbians for public health research: a review of the literature from 1990 to 1992', *Journal of Homosexuality*, 30 (4): 31–47.

Sell, R. L., Wells, J. A. and Wypij, D. (1995), 'The prevalence of homosexual behavior and attraction in the United States, the United Kingdom and France: results of national population-based samples'. *Archives of Sexual Behavior*, 24 (3): 235–48.

Simons, G. F. and Zuckerman, A. (1995), *Sexual Orientation in the Workplace*. Thousand Oaks, CA: Sage.

Singer, B. and Deschamps, D. (1994), *Gay and Lesbian Stats*. New York: The New York Press.

Snowdon, R. (1996), 'Virgin TV ad to show gay kiss', *Marketing*, 1 February: 1, 13.

Stuber, M. (1998a), 'Unternehmen ignorieren Schwule – selbst schuld?', *Männer Aktüll*, June: 16–19.

Stuber, M. (1998b), 'Schwul arbeiten und schwul einkaufen?', *Männer Aktüll*, July: 14–17.

Stuber, M. (1998c), 'Gay marketing – considerations for the travel industry in Europe', presentation at IGLTA Regional Conference, Cologne, 4 July.

Stuber, M. (1999), 'Millionen unentdeckte KundInnen – Die Erschliessung homosexueller Marktsegmente', Presentation at the Cologne Travel Fair, 28 November.

Stuber, M. (2000), 'European trends in gay/lesbian tourism', presentation at the First International Conference on Gay Tourism, New York, 7 April.

Stuber, M. (2001a), 'Rosa Randgruppe oder Coole Cash Cow?', presentation at the University of Cologne, 22 January.

Stuber, M. (2001b), 'Kratzer am Kitschbild', *Horizont*, 10: 16.

Susser, P. A. (1986), 'Sexual preference discrimination: limited protection for gay workers', *Employment Relations Today*, 13: 57–65.

Tilsner, J. (1994), 'Gold in the gay games', *Business Week*, 4 July: 34.

Wagner, R. (1997), 'Benefiz und Unternehmer', *Vary*, 6: 23–7.

Wardlow, D. L. (ed.) (1996), *Gays, Lesbians, and Consumer Behaviour: Theory, Practice, and Research Issues in Marketing*. New York: Haworth.

Wharton, S. (1995), 'The pink economy', 7th International Conference of the Society for the Advancement of Socio-Economics, University of Bath.

Wilke, M. (1996), 'Gay press sets pace with 19.6% ad increase', *Advertising Age*, 67 (37): 54.

Zillich, N. (1988), *Homosexuelle Männer im Arbeitsleben*. Frankfurt am Main: Campus.

WEBSITES

Gay Britain website (established by the BTA): *www.gaybritain.org*

Gayjet website (company donates 10 per cent of profits to community causes): *www.gayjet.com*

Out&About Tour Company: *www.out&about.com*

QT Magazine (information on gay and lesbian travel): *www.QTmagazine.com*

British Tourist Authority (BTA) (contains no references to gay events or issues, but see the Gay Britain site): *www.visitbritain.com*

CHAPTER 5

A Place for Us 2001: Tourism Industry Opportunities in the Gay and Lesbian Market

(An Interview with Thomas Roth of Community Marketing)

THOMAS ROTH AND MICHAEL LUONGO

INTRODUCTION (MICHAEL LUONGO)

'There's a place for us.' You don't have to be a Broadway Show Queen to know where that phrase comes from.[1] But for gays and lesbians who travel, that song takes on a special meaning. Yes, somewhere there's a place for us – but where is it? And more importantly from Tom Roth's point of view, if you are that place, how do you let gays and lesbians know you're somewhere out there?

Tom Roth is the President of Community Marketing, a travel consultation firm helping companies, tour operators, travel agents and government tourism boards gain access to the gay and lesbian travel market. Each year, Community Marketing undertakes a large survey of gay men and lesbian women, and makes recommendations based on the results, suggesting how businesses and destinations can increase their share of the gay and lesbian travel market. For this chapter, I sat down with Tom Roth to discuss his company and the implications of his most recent survey: what it means for today's gay and lesbian travellers, for tour companies, cities and other destinations, and where the information fits with some of the other material in this book.

INTERVIEW WITH THOMAS ROTH[2]

Tom, before we get started, tell me a little bit about yourself. How did you get started in the travel field to begin with, when did your interest in the gay and lesbian market develop, and when did you start Community Marketing and its sister company, the Travel Alternatives Group (TAG)?

I started becoming interested in travel when I was nine when my family went down to Mexico for a month. My father was a doctor, and we went to a small poor neighbourhood and gave tuberculosis vaccinations to kids and I started speaking Spanish and playing with the local kids – and I just loved it. And so that kind of started my interest. Then we went on a family vacation to Europe when I was thirteen and I was sold on travel. Over the course of my life and career, I've been to about 60 countries – travel is just in my blood. I started going in the direction of the community marketing angle in 1992. I had a background as a travel agent and also corporate travel, arranging seminars and so forth. It came to reassessing what I really wanted to do and I knew that selling airline tickets was *not* what I wanted to do. I really wanted to facilitate communication to the gay community from the travel trade. I took an assessment of what was out there and there was nearly nothing in 1992. IGLTA [International Gay and Lesbian Travel Association] was still a very small organization and they had little to offer in terms of marketing. The only other way to reach the gay market was through *Our World*, which had just started, and the *Advocate*. Otherwise, there was nothing. With my travel background, I knew that trade shows were important to the travel industry and so that's when I launched Community Marketing in 1992 [see website, details below]. Our first promotion was the first International Gay and Lesbian World Travel Expo at the Sheraton Palace in May 1993 in San Francisco. It was nerve-wracking because in '92, and early '93 when I was sending out invitations to the airlines, these people, they didn't know what to think. And most of them responded with 'no response'. So, I was nervous. I had rented this big beautiful ball room at the Sheraton Palace. What ended up happening was coincidental, and helped to launch the Expo. American Airlines had its incident.

Can you explain that 'incident'?

After the March on Washington[3] in April 1993, a flight full of gay and lesbian travellers on an American Airlines plane stopped through Dallas. And a very insensitive flight attendant, recognizing that there was a gay population on the plane, radioed to Dallas and asked them to please remove all the pillows and blankets so that the next passengers didn't catch AIDS from these people. That caused a real uproar – word got out. American Airlines at that time was already probably one of the largest employers of gay and lesbian people. They provided sensitivity training, they also had a lot of community support programmes in place. So, they wanted to communicate. So it was perfect. I had the perfect venue for them to communicate to the gay community: 'Look, we're not the bad guys. There was a small incident. We've taken care of it, we apologize.' So, they took a front booth at the Expo. By them signing up to the Expo, we got press in the travel trade publications. The travel trade publications are looked upon as authoritative by the travel trade. Other people started calling and saying: 'You know, by the way, we got your invitation to exhibit and we'd like to give it a try.' And it filled up with exhibitors and it filled up with people. So it was a really interesting start. I don't know what would have happened otherwise.

About how many people exhibited at that first Expo?

The first one we had about 55 or 60. A wide variety of people from small travel agents and B&Bs all the way to American Airlines.

And that same Expo has now been expanded to how many different cities?

Now we're in four cities, consistently. We've been to a variety of cities over the years. We've done it in Atlanta and Houston and Chicago. But we've found that over the years, by trial and error, the cities that really deliver the local community are those four cities – which is New York, Washington, LA [Los Angeles] and San Francisco [see Figure 5.1].

What types of things would a client in the travel industry expect with a marketing contract with Community Marketing? What do you do besides the Expo?

Great, and this also leads into the Travel Alternatives Group. The Expo is attended by consumers, and it is targeted at consumers, but it also drew the travel trade, because we got travel trade press. The travel agents that came said: 'This is great. We need to know more.' So we started a workshop series. And the workshop series was successful. The travel agents then said, 'We need to do this more than once a year. Is there any kind of communication that you can do?' So

Figure 5.1 Sponsors of the ninth International Gay and Lesbian World Travel Expo, New York. *Source*: Thomas Roth, Community Marketing Inc.

we started a newsletter and it started to become more and more involved with the travel agents. They needed a consortium-like kind of organization that would help them identify gay-friendly suppliers, help them negotiate override commissions, and help them be a strong contender in the gay community, and so that's how we launched the Travel Alternatives Group in 1997 [see Figure 5.2]. So, what Community Marketing does for a client is to deliver three different angles. One is for suppliers to reach travel agents, another is for travel suppliers or destinations to reach consumers directly, and the third is to reach the community via the media. With every client, we sit down and we say: 'You need this three-pronged approach.' And the Internet, it wasn't around when we first started, but now it's kind of laced through all of those, because we can now communicate of course through the Internet.

Actually, earlier you started to talk a little bit about the surveys, and that's really what we are here to discuss. You had given me a copy of the most recent survey Tourism Industry Opportunities in the Gay and Lesbian Market 2001[4] *and I see you've also got a new survey that you've done online which is sort of an adjunct to it – some of the same questions, with slightly different results. Tell me a little bit about the surveys, and how long have you been doing the surveys,*

Figure 5.2 Travel Alternatives Group desk resource. *Source*: Thomas Roth, Community Marketing, Inc.

and tell me about the men and women in it – from where did you draw the survey participants?

We started doing the survey in 1994, which makes us really quite distinct not only in the gay travel niche, but also in the gay market. There's never been, other than this, any consistent research on gay and lesbian buying habits, preferences and sensitivities. Really, we started it just so we could identify the needs of gay and lesbian travellers as distinct from their mainstream counterparts, and communicate that to our clients. And it was launched in 1994, and what we've been able to do, which has been remarkable, is to compare year after year the trends that are changing the face of gay and lesbian travel. When we first started doing the surveys, there were very few destinations that were doing what we call 'rolling out the pink carpet' for the gay market. That's a night and day difference from now. Now they're competing with each other to try and get our attention.

Definitely, definitely. One thing I wanted to say before we start talking about the individual surveys is that there is some discussion on the biases of surveys of the gay and lesbian community. In another chapter of this book, Michael Stuber challenges some of the basic assumptions of these surveys, differentiating for example, between gay men and openly gay men who participate in them. How do you go about comparing your survey results to the general population? Where does that data come from that you are comparing this with?

OK. Number one, we're very out. Right in our survey we say these are active, gay and lesbian consumers. We don't ever represent that this is a slice of the gay population, because we can't reach that. And there's no way to really track that. So we've distributed the survey through gay media, essentially. Through gay travel publications, through direct-mail opportunities, at Gay Pride and our gay travel expos. And largely through direct mail. We're pretty consistent in bringing in anywhere from 1500 to 2500 surveys a year. And that's increasing now that we have the online surveys, so there will probably be over 3000 responses this year. It's a pretty wide coverage compared to other surveys, also, but it is distinctly gay and lesbian consumers. And that's what we want. I mean we communicate that to our clients, this does not represent every gay and lesbian person. Our clients are targeting self-identified, motivated gay and lesbian people who read the publications, who look for a gay-friendly, welcoming environment.

Perhaps have a higher income?

So, for us, it really suits the need. There's always a lot of disputes about research. And one thing we can say with confidence is that we have distributed the survey to a wide variety of people over seven years, and the results are consistent. So it validates itself. The first time we did the survey we asked: 'Have you taken a cruise in the past year?' That was extraordinary, that 15 per cent said they had taken a cruise in the past year! And I didn't personally believe it, although I looked at the statistics myself three times, and found that to be the case. The next year it came out to be 14 or 15 per cent. The next year again, the next year again. Now we're up to about 20 per cent, mostly because of the variety of opportunities out there, but still it's in the range. So we're confident in the research because it proves itself over the years.

Are most of the people who participate in this survey from the United States and Canada, or elsewhere?

Mostly from the United States.

And then when you compare the results to the general public?

Every two years, *Travel Weekly* commissions Plog Research to do a study on mainstream travel trends, and so wherever possible, we compare our results to theirs. So, 'Did you take a vacation?' we can compare; 'Do you have a passport?' we can compare. There are some things that we can't compare. We ask: 'Did you take three or more vacations last year?' That's something that is distinct to the gay market, and we found that 50 per cent or more take three plus vacations. We can't find any research similar to that. But we can compare international vacations, and it is a huge disparity between the two.

Which kind of brings me to my point about looking at some of the actual comparisons in the recent survey. One finding is that 54 per cent of participants in your survey took a recent international vacation, compared with the mainstream average of 9 per cent. Why is there such a huge difference between the gay and lesbian and the mainstream population?

It's a few factors. Number one, I think it's money. Gay and lesbian people by far have more discretionary income. We find that the income range is more or less the same, but the discretionary income is far more. So, travel in the case of the gay and lesbian community is more or less a lifestyle issue. At cocktail parties and at clubs, people are talking about where they've been and where they're going. And it's a large part of our lifestyle; we'll give up coffee before we'll give up travel, I think. So, there's that. There's also a high level of education, which I think makes people more aware of the world and what's available out there, and also leads to an interest in cultural destinations and wanting to experience other cultures and other places. And third, I think it's just a general comfort. I think we start travelling when we're really young, and because we have the propensity to travel and the money, we have that comfort level. So travelling overseas is just like getting on a plane and going to the next town.

And what about children, that's another thing that often comes up?

Yes, of course, that's right. And that also points to the research that shows that September and October are by far the most popular times for gay and lesbian people to travel. And that's of particular interest to tourism boards because that's shoulder season. And the other preferred time-period is February, March and April.

Also shoulder season.

Yes, our focus groups have told us, the reason is just what you've said. We don't have kids, 'we can'. We don't need to stay in line. We get better value.

We don't have to wait till the kids are home from school on vacation.

That's right and when we do travel we don't have to wait in the long queue to get into museums, and deal with the crowds.

Sort of touching on that, you said that gay and lesbian travellers are less likely to plan 'once-in-a-lifetime' vacations. How did you come to this observation, and what does it mean for destinations interested in the gay and lesbian market?

I think that destinations which are mature in the gay market need to constantly reinvent themselves. SF [San Francisco] is a good example of a destination that can lose market share because it just assumes that gays and lesbians will be coming in droves.

And they have been coming in droves.

And they *have* been coming in droves, so they haven't had to do anything. But now there are so many destinations that are coming onto the market, and really positioning themselves well. And people will go there and try them. So the mature destinations need to reinvent themselves. They need to communicate to the gay market what's new; they need to emphasize events and catalysts to bring gay and lesbian travellers back. So in the case of San Francisco or New York, or Miami, 'come back', because you have to assume that most have been there before. And for new destinations, Australia, for example, is not the destination of a lifetime. I think gay and lesbian travellers will go there maybe three or four times in their lives, if not more. It's such a great place, we don't mind getting on a plane and having a few drinks, and arriving in Sydney – it's just not an issue. So, I think that the 'vacation of a lifetime' concept – and also saving up for it – is not such an issue as it is with the mainstream with four or five kids: planning and planning, and saving and saving, and then finally . . .

Waiting until the kids grow up. Some people have once-in-a-lifetime vacations every year.

Exactly, or more.

In your recommendations to prospective clients, you talk about developing new destinations, and making sure that they are gay-friendly. How does one go about this? Is there a way to make even a determinedly anti-gay destination like the Cayman Islands gay-friendly for individual tour groups?

I think that the Cayman Islands, since you brought up that example, is such a real challenge. I think that the Cayman Islands have such a bad reputation in the gay community that I could not recommend that anybody develop a gay tour group to the Cayman Islands. There are cruise ships that go there, and if you happen to be on that cruise ship, you're going to go there, but I don't think it's a destination to promote. But for other destinations, what is the angle you're trying to get?

I mean, how do you make something gay-friendly? I mean some people often point to the Muslim World, and I think it's the same for women's travel, as well.

I agree. I would never recommend a Muslim country to gay people who care about how locals are treated, who care about the government policies and who

133

care about what could happen to them if it were ever discovered that they are gay. We have too many great options to select from. I don't recommend going to places where we are not welcome.

Otherwise if a destination is *new* to the gay market and is otherwise neutral in terms of its perceptions, one real key element is to involve the local gay community. We really recommend that. Bloomington, Indiana, is a great example. They are really involving the local gay community via the gay market. Minneapolis, Philadelphia, New Haven. These are not key gay meccas, but they have huge potential in the gay community, especially for regional travel, and also for event and meetings kind of travel. Bloomington is positioning itself as a welcoming destination for gay and lesbian meetings. Nobody else has really ever done that, so they're really reaching out to meeting planners. They're a college town, they've got facilities. They have a gay-friendly community. And as an example of how you better position yourself as gay-friendly, the Bloomington CVB [Convention and Visitors Bureau] executive director went to the Mayor's office and said, 'we want to position Bloomington as a gay-friendly destination. We notice that the hiring practices and policies for the city do not really recognize gay relationships. We want that changed.' And they did it. They just said: 'Yes, we'll do it.' And that's a sweeping change, I think. Recognizing the value of gay tourism and making social and economic decisions based on that. We're very proud of Bloomington.

And how laws affect tourism, and how a liberal environment can affect tourism?

Absolutely, so communicating that to these meeting planners, they'll generate some good business. And we've also recommended that they go to the local community and try to involve them in the tourism outreach. They started with a focus group with only six or eight people and it's grown to 30 or more. All from the local gay community. So, from their local organizations, from their local clubs, and charities and so forth, they're all saying 'yeah, let's get together and do this'. So, they have really created a catalyst effect, where the community is involved in marketing and distribution of Bloomington to the gay and lesbian market.

And that can work for almost any community?

It can work for any community that has a gay element to it. We also really recommend positioning whatever gay events that they've got as 'gay tourist attractions'. So that would include a gay film festival, gay pride, gay street parades, gay street markets and other festivals.

I wanted to get back a little bit to the airlines because they are some of the biggest and most visible components of the travel industry. In question six of your survey, your participants ranked their favourite airlines, and for the sixth year in a row, American Airlines is ranked number one. We have already talked a little about their early marketing in relation to the pillow incident. What is it that American Airlines is doing so well to hold this position?

Well, first of all, they were the first. In any marketing challenge, that's the place to be. They've been unbeatable since then, and the reason is that they've done it right. Again, involvement in the local community has been their ticket. They didn't just come in with a big budget and start advertising *at* us, they came from *within* us. They got involved with gay associations, charities and non-profit-making organizations. Through sponsorships and community support they've been able to win the hearts of the gay community, and the gay community recognizes that. In the same light, in every survey where we ask 'Does giving back to the gay community make a difference in your decision-making process?' 89 per cent or more say yes, it does. So they've done that right. And they've done it very cost-effectively, too. They haven't had to dump a ton of money at marketing. It's really been working for them.

Having a few key people like Michael Fricke[5] and some others.

And that's another first. They're the first Fortune 50 company to have established a gay and lesbian marketing team. On their business cards, I know it was ground-breaking when they did it, it said: 'Rick Cirillo, National Sales Manager, Gay and Lesbian Community'. That sent ripples through the whole travel industry that that *could* be done, especially by a conservative, Dallas, Texas-based corporation.

Sort of again about the airlines, in the survey, United is ranked two. I know that United received a lot of bad publicity, especially in San Francisco, when it did not want to treat its gay and lesbian employees equally to their straight counterparts. To some degree, United received a backlash for that, marketing to the community on one hand, and then doing that on the other. How does United still succeed in getting such a high rating?

What we hear from our focus groups is that they are winning that by default. That they don't have the brand loyalty, but the fact that they own a lot of major markets, including San Francisco. They have more than 50 per cent of the market share in San Francisco, so therefore by default, people belong to their frequent flyer programme. If they want to get anywhere non-stop, they have to fly United, but it is almost begrudgingly. I was told in the focus groups that they do that just out of need. When they can choose another airline, particularly American [Airlines], and apples are apples, they definitely will go with American. Our online survey found American at 32 per cent and United at 18 per cent, which shows an even wider gap.

Very different.

Yeah. Even more than the other, American is more and United is less.

Here American is ranked number one, but United is ranked?

It's still two . . . 18 per cent is two. And Delta has 16 per cent. Now that's a good comparison. Delta has never done a thing for gay and lesbian marketing, and they're only two points behind United.

And Continental is doing stuff and they are at 12 per cent?

Yeah, they're starting to, but you also have to consider the size of the airlines. United, Delta and American are pretty much parallel, though they always kind of vie for who's the biggest. Continental is a much smaller airline. They don't carry 12 per cent of US passengers, so the fact that their market share in the gay community is bigger than their national market share is what you have to look at. And American's in this case is much higher, because American's market share is somewhere around 18 or 20 per cent, but they're 32 per cent in terms of favourite [judged by gay and lesbian travellers]. Now that doesn't mean market share, but it's certainly preference.

That's interesting, because that isn't something I would have thought to look at.

And US Airways is new to the market, but they're already gaining ground. Their market share as a national percentage is much less than 13 per cent, but still they have shown strength recently. And they are the second airline to dedicate staff to the gay and lesbian community. And a marketing plan and the corporate will behind it to make a difference. Comparing United and US Airways is like David and Goliath, but there's only a 5-point spread there in terms of their preference. US Airways is making huge strides.

Coming off of the airlines a little bit, travel agents have been hit hard by recent travel market trends.

Travel agents hate airlines.

Yeah, they're taking their commissions away! You do mention, however, in the survey breakdown that in terms of the gay and lesbian market, there is good news. More gay and lesbian travellers use agents than mainstream travellers, and that's in spite of an increase in Internet usage which you think would play out the opposite. How does this seemingly contradictory pattern emerge?

Again, we are able to get qualitative information on this from our focus groups, and we ask that very question in the focus groups. 'Why are you researching on the Internet, and talking to your friends, and reading every gay and lesbian newsletter and magazine and guidebook, and so forth, and still bringing your business to the travel agent?' And there's a couple of reasons for that. Number one, they trust the experience of their travel agent, especially for destinations they've never been to. And secondly, they want to support their local community, which I think is something way beyond what the mainstream would consider in terms of a purchasing decision. They know that their business means that their friends who work at that agency will continue to have jobs, and that business won't get boarded up. So there's a sociological interest to support those businesses. Again another parallel is when we ask: 'Does it make a difference in terms of a purchasing decision whether a company has good gay corporate policies?' I don't think that John and Mary Smith from Omaha are going to look at the corporate policies of X airline and see whether they want to go on that airline. The gay community is much more savvy to that and really pays attention to news, whether it's beer, or car companies, or airlines. Who's friendly and who's not, and we support those with our wallet.

Excellent. I think one of the most important aspects of your survey is the section on where people have visited in the last three years and where they

plan to visit. We sort of touched a little on this with San Francisco's market-
ing. There are some interesting patterns developing out there. For instance
the four most important gay destinations in many people's minds – New
York, San Francisco, Miami and West Hollywood/Los Angeles – all show a
flattening of current interest among gay travellers, and a decline in future
interest – Miami a 23 per cent decline. At the same time, other cities are
showing a huge increase in interest among gay travellers. For instance, Mon-
treal, a 76 per cent increase. Maybe ten years ago, Montreal was not con-
sidered such an important destination. How did this change come about –
how were you involved in this? How does Montreal serve as an example to
other destinations looking to increase the amount of gay and lesbian travel
within their borders?

I think Montreal is distinct in terms of its commitment to the gay market. From
the first time that they decided in 1994 to exhibit at the Gay and Lesbian World
Travel Expo, they have never slowed down. They've been dynamic in the market,
and along with the provincial tourism office, Tourism Quebec, they have been
real examples for the travel industry [see Figure 5.3]. And especially the fact that
Montreal was suffering from some hard economic times during that period.
There was the whole vote for secession and all that, they recognized the potential
value of the gay market, and so they went for it. And they have been very
comprehensive in their push, in terms of press. We have 34 media going there in
a couple weeks for Diverscite [Montreal Gay Pride]. So their focus on the press
has been significant and consistent. Their approach to the travel trade is also
great. They travel around the country meeting with travel agents on a regular
basis, invite them to come on FAM [familiarization] trips to show them a good
time. The travel agents go back and talk it up. Their approach directly to the
community, as well, has been strong and non-stop, in terms of their consistent
approach to positioning Montreal as the gay-friendliest destination in North
America. So, if I'm in San Francisco, it's really interesting to see it's not that
much of a difference to go to Miami or to go to Montreal or go to New York.
Why not go someplace which really has aggressively said: 'We're gay-friendly.' It
goes beyond that. The province of Quebec has passed a resolution, which
virtually brings equality or parity to gay and lesbian couples with their straight,
heterosexual couples. And that again has won the interest and the attention and
the hearts of gay and lesbian consumers. 'I want to go and support and be part
of an environment like that.' And there are other places on earth that are like
that, as well, and they are getting notoriety for it [Toronto has also advertised
itself as 'gay-friendly' – see Figure 5.4].

Figure 5.3 *Gay travelnews* feature on Quebec, spring/summer 2001. *Source*: Thomas Roth, Community Marketing Inc.

Again it's sort of like with Bloomington, Indiana, where the changes in the laws and the social atmosphere really play out into tourism.

South Africa is another great example. Ten years ago, if I asked at a focus group, how many gay people want to go to South Africa, a chill would go through the air. Now, everyone would raise their hands, because South Africa was the first country to write into their constitution equality and protection for gay and lesbian citizens. That opened the doors to their own community coming out and starting to thrive, which in turn brought European visitors down there in droves [but see Want, this volume, for an account of opposition to gay tourism in South Africa]. And that's sort of catching on. And European and Australian destinations are taking more steps to bringing these kinds of changes about. It's tremendously interesting right now. Belgium has just brought gay and lesbian marriage rights to their citizens like Holland, and Sweden, Denmark, Germany, France and

Figure 5.4 You're here, you're queer, let's go shopping! *Source*: Vals Fauquier, Tourism Toronto.

Spain. They're all in various degrees of doing that. Quite the opposite of our own country.

Well, and Vermont?

And, Vermont, absolutely. [See Link, this volume, for details.]

More people are going there, but again it all relates to the laws and changes.

Certainly, because it's a matter of feeling welcome. We're spending limited funds. However much anybody has, it's limited, and I want to go some place where I feel welcome. I want to go some place that doesn't give me attitude when I check into a hotel for example, and that goes into the selection process.

Or when you walk on the street.

Exactly.

You have said that there is a limited amount, and ultimately there can only be so many destinations and so many dollars spent on travel. In the future, how do you see traditional gay destinations like Provincetown, Fire Island, San Francisco, or Brighton in the United Kingdom competing with these up-and-coming destinations?

Keeping it fresh; giving people a reason to come back. I sort of touched on that with San Francisco, but it's parallel with these other destinations. They have to recognize that there is competition out there now, they can't be complacent and just say we are a gay mecca and everybody will come, let's put our attention elsewhere. They have to put their attention on the gay market. They have to look at their own policies, and make sure that they are constantly updating their own backyard to make sure that people don't compare and say: 'Wow, Brighton doesn't even have domestic partner benefits, why would we want to go there?' So there is going to be more such scrutiny as more choices come onto the market.

Speaking of limited dollars to be spent on travel, here in mid 2001, the world's economy is softening. When I first started writing on the gay travel market in the early 1990s there was another economic slowdown, and this market was constantly touted by people in the industry as 'recession-proof'. With the decline in consumer spending here in the United States and the drop in value of the Euro, how do you see the gay travel market over the next few years? Will it still be that type of recession-proof niche?

No, I would never say 'recession-proof'. I always say 'recession-resistant'. There are still people who will be hurt by this and they'll travel less. But even in those cases they will still travel. If they have to skip a mortgage payment, they will still go on a vacation. And for that, my answer is the regional destinations have a much better shot at it. Montreal is a perfect example. It's a foreign experience, it's a flavour of France, but it's very inexpensive to be there and it's relatively inexpensive to get there. I think Quebec and Canada in general have a tremendous opportunity to capitalize on the soft economy and the gay dollar. Other places, going to Sydney for the Mardi Gras, for example, may be less popular over the next few years. But at the same time, they've got the Gay Games. Sydney, particularly, offers a big draw and people will make an effort to go.

Another intriguing area the survey touches on is how gays and lesbians gather travel information. While local gay publications and Damron's *serve as important guides, it seems more gays and lesbians read* Condé Nast Traveler *or* Travel and Leisure *than* Our World *magazine, for example. How do you explain this trend, and does it mean that even 'mainstream' outlets might be good advertising vehicles for companies seeking gay and lesbian clients?*

I think there's a line to draw here. For mainstream advertisers to the gay community, they need to focus on gay media. For gay suppliers to the gay community, they need to expand into mainstream channels. One example would be a gay tour operator who has just advertised in *Our World* exclusively. In order to kind of break beyond our 'triangle', they need to get out. They need to advertise in the Sunday travel section, or put a small classified ad into these larger more mainstream publications, because just the word 'Gay Adventure' or 'Gay Travel' in those classifieds will make them stand out. We see 25 per cent are reading those magazines. So it's a good opportunity to grow their market share.

You don't really touch on this in the survey, but do you see a difference in the ways gay men travel versus how lesbian women travel?

I don't touch on it in the survey, because to be fair, our surveys are so heavily weighted towards gay men that it wouldn't be fair to take the 5 per cent of women that answer our survey and separate them out. It's not enough numbers. I can only speak about anecdotal experience and focus groups. The stereotypical concept is that a lesbian traveller goes camping, but we found there are very wealthy lesbian women who go luxury all the way, and they don't stop. So I think there is every shade of grey in both communities. I think gay men are much less likely to do adventure travel, for example as a stereotype, than woman are. Women seem much more open to that. But otherwise, I think there's a lot of similarities, more similarities than differences. And those differences would be pretty parallel to mainstream men and women. A lesbian woman is not going to feel comfortable where a straight woman is not going to want to be travelling alone. So, if they don't feel welcome, if they don't feel equal, they are going to be reluctant.

So it's other social issues that are associated with women's travel.

Yes, other social issues, more than the difference between gay men and lesbian women.

What types of things might you include in future surveys – such as how gay families with children travel as an example – or other niche markets within niche markets?

We want to develop that further, and as the number of survey participants grow, we'll be able to. We ask this question in this survey: 'do you have children living at home?', and 3 per cent said 'yes'. That doesn't mean it's not a market, it means it's a really distinct niche-within-the-niche. And right now we are helping to promote a Carnival gay family-friendly cruise, because it's something that is not offered. We had so many calls from travel agents, and from individuals, asking 'Where can we bring our kids? You know we are a lesbian couple, we have kids, we're a gay couple, we have kids. What kind of gay-friendly experience can we do together?' – and there isn't anything. That is why we're promoting this family-friendly cruise, it's in December. It's the first one. We don't think it'll be huge, but it will be a start. Just so that there are outlets for those niches-within-the-niche.

One of the things that you have talked about was lifestyle, and how travel is part of the gay and lesbian lifestyle. Martin Cox, one of the authors in this book, discusses how gay travel is an inherent part of establishing gay identity. Living in San Francisco, it may be hard to put yourself into the mind of someone who is not surrounded by all things gay, but do you have any stories or examples of this connection between gay identity and travel to gay destinations?

It's a coming-out experience for most gay people, and that's why there are gay 'meccas': they are magnets for people who live in a closeted situation or in an unfriendly community. Travel can offer an opportunity for them to be the majority. If you visit the Castro District of San Francisco, you're not 10 per cent or less, you're 90 per cent or more, and it's an enlightening experience for gay and lesbian visitors. And in a lot of ways it helps them change their perspectives on where they want to be in their life and how they want to live their life. So it can be a transformational experience. And gay travel, whether it's coming to a big city like San Francisco, or going on an RSVP cruise, again it's an experience that is heavenly for people who don't otherwise have that experience or ability.

What is your biggest success story? And what was your most reluctant client? This is where you really talk about you and your company.

I don't think we have any reluctant clients because we don't really go out cold-calling. Most clients come to us, based on our reputation and market leadership position. We know that they are warm and receptive before they even pick up the phone. I think the best success story is Montreal and Quebec, because they've gone from zero to 60 in such a short amount of time. We're really proud of being there to support them. And right now we're supporting their bid for the 2006 Gay Games [see Stuber, Chapter 4 this volume]. We're not sure that they'll get it this time, but they will get it, it's a fantastic destination. It's going to be an amazing host city for whenever they do get it. We're also really proud to be part of the American Airlines success story. We kind of 'touch the lives' of any supplier or destination that gets involved in the gay market. Yes, we're in business and business is supposed to make money, but we put ourselves through amazing amounts of stress and in the early days, a lot of austerity, because we're so committed to doing what we do. We love doing what we do.

I was going to ask where does the International Gay and Lesbian Travel Association (IGLTA) fit into all of this? You sort of touched on this. What is the difference between services that your company offers, versus what membership in the IGLTA offers to a company or destination?

Anybody in the travel trade would recognize the difference, but maybe others don't. In the travel industry, there are trade associations, most noticeably ASTA [American Society for Travel Agents], as well as USTOA [United States Tour Operators Association] and PATA [Pacific Asia Travel Association] and other sorts of regional trade associations. A trade association's purpose is to facilitate education, networking, hopefully influence government policy, and those kinds of things. They can't really have a 'preferred supplier' or help someone market themselves, because that shows preference. And a trade association, being a membership organization, has to be equal to all. Community Marketing, and in particular the Travel Alternatives Group, has been able to do something very distinct [see Figure 5.2]. In the travel industry, there are what's called 'consortia', and those 'consortia' are groups of travel agencies that band together to strengthen their negotiating power by pooling their resources. So, 'Joe's Travel Agency' that brings in a million or two a year, they can't really knock on the door of Carnival Cruise Lines and say, 'we want higher commissions'. But pooling them all together, 200 or more travel agencies that represent the gay community, and having us represent that buying power to Carnival Cruise Lines, or Cunard or a Seaborne, or American Airlines, we are able to really move some incentives and override commissions to these agencies. So we help destinations market themselves. We have developed a powerful portfolio of marketing services that help them avoid reinventing the wheel. We provide market research, strategic sessions for executives, and a wide range of promotions to reach the gay market.

Excellent. Excellent. What do you see as the future of gay travel – will it increase, or will we begin to see it as a non-issue in the upcoming years as gays and lesbians assimilate into the mainstream?

I think there is a polarization, the distinction between gay-friendly and not gay-friendly. And it's already happening. We just see in terms of marriage policies and AIDS policies and issues that are coming up, that there is a stronger colouration of 'pink' and 'non-pink'. Ultimately, our goal is that it will be a non-issue. That gay and lesbian people will be free and happy and welcome everywhere that they want to go.

And you'll close shop.

And we'll just close up because we'll just be able to say we've done what we set out to do. But until then, we're working to help. The motto of our company is:

'Opening doors around the world for the gay and lesbian community.' So the more doors we can knock on and enlighten, the more fulfilled we'll feel, and then it's all done and we're happy.

It's like converting, or missionary work. Eventually you don't have to do it anymore.

Right, and I think what is also fulfilling is to see what happened in Bloomington, Indiana, and what happened in Quebec, and what's happening across Europe, is the recognition that either as a by-product, or in spite of, or separate from gay tourism, they recognize that they have to do their homework. They have to create a genuinely gay-welcoming destination, and that means: 'Are your own people welcome in your own country?' And once they've achieved that, then they've got the foundation for gay tourism.

Thanks, Tom.

Thanks, Mike.

NOTES

1. 'Somewhere', *West Side Story*, Stephen Sondheim (1957/61).
2. This interview took place at the World Trade Center Marriott, New York City, on Wednesday, 25 July 2001.
3. The March on Washington [MOW] is a recurring gay and lesbian civil rights march in Washington, DC held every six to seven years. The previous MOW was in 1987, and the most recent was in 2000, dubbed the Millennium March. Statistics vary, but several hundred thousand people attend each of these marches. For more information, visit *www.millenniummarch.com*
4. For a complete list of all *A Place for Us 2001* survey questions and results, see the Community Marketing website.
5. Michael Fricke is a National Sales Manager to the Gay and Lesbian Community, American Airlines.

WEBSITES

American Society for Travel Agents: *www.astanet.com*
Community Marketing Inc.: *www.mark8ing.com*
Gay Quebec: *www.visitgayquebec.com*
Gay Travel News (site of the Travel Alternatives Group): *www.gaytravelnews.com*

International Gay and Lesbian Travel Association: *www.iglta.com*

Pacific Asia Travel Association: *www.pata.org*

Toronto Tourism site (information for gay and lesbian tourists under 'What's Hot': *www.torontotourism.com*

United States Tour Operators Association: *www.ustoa.com*

PART 2

Identity, Choice and Resistance

CHAPTER 6

The Long-haul out of the Closet: The Journey from Smalltown to Boystown

MARTIN COX

INTRODUCTION

One often has to leave 'home' to find a queer home (Binnie, 1997: 240).

Gay identities are a matter of geography in that the spaces and places in which homosexually inclined people move have a direct and profound influence on identity construction. Rather than presenting holidaymaking as 'a trance-like suspension from the everyday' (Craik, 1997: 114) it is argued in this chapter[1] that holidaymaking plays a significant part in providing important opportunities to explore the 'rainbow' of gay cultures. Holidays provide a context where gay, non-gay and non-sexual cultures become entangled. It is in the midst of such cultural complexities that holidaymaking plays a significant part in constructing ever-changing gay identities that enable some gay people to proclaim, 'I am what I am' (sung by Gloria Gaynor). This relationship between holidays and identity may be understood within the context of the argument of Glennie and Thrift (1992: 435) that identities have 'become more tightly drawn to particular life-styles'. However, this association should not be seen in over-romantic terms, since holidaymaking is not always a matter of free choice, but may be constrained by factors of sexuality, class (see McIntosh, 1997), race (see Skelton, 1995 on the interplay of race and sexuality), disability (see Butler, R., 1999 on disabled bodies and gay spaces) and the fear of homophobia.

In this chapter I am concerned with the ways in which the practices of holidaymaking may play a significant role in the cultural construction of differing gay identities. In particular, I focus on the ways in which holiday experiences assist in enabling gay people to identify with others through the performance of gay cultures. I argue that such identifications assist in what those absorbed into gay cultures commonly refer to as 'coming out'. This exploration of the interrelationship between the practices of holidaymaking and gay identities should be seen in the broader context of debates about a shift from work to non-work experiences as being the basis of people's sense of identity (see Urry, 1990: Chapter 5). Holidays are a significant part of a broad range of non-work experiences and should be set apart from leisure experiences that are local and contribute to a sense of being 'at home'. Far from being an extraneous pursuit, holidaymaking has the potential to take people away from the parochialism of home and then bring them back again, having absorbed something of the complexity of a larger world (see Munt, 1994). Gay people, of course, are not set apart from this process and it is important to begin to understand how our lives at home are touched by travel for pleasure. In this sense, holidaymaking is a serious business that may challenge and change our identities and sexual cultures before sending us back to our work-aday lives.

The journey from a small provincial town (Smalltown) to a large and thriving, overseas, metropolitan gay area (Boystown), such as the Castro in San Francisco or the Shinjyuku-ni-chome in Tokyo, is, arguably, the longest single step that can be made in the much longer journey out of the closet and should be understood in the context of the view that 'Coming out is a central feature of the experience of lesbians and gay men in the western world' (Davies, 1992: 75). The journey from Smalltown to Boystown could be interpreted as a metaphor for coming out of the closet, but here I use it as an example of one journey that can be made as part of the longer voyage towards achieving the identities of an out gay man that is grounded in metrocentric gay cultures. Accepting that different gay people will make their own unique journeys and that the travels associated with gay holidaymaking can contribute to identity development in a variety of different ways, the journey from Smalltown to Boystown is one among many important gay holidaymaking experiences.

For Brown (1999:187), the 'closet is a bounded physical space' which serves to constrain same-sex desire. More poignantly, for Signorile (1994: *xxi*), the closet is a 'wretched' place of 'tyranny', 'pain and torture'. The journey out of the closet is as complex as it is unique to each gay person. This complexity is reflected in a variety of differing studies, each attempting to make sense of gay and lesbian departures from closeted spaces. For example, Sinfield (1997) argues that in some east Asian cultures coming out is not a significant rite of passage; a point that serves to highlight the centrality of coming out among Western gay cultures. The spatial metaphor of the journey is emphasized by Herdt's (1992) conceptualizing of coming out as a 'rite of passage': 'Today, the political power of the gay and lesbian community suggests that coming out is more of a collective initiation rite, a public coming-of-age status-adjustment transition into the adult gay community' (Herdt, 1992: 31).

The journey across a 'threshold' suggests a binary distinction where gay people are either in or out of the closet. This is an understanding that is replicated by Signorile (1994). In stark contrast, Sedgwick (1990: 67) challenges the usefulness of such binarism and argues that there are few openly gay people who are not deliberately in the closet with someone in their lives. The spatial implications of this complexity of being both in and out of the closet at the same time is highlighted by Valentine (1993: 241), who asserts that the journey out of the closet is more akin to 'an unfolding narrative as the person "comes out" in more and more spheres of their life'. Hence, someone may be gay in his or her own home, 'straight' with their parents, and asexual at work. This approach supports the work of Davies (1992: 79) who argues that gay men manage coming out by geographically compartmentalizing their lives so that the disclosure of their gay identity only occurs where it is judged to be safe.

For Altman (1971), Jenness (1992) and Savin-Williams (1998), coming out is about much more than issues of disclosure and secrecy. In each of these studies, coming out is about the search for a gay identity:

> The expression 'coming out', common among homosexuals, implies much more than a first sexual act with another man or woman. Rather it is bound up with the whole process whereby persons come to identify themselves as homosexual, and recognise their position as part of a stigmatised and half-hidden minority (Altman, 1971: 22–3).

Altman's early work is important, as it recognizes that the journey out of the closet is also about a journey of 'discovery' into the 'gay world' (Altman, 1971: 26). Altman maps out a journey of discovery through the often twilight spaces of America's emerging gay cultures in the late 1960s. For Savin-Williams (1998), the final destination in journeying out of the closet is to be able to achieve a *positive* gay identity. He argues that finding a positive gay identity is part of a 'developmental trajectory' through 'time and space' which includes 'exposure to gay culture/communities', culminating in the discovery that there are a multiplicity of gay scenes, each offering, potentially, positive identifications (Savin-Williams, 1998: 188).

For Weeks (1971: *xii*), coming out is not only a 'personal process' but, as his work suggests, it 'can also be seen as a historic process', resulting in 'the gradual emergence and articulation of a homosexual identity and public presence'. Indeed, one is struck by the contrasts that emerge in the quality of gay experience that separate the work of Altman (1971) and Savin-Williams (1998). Crudely put, the gay community is making its own, collective journey out of the closet. Acknowledging this collective journey provides a context for the individual stories of journeying out of the closet and so highlights the *quality* of the gay spaces that gay men journey through which are vital to understanding the geographies of developing a particular gay identity.

Sinfield (1997) challenges how we should make sense of these predominantly metropolitan gay spaces with regard to the issue of coming out: 'If there is one thing that characterises metropolitan lesbian and gay identities, it is 'coming out'. However, the term is misleading, in so far as it allows the supposition that this kind of gayness was always there, waiting to be uncovered' (Sinfield, 1997: 210).

HOLIDAYS TO THE METROPOLIS

When trying to grasp geographies of coming out, it is important to understand the sexual culture in which a person is coming out. Sinfield (1997) reminds us that metropolitan gay cultures are the most powerful. However, whilst queer theorists seek to de-centre metropolitan gay cultures (see Phillips, *et al.* 2000), my urbanite interviewees illustrate the hegemony of such cultures in their holidaymaking:[2]

> *Anthony*: At that time we were living in the Midlands and there was no gay scene there to speak of. So going to San Francisco was a great experience to be able to bump into one of the world's largest gay scenes. At the time, I think it was described as the gay capital of the world. So you can imagine what it must have been like to have gone from a real dead-end sort of place in the . . . you know, to then end up in the world's gayest place.

In Anthony's story, the urban gay scene is presented as the only significant way to be gay. San Francisco is described as the polar opposite to his own 'dead-end' experiences away from metrocentric gay cultures. In a similar account, James tells a story of how his holiday experiences in Sydney contrasted with living a suburban life in Essex:

James: Sydney for me was the most marvellous place I'd . . . ever been to. I lived in Essex at the time and hadn't been out very much, so it was the wildest place that I had ever been to. Such a contrast going from a really tame place like Essex to the centre of the gay universe . . . well that's what it seemed like at the time. At the time I was still living with my wife . . .

James's casting of Sydney as 'the centre of the gay universe' concurs with notions of 'gay capitals', a feature picked up by the gay travel industry as a means to market holidays to particular cities. The *Spartacus International Gay Guide* labels many large urban areas such as Amsterdam, as 'gay capitals'. Indeed, *Spartacus* maintains that Amsterdam 'has, without a doubt, earned the title of the gay capital of Europe' (Bedford and Rauch, 2000: 709). This notion of a transnational gay capital is a further indication of the dominance of particular gay cultures in the holidaymaking practices of some gay people. For those gay people who are attracted by the possibilities of such a journey, the contrasts between home and away are so immense that when such differences are sampled for the first time, it is possible for gay people to experience a particularly profound emotional response. In constructing a successful holiday experience, the sense of being away from home is an important ingredient. The issue of gay sexuality, as expressed by my informants, serves to contrast home and away as polar opposites. From tame to wild, from no gay scene to the world's largest gay scene; individual people are faced with making sense of sharply contrasting experiences.

The following extracts illustrate something of the way three informants, Anthony, Alex and James, experienced a great tension between their lives at home and their unfolding experiences of gay commercial areas away from home. Alex lives in a suburban area on the edge of London. He has been in a stable relationship with his boyfriend for the past six years. He is an office-worker in central London and is in his early thirties.

Alex: When I went there [Amsterdam] it did come as a surprise . . . even though everybody has been telling me for god knows how many years . . . Actually seeing it . . . was a surprise . . . especially coming from somewhere like here in England . . . it was a surprise . . . the way that, you know, everybody was so open and everything.
Martin: What makes you say that?
Alex: For example . . . we went into the red light area in the evening and, you know, there was everybody holding hands and kissing and everything and it

wasn't men kissing girls – it was girl kiss girl and boy kiss boy, you know, and nobody seemed to be batting an eyelid.

Anthony: So, yeah, you can imagine I was in seventh heaven. I felt as though it [San Francisco] was some kinda dream, you know ... ordinary things like walking down the street seemed so fucking brilliant.

James: God it [Sydney] was like ... well I was shocked at the number of attractive, really muscular, heavy, blokes who were just having a real good time. It was *wild*, yeah, for me it was wild because I hadn't been to London before I'd been to Australia.

Each of these short extracts of gay holidaymaking experiences illustrate something of the emotional or affective nature of a first experience of gay places abroad. It is, perhaps, the unexpectedness of my informants' holidaymaking experiences that is most striking. Feelings of surprise, shock and amazement serve to destabilize pre-existing identities. It is an experience that marks a stark contrast between being at home and being away on holiday. In particular, it is important to grasp how emotions heighten the distance between home and away and transform otherwise 'ordinary' events so that they appear extraordinary: 'Ordinary things like walking down the street seemed so fucking brilliant.' This gives the impression of a holiday experience characterized by a heightened tourist gaze: a gaze that notices the otherwise 'taken-for-granted world' and subjects it to critical analysis. For the gay holidaymaker who is propelled into an emotional critique of their personal lifestyle, the tourist gaze may become an introspective gaze upon the self.

The shock and surprise experienced by gay holidaymakers who make the journey to gay places for the first time suggests a lack of preparedness. For Anthony, life in a small town failed to prepare him to understand his sexuality and the variety of metrocentric gay cultures. Even where gay people are informed by other gay people, it may not be sufficient to compensate for the lack of media and other educational experiences that are, so often, an integral part of many mainstream holiday experiences. Shuttleton (2000) considers the significance of gay images in the media by focusing on Hettie Macdonald's film, *Beautiful Thing* (1995) and shows how the film was written to reach out to working-class gay youth. *Beautiful Thing* is an urban story of young love, and may be seen as a further indication of the hegemony of metrocentric gay cultures. So, although media images of gay people are beginning to make gay cultures visible, such images often arise from the paradigm of metrocentric gay cultures. From my interview with Anthony, it became apparent that his experiences of such cultures in San Francisco were instrumental in his decision to move to London. Such migratory experiences not only serve to maintain metrocentric gay culture, but also contribute to 'straightening' out the countryside, depriving rural areas and small towns of people who may have otherwise contributed to a local diversity of sexual cultures.

Many holidaymakers may indeed delight in and crave the novel and the unexpected when on holiday, often seeking such experiences through the cultures of an authentic 'other' (see Hetherington, 1998: 120–1). In contrast, the gay holidaymaker who makes that initial journey to a gay metropolis is confronted with the shock of trying to make sense of his own gay identities through a culture that has the potential to become his own. Among my informants, it was the shock of seeing one's self, rather than the voyeurism of gazing at others, that characterized their holidaymaking experiences.

Holy days at the shrine

It has been argued that 'in contemporary society tourism has become another form of religion' that contrasts with profane elements of life at home (Tresidder, 1999: 138). Indeed, travel to a gay place far away from home evokes interesting parallels with Turner's (1973) argument that travel may become a rite of passage that has parallels with a pilgrimage to a shrine. If a shrine is a place of some symbolic significance to people who are marginalized (Shields, 1991), then it is possible to portray cities with a significant gay population as 'meccas'. Whilst it is possible to appreciate how 'gay-meccas' lead to 'social dramas' (Turner, 1976) that disrupt the routines of life at home, the experiences of the gay holidaymaker do not entirely map on to Turner's pilgrim who is reintegrated back into society on returning home (Turner, 1982: 69). In Turner's work there is little sense of the pilgrim being held in a dialectical relationship between the routines of home and the drama of the shrine.

Participant observation
Ibiza Town, August 1997
At 11.00 p.m. the bar tour began. We were a group of a dozen gay men, brought together by Ben, our holiday rep. Together we walked in convoy, heading for the gay bars found along the Calle de la Virgen. It was an opportunity to make friends and soon I found myself chatting to Roger who was keen to tell his story. He was a frequent visitor to gay resorts since he found life at home problematic. He explained to me the difficulties of being gay as the manager of

a country pub in the north of England. He told me that his only free-time was during the afternoon or very late at night, which meant that a trip to his closest gay bar was a 20-mile drive to the nearest city; worse still, driving meant that he would have to return home sober. Roger explained that he had to be careful about being gay because of his job, which also provided his home. His domestic privacy was further eroded by having to share his accommodation with the relief manager. Roger stressed that he spent all of his holiday-time in Ibiza, where he had established a network of holiday friends.

Using Roger's story, it is possible to begin to appreciate that reintegration, after a 'gay holiday', back into the routine of daily life at home may be a particular problem for some gay people, especially those who do not have easy access to places where they can meet with others who wish to participate in the same sexual cultures. Furthermore, as Phillips, *et al.* (2000) argue, metropolitan sexuality does not transplant well into the countryside, since rural sexualities form a distinctive paradigm that is not always congruent with metropolitan sexualities. Given this cultural divide, it is possible to appreciate that the emotional distance between home and away does not always subside due to a process of reintegration as Turner (1982) suggests. Rather, as in Roger's case it is possible to appreciate how gay holidaymaking is used as part of an inter-national 'time–space strategy' (see Valentine, 1993) that manages one's gay identities. Whilst Valentine's study looks at intra-urban lesbian experiences, here it is possible to appreciate how holidaymaking becomes an important element of some gay people's identity management.

Whilst Roger used his holidaymaking experiences to maintain a multiplicity of sexual identities, for Andrew his 'pilgrimage' to San Francisco brought about a paradigmatic shift in his identities. Andrew was in his mid thirties when he told me his story of travelling to San Francisco for the first time:

Martin: Going back to when you were a teenager . . . what were your first experiences of going to gay places?
Andrew: Pretty good. Well, when I came out I was in San Francisco, I was about twenty-one, it was about ten or twelve years ago. . . . that was like a bloody sweetshop, it was amazing, of course. San Francisco is so out.
Martin: Why did you describe San Francisco as being 'like a sweet-shop'?
Andrew: Well because it was so kinda, like guys walking hand in hand and arm in arm down the street and there were so many bars. I had never been to a place where there were so many different bars. So, . . . it was an opportunity. It was very easy to pick people up as well.

Martin: So what did it feel like when you saw people who were so openly gay walking down the street?

Andrew: Amazing really! Complete, so unusual, it was, like, so amazingly liberating.

Andrew's story of his first visit to San Francisco reiterates the shock and amazement of finding metrocentric gay cultures expressed on the streets and in the commercial spaces of San Francisco. However, his comment that seeing openly gay people walking down the street, was so 'complete, so unusual, it was, like, so amazingly liberating' suggests an experience that marks the beginnings of a distinct phase of identity change. Hetherington (1998) uses Turner's work to argue that liminality, or 'passing moments of release' when the rules of society are 'reinvented' (Hetherington, 1998: 113), affords the 'traveller a means of breaking with their existing society and identifying with another. In so doing they become integrated into a new way of life, with a new lifestyle and a new identity' (Hetherington, 1998: 118). Hetherington's work is important since it explores the relationship between travel and identity through an engagement with liminality.

Wide-eyed at the carnival

From Andrew's account it is possible to gain a sense of his holidaymaking being brought alive by experiences of excess in so many gay bars with so many easy 'pick-ups'. For Shields (1991), excess is associated with the freedom of liminal spaces, since these have the potential to become spaces of carnival. Experiences of Sydney as 'wild' and San Francisco as 'a bloody sweet-shop' provide a sense of the carnivalesque, which, as Jackson (1989: 80) points out, 'may provide a relatively harmless and ritualised way for subordinate groups to express their sense of injustice'. For Bakhtin (1984: 33), the spirit of the carnival is 'freedom': a freedom that Andrew expresses as being 'so amazingly liberating'.

Carnival is also characterized by hyperbolic performances (see Lewis and Pile, 1996) and provides a space where 'the spirit of play escapes' (Lancaster, 1999: 110). Playing in a symbolic sweetshop provides an important space for the development of new gay identities. Whilst the case has already been made for drag as a hyperbolic identity (see Bell *et al.*, 1994, and Butler, 1990), it is important to recognize that exaggerated gender performances may be liberated by the spirit of the carnivalesque. Lancaster (1999: 110) makes the case that transgressive gender performances come about during playful times of carnival: 'On the public occasion of the carnaval [*sic*] and in other carnivalesque festivities, the official body is travestied and a rebellious libidinal body is liberated.' The following extract from my research diary allows a glimpse at the body of a gay holidaymaker as he performs with a 'rebellious libidinal body':

Participant observation

Ibiza Town, August 1997

It was around midnight and I joined the crowds promenading along the Calle de la Virgen in the heart of Ibiza Town. I especially remember the spectacle of a Danish holidaymaker who was standing, grinning, in the middle of the narrow, pedestrianized street outside a German gay bar. His attractive muscle-toned, youthful body had been prepared with the necessary physical exercise to achieve a hardened masculine physique. In line with the contemporary fashion, he stood in heavy black platform boots. Around his middle he wore a black leather apron, studded in the style of a Roman Centurion. Somewhat provocatively, his buttocks were visible and sun-tanned. Heavy metal bolts penetrated his nipples and complemented the industrial look of the shiny heavy metal chain hung around his neck that supported a steel padlock as if it were a gemstone. A pair of sinister looking, black, designer sunglasses were matched with a black stocking that covered his hair (something about him suggested 'Robo-Cop'). Attached to the top of his head was a long black, 'girlie', hairpiece. As other holidaymakers walked past, he would deliberately strike a defiant pose in their path. He frequently smiled, boyishly, with the delight of entertaining the steady flow of passers-by with his outrageous outfit. Some holidaymakers photographed him, whilst others dragged their wide-eyed children away by the hand.

There are many issues raised by this particular performance, but here I am especially concerned with the implications of this form of the carnivalesque for those gay holidaymakers who are struggling to make sense of their own sexual identities. Bakhtin argues that 'carnival is a spectacle lived by people who are all participants, actors, not spectators' (Bakhtin, 1984: 7). Indeed, it is possible to appreciate how a collage of genders becomes a spectacle for all to appreciate, but for the 'wide-eyed children' this part of the carnival became a learning experience that intruded into the family holiday. For those (gay) holidaymakers who are trying to make sense of themselves and gay cultures, the spectacle of transgressive gay bodies may indeed position them as 'wide-eyed children'. For some, carnival provides a 'sweetshop' of risqué experiences where (gay) holidaymakers may explore the pic-and-mix of gender performances.

The significant emotional distance between home and away that may arise when gazing as wide-eyed spectators has a complexity that is rooted in carnival-esque experiences of excess. In this regard, the excesses associated with hyperbolic gender performances may challenge and disrupt gay people's existing senses of identity. For Lett (1983: 48), liminality has the potential to strip tourists of their identities from back home so that new 'bonds of friendship' or 'communitas' may develop. These emotional experiences may be understood in the context of Maffesoli's broader observation that 'we are witnessing the tendency for a rationalised "social" to be replaced by an empathetic "sociality", which is expressed by a succession of ambiences, feelings and emotions' (Maffesoli, 1996: 11). For Maffesoli, sociality is a matter of 'emotional community' and in this regard, it is possible to see how the emotional distance between the sociality of home and away can cause an emotional instability which gay holidaymakers need to address if they are to be able to achieve emotional coherence after returning home.

Developing Maffesoli's notion of 'emotional community', in the section that follows, I wish to explore how individual gay identities are constructed through the performances of being with other gay people in places abroad.

LEARNING HOW TO BE GAY

We travel great distances in order to live in the ways that enhance fuller contact with one another. The spaces that we cross and in which we live – to which we adapt, create, and sometimes reconstruct – have great bearing on how we come to express ourselves (Ingram, 1997: 27).

For Ingram, how we express our sexual identities is inherently bound up with the spaces that we travel through. Here I am concerned with the ways gay people choose to perform as being gay among a multiplicity of differing options open to them. As Ingram notes, the spaces that are used to 'express' a particular gay identity are of critical importance for the development of an individual's sense of gay identity. The wider significance of space for identity development is acknowledged by Hetherington: 'Almost a hundred years of sociological writing on subcultures, gangs and political groups shows us that making a space for oneself – a turf – is a major source of identification within identity practices' (Hetherington, 1998: 18). For those gay people who are denied space to be gay in their lives at home, finding gay spaces on holiday may provide 'a turf' – a space to identify with other gay people in ways that may not be possible at home. Hetherington's observation that 'a space for oneself' is integral to a wide range of identity practices is significant, not only in the context of the gay holidaymaker but also for wider debates in queer theory that often disregard commercial gay spaces as inward-looking ghettos (see Davis, 1995: 287). Contrary to arguments that have been made against the commercialization of gay cultures (see especially Whittle, 1994; Tatchell, 1996; Field, 1995), it is nevertheless important to recognize that commercial space is part of a repertoire of spaces claimed by gay people as their own. In the interview extracts quoted above, it is possible to observe how commercial gay space has had a significant influence over the lives of some gay people. Queer theory at its best is inclusive, but needs to be able to find value in all the spaces that are symbolic to people of a dissident sexual identity, since, as Maffesoli argues, it is where 'there is a sharing of the same territory (real or symbolic) that the communal idea and its ethical corollary are born' (Maffesoli, 1996: 16). Yet the greatest dilemma facing gay cultures is how to create a 'turf' for gay people that is not also a closet. For some queer commentators, such as Whittle (1994) and Désert (1997), notions of a gay village are synonymous with confinement. However, to understand gay cultures in this way relies on a fundamentally flawed notion of cultures being neatly bounded and internally homogeneous (Crang, 1999).

I didn't know how to be gay

Before expressing a sexual identity, in whatever spaces gay people find themselves, a process of learning has to take place. Here I wish to make the case that since expression is about performance (see Goffman, 1959), it is necessary to learn the performances in order that a gay identity may be articulated. Rob is in his late thirties and talks here of his early experiences of gay culture:

Martin: Right ... and how much of that finding yourself is related to your sexuality?
Rob: I think quite a lot of it ... it was especially in the early days, I mean, I knew there was something different ... I think I knew from a very early age that I was probably gay ... [Yeah] It was ... one of those bizarre situations ... I didn't know what being gay meant ... how ... well, I didn't know how to be gay ...
Martin: And so how did you find out?
Rob: Literally just by trying ... trying out different scenes and scenarios and trying a few different things out ... on holiday was the best option for that ...
Martin: Why ...?

Rob: 'Cause you weren't ... there was very little risk of you bumping into someone you knew or ...
Martin: And ... would you have done this at home?
Rob: No, never ...
Martin: So what's the difference ...
Rob: There was no risk of anyone that I knew finding out ... [Right] ... Especially there was no risk of my family finding out ... [Right]. Or the Marines ... It made me more confident about myself ... more than anything ... so that I could go out and do gay things and not worry.

Rob works as a shop manager in London, having been 'encouraged' to leave the military because of his sexuality. In the above extract he is talking in the context of recounting his first holiday experiences as a young adult when he was able to travel, alone, across Europe in a journey that took him away from the confinement of his biological family. Rob 'knew from a very early age' that he 'was probably gay' but was faced with the difficulty of not knowing 'how to be gay'. The journey out of the closet requires increasing levels of proficiency in performing as a gay person. A gay identity is learned and performed in a variety of spatial contexts and 'trying out different scenes and scenarios' is an important part of that learning process. In the parlance of the homophobe, Rob's holiday experiences had been instrumental in 'corrupting' him into a gay lifestyle. It was a holiday that enabled him to de-centre the sexual cultures associated with the heterosexual family he had grown up within.

As Rob's account reveals, it is the imagined distance between home and away that may provide holidaymakers with the confidence to feel able to take *risks* in the holiday performances in which they choose to participate. On returning home, the gay holidaymaker may feel a desire to make repeat performances and to make changes to their lifestyle at home. Since the distance between being home and away may be imagined rather than simply measured, crossing a national boundary may assist in extending that imagined distance. Away from home, this low-risk 'gay environment' affords the opportunity to be less inhibited, thereby enabling the holidaymaker to experiment and refine new performances associated with particular sexual cultures. This is a point that is further elaborated by Andrew's experiences of San Francisco:

Andrew: It [San Francisco] just sort of made it easier really, it just sort of made being gay less of an issue. You felt that you could easily belong, even if you weren't part of that community. It made you feel that you could totally be yourself.

Martin: You say you felt as though you could belong . . .?

Andrew: Well, you sort of belong to a group, the fact that you are not totally isolated. You know that you are one of so many people, so you could really be yourself . . . and the fact that you are in a different country meant that you could reinvent yourself because no one knows who you are.

Martin: How did you reinvent yourself?

Andrew: I slept with a few people. Just that whatever you did didn't matter; wherever you were, whoever you were with – because no one knew you. It was during the summer holiday when I was at college, so I knew that I would be coming back studying, so I thought that I would make the most of it, just go for it.

When you are in a different country, released from the strictures of being at home, you can 'reinvent yourself'. The desire and the ability of gay people to be able to reinvent themselves on holiday raises questions about the formation of a person's identity, suggesting that identity can be formed and then reformed, thereby supporting notions that sexual identity is fluid and ever-changing. In Andrew's case, his first visit to San Francisco resulted in a paradigmatic shift in sexual identity. Such a major change in identity occurs where the meanings attributed to one's identity no longer enable holidaymakers to make sense of the performances that are appropriate to the new spaces in which they find themselves. Of course, when sexual identity is so fundamentally challenged it is possible for the self to be maintained by rejecting the shared meanings attributed to a particular place. However, Andrew felt that he 'could easily belong' to what he perceived as a gay community. In this regard, he was able to feel that he belonged to a group. Belonging is a matter of identification.

Finding new identifications

Using a Durkheimian perspective, Weitman (1998: 71) argues that religion amounts to 'getting individuals to reidentify themselves as members of a collectivity'. Likewise, holidaying at a gay-mecca invites gay people to become part of a greater collectivity by reorienting existing sexual identities away from an individualized self. Yet there was a sense among some of my informants, that identities, especially their sexual identities, should be regarded as an intensely personal and private matter. However, identities do enter the public domain when people seek to identify with others. For Maffesoli, identification is a matter of 'elective sociality' (Maffesoli, 1996: 86) where people may associate with others as a matter of choice rather than being ascribed to any particular form of community. Here I wish to show how holidaymaking enables gay people to encounter other gay people, permitting new identifications to be made in the spaces travelled.

First, let me introduce Carlo, who is a retired office-worker in his late sixties. He is a keen naturist and now works part-time as a masseur. He lives alone in his own home. In the next interview extract, he talks about his experiences of visiting Amsterdam for the first time:

Martin: What was your most memorable holiday?

Carlo: Let me see . . . I suppose it would have been the first time I went to Amsterdam about . . . which must have been 20 to 22 years ago . . .

Martin: The first time you went, can you remember how you, sort of, felt. What was it like . . .?

Carlo: Well, I quite enjoyed it and I went to . . . er . . . went to one or two of the bars there and looked round the umm . . . the museums, I really liked the Rijksmuseum, [Yeah] and one or two other things . . . and generally, you know, the only thing that spoiled it was that I was . . . I went with a rather unsatisfactory companion . . . who . . .

Martin: Another gay man?

Carlo: Yes, yes . . . and he turned out to be a rather unsatisfactory . . . companion . . . which spoilt it a little bit . . .

Martin: Because . . .?

Carlo: . . . sort of, . . . yes, yes, he wanted to . . . sort of, run around looking in porn shops and they didn't appeal to me at all.

Martin: Did you go into any of them?

Carlo: Yes, briefly, with him, but er . . . he . . . I felt that once he got there . . . I, I like, if I'm on holiday to be with a companion, you know, to go . . . and he tended to roam, sort of, go round and do his own thing which I hadn't expected.

Martin: What about, sort of, nightlife?

Carlo: Then we did, sort of, go in the bars and things, I didn't . . . I didn't really go for the nightlife much but next time, er . . . I used to go . . . I didn't particularly [like] the leathery bars but I liked the ones, I think, by the Amstel 'cause you probably know . . . you've been to Amsterdam I expect . . . [Yeah] It's in three parts, the gay scene, your leather bit, sort of, quiet bit and I can't remember what the other bit is, but the quiet bit is the nicer, I think . . . we used to go to the Amstel Bar [that] was the one I liked.

Martin: Yeah, I know it . . . why did you like that?

Carlo: Well, just because it wasn't too noisy and it wasn't . . . people there weren't too way out they were just nice ordinary people, you know, like you and me, sort of thing. [Yeah] . . . Without being too way out or . . .

Martin: What do you mean by 'way out'?

Carlo: Well, I mean, they weren't sort of, dressed up in outrageous, er . . . leather gear, or with rings through their noses, sort of thing. [Yeah . . .] Which I don't altogether go for, sort of. I mean you may have rings through all sorts of bits of you, I don't know, but . . .

Martin: No, I'm not into pain!

Carlo: No . . .

Martin: Yeah, so were you, sort of, kind of, like 'out' when you went to Amsterdam first of all?

Carlo: . . . not really, no, no . . .

Martin: So was there any sense of like, sort of, escaping from . . .?

Carlo: Well I think it was more a sense of, sort of, exploration. [Right] . . . I thought, I've heard about Amsterdam . . . I thought it would be nice just to go and see what it was all about . . . like. [Yeah] Not so much escaping as exploration, I think.

Simply being gay is not an adequate basis for identifying with another gay person. Carlo's unsatisfactory holiday experiences stem from differences in gay identity. His exploration of Amsterdam highlights a spatial complexity that arises from a fragmentation that reflects a multiplicity of metrocentric gay cultures. For Carlo, each identity had its own place in Amsterdam: 'It's in three parts, the gay scene, your leather bit, sort of, quiet bit and I can't remember what the other bit is . . .' For the gay holidaymaker to be able to make sense of urban sexual cultures in a city such as Amsterdam requires particular skills and experience in being able to grasp the cultural landscape. In looking for 'nice ordinary people', Carlo clearly felt the need to associate with other gay people with whom he could identify, and did so by focusing on particular social spaces. In addition to the bars on the commercial gay scene, Carlo's holiday experiences illustrate how many gay people choose to combine 'non-gay' tourism attractions alongside the gay scene. For example, he illustrates a preference for the art of the Rijksmuseum (and the people who share an interest in such art) over the porn shops that punctuate the gay scene in Amsterdam. There is a sense in Carlo's account that Amsterdam was understood according to a binary taxonomy of gay and non-gay spaces, so that the Rijksmuseum became a place of respite from gay culture.

Finding real men and sissy boys

> The links between sexuality and gender have begun to fray, and many men, who were always 'macho' rather than 'sissy', have come out and become gay (Segal, 1990: 149).

Holidays provide important opportunities for gay people to broaden their understandings of sexual cultures through meeting others beyond their 'everyday' social spaces at home. Meeting new people and attempting to identify with their cultures emerged as a strong theme in the course of my research. For many of those gay people, like Carlo, who were looking for 'ordinary people' akin to themselves with whom they could identify, gender performance arose as an issue that 'troubled' them. Butler (1990) has argued that gender is a troubling issue for feminists. Here, in the two short accounts that follow, it is possible to see how gender and identifications form a significant issue among gay people. First, James tells a story of how his experiences in Australia enabled him to distinguish between sexuality and gender:

Martin: Can you explain what happened to you on holiday [in Australia] that enabled you to stop pretending you were straight?
James: I, I think it was ... before I went to Australia I thought that I was straight ... well ish ... because I thought of gay men as being limp-wristed sissy boys, who wore women's clothes and camped about. You know the type ... when I was at school they used to be the ones who got teased and called poof. At school I would join in on this ... this gay bashing ...'cause it never occurred to me that I was a poofter, even though I got a thrill from looking at the other boys in the school showers. [So ...] So, yeah, I'm still not really interested in that sort of 'Nellie' type of gay man. I have to say, being gay in that way ain't me guv ... What I discovered in Australia was that there are plenty of men ... men like me who are like ... real men and are gay at the same time ... if you see what I mean.
Martin: Yeah ... what do you mean by real men?
James: Masculine ... not camp. In Sydney I noticed that there were plenty of tough guys on the gay scene. There are plenty of butch guys in London ... but, I first noticed that type of gay man in Sydney.

Prior to his holidaymaking experiences in Sydney, 'gay masculinity' seemed something of an oxymoron for James who, prior to travelling, had a limited understanding of metrocentric gay cultures. Living in suburban Essex, 'cottages' (public toilets) were the only places in which his male-to-male sexual experiences had taken place. His experiences in Sydney precipitated a desire to identify with a new group of people and make a break with his past. His journey to metropolitan Sydney afforded the possibility of encountering, not just a singular gay role model, but a choice of metropolitan gay identities that could be explored and experimented with. Masculinity in its various forms, which James describes as 'butch' or 'camp,' is often the public performance of gay identities and provides a focus for identifications.

A different perspective on the relationship between gay sexuality and gender is provided by Phillip, a student in his early twenties. In the context of discussing holidays to places in England, Phillip evaluates a holiday resort according to his experiences of the gay gender performances that he associates with a particular place. Here he discusses the English seaside resort of Brighton:

Phillip: Brighton's OK . . . but it's not my favourite place . . . it's . . .

Martin: What didn't you like about it?

Phillip: Just some of the people there. You go down there and . . . you see them first and then . . . when they open their mouths you think, yuck! [Really?] Yeah, because they look cool to start with and then as soon as they speak to you, my heart sinks . . . [Why?] Because I think gay men should be more straight-acting . . . I don't like all that fluffy stuff, especially when gays talk about 'she' instead of 'he'.

Gender performance is complex and, as Phillip points out, speaking is part of the performance. Developing this point, Delph-Janiurek (1999) argues that our voices can be stylised to become a form of drag in which idealizations of masculinity or femininity can be parodied. For Delph-Janiurek, voice is an important element of performing gay identities. For Phillip, voice is a significant part of being able to identify with those identities. Gender and gay sexuality emerge not only as intricate but also as contentious and politicized issues. Among some gay people, camp is regarded as an inadequate gender performance that is too closely associated with homophobic representations of gay men. More broadly, Segal (1990: 16) argues that homophobia has resulted in the 'forced repression of the "feminine" in all men'. Developing this point, Clatterbaugh (1997: 138) observes that to be gay is often regarded as a failure to be masculine. Yet, far from being a failed performance, camp may be portrayed as 'a screaming great laugh', a 'playful performance' that is 'a declaration of effeminate intent' (Medhurst, 1997: 274–93). Significantly, in searching through my interview transcripts, I was unable to find stories of gay men who did much to defend the 'sissy-boy' gender performance. Ironically, however, although many gay men may aspire to get 'butch', Silverman (1992: 346) argues that 'virile displays always seem so feminine' and points to the way some gay men wear masculine clothes with female precision.

So it would seem that gender is a troubling issue for many gay people, not least because metrocentric gay culture is diffracted into a multiplicity of gender formations, each carrying the potential for conflict with and rejection from other gender performances. Among the most dominant are those gay people who consider themselves to be 'straight-acting' and privilege themselves as being 'normal'. More broadly, those who hold this position are part of a cultural politics that values masculinity over femininity. Further, the straight-acting gay male may be deconstructed as being involved in a project that ties gender to biological sex (male *or* female), whilst constructing sexuality as a separate layer of the human self. Here, Butler's (1990) notion of performativity strips 'straight' gender performances of any sense of authenticity.

CONCLUSION

Overall, it can be appreciated that there is a strong association between holidaymaking and changes in gay identity. As an exploration of gay identities, there is a sense that this chapter represents a journey through a range of spaces found on the Western gay scene. Initial experiences of metrocentric gay cultures, by men whose knowledges of gay performances may arise from provincial areas of Britain, provide a profound illustration of the impact of gay spaces on identity change.

A point that seems to characterize the long-haul out of the closet is the emotional distance from being at home. This emotional geography represents a development of Urry's (1990: 11) understanding that 'tourism results from a basic binary division between the ordinary/everyday and the extraordinary'. Here I have endorsed this binarism of home and away. However, through an engagement with Maffesoli's (1996) notion of an emotional community, I have suggested that holidaymakers experience this divide emotionally and that this yields an important *emotional distance* as they move between being at home and away on holiday.

Away from home, gay men may develop competency in performing their gay identities. The acquisition of such skills underlines the importance of holidays as opportunities for learning experiences that may equip gay men to manage their sexual identities and cope with the issues associated with homophobia.

Accepting this to be the case, the educational value of gay holidaymaking arises, not only from travelling through spaces that are different to home, but also comes from the sense of emotional freedom that such a distance may grant. This, however, is not to suggest that such freedom inevitably brings about opportunities for greater agency of the self but may also be allied to an engagement with alternative forms of performativity not previously experienced at home.

Furthermore, it would seem that the emotional geographies of gay holiday-making might vary according to previous experiences of gay cultures. This is an important factor since repeated experiences may serve to reduce the emotional distance and, thereby, alter the relationship between Urry's (1990) 'basic' binarism of ordinary (home) and extraordinary (away). Here it is possible to extend this understanding of tourism if we accept that experience has the capacity to erode the sense of novelty and wonderment that the tourist gaze may initially bring. For example, in this chapter, the 'mundane' experience of walking down the street became extraordinary because it was a street in a gay locale; yet, this is an experience that may lose its emotional distance from home with further experiences. Whilst the relationship between being at home and away on holiday is at the heart of holidaymaking experiences, it is important to recognize that 'home' is as much about being 'away', since the two are held in a complex dialectical relationship where it may not always be possible to differentiate clearly between the two. To sum up, I would stress that the distinction between home and away is as much about emotional experiences that are embodied and performed as it is about a tourist gaze. Gazing, of course, is an embodied performance that is fundamental to the emotional experiences of the gay holidaymaker.

Finally, the long-haul out of the closet is about how homosexually inclined people learn to participate in particular gay sexual cultures through the spatialized practices of holidaymaking, which may provide the emotional distance from home that facilitates identity change. In this chapter, the ethnographer's gaze has focused on some of the positive aspects of gay cultural identities and as such serves as a deliberate rebuff to homophobes and over-zealous queers who see little value in the apparent hedonism of the metrocentric gay lifestyles found in Boystown.

NOTES

1. I am grateful to Judy Hemingway, Phil Crang and Hugh Clout for their comments on an earlier version of this work. Note that 'Boystown' is a term used by American gay men to describe the gay area of West Hollywood (Le Vay and Nonas, 1995).
2. Names of all interviewees quoted in this chapter are pseudonyms.

REFERENCES

Altman, D. (1971), *Homosexual Oppression and Liberation*. New York: New York University Press.

Bakhtin, M. (1984), *Rabelais and his World*. Bloomington, IN: Indiana University Press.

Bedford, B. and Rauch, R. (eds) (2000) (29th edn), *Spartacus International Gay Guide: 2000–2001*. Berlin: Bruno Gmünder Verlag.

Bell, D., Binnie, J., Cream, J. and Valentine, G. (1994), 'All hyped up and no place to go', *Gender, Place and Culture*, 1, (1): 31–47.

Binnie, J. (1997), 'Invisible Europeans: sexual citizenship in the new Europe', *Environment and Planning A*, 29: 237–48.

Brown, M. (1999), 'Travelling through the closet', in J. Duncan and D. Gregory (eds), *Writes of Passage: Reading Travel Writing*. London: Routledge.

Butler, J. (1990), *Gender Trouble*. London: Routledge.

Butler, R. (1999), 'Double the trouble, twice the fun? Disabled bodies in gay spaces', in R. Butler and H. Parr (eds), *Mind and Body Spaces: Geographies of Disability and Impairment*. London: Routledge.

Clatterbaugh, K. (1997) (2nd edn), *Contemporary Perspectives on Masculinity: Men, Women, and Politics in Modern Society*. Oxford: Westview Press.

Craik, J. (1997), 'The culture of tourism', in C. Rojek and J. Urry (eds), *Touring Cultures: Transformations of Travel and Theory*. London: Routledge.

Crang, P. (1999), 'Local–global', in P. Cloke, P. Crang and M. Goodwin. (eds), *Introducing Human Geographies*. London: Arnold.

Davies, P. (1992), 'The role of disclosure in coming out among gay men', In K. Plummer (ed.), *Modern Homosexualities: Fragments of Lesbian and Gay Experience*. London: Routledge.

Davis, T. (1995), 'The diversity of queer politics and the redefinition of sexual identity and community in urban spaces', in D. Bell and G. Valentine (eds), *Mapping Desire: Geographies of Sexualities*. London: Routledge.

Delph-Janiurek, T. (1999), 'Sounding gender(ed): vocal performances in English university teaching spaces', *Gender, Place and Culture*, 6 (2): 137–53.

Désert, J. (1997), 'Queer space', in G. Ingram, A. Bouthillette and Y. Retter (eds), *Queers in Space: Communities, Public Spaces, Sites of Resistance*. Seattle, Washington: Bay Press.

Field, N. (1995), *Over the Rainbow: Money, Class and Homophobia*. London: Pluto Press.

Glennie, P. and Thrift, N. (1992), 'Modernity, urbanism and modern consumption', *Environment and Planning D: Society and Space*, 10: 423–43.

Goffman, E. (1959), *The Presentation of Self in Everyday Life*. London: Pelican.

Herdt, G. (1992), '"Coming out" as a rite of passage: a Chicago study', in G. Herdt (ed.), *Gay in America*. Boston, MA: Beacon Press.

Hetherington, K. (1998), *Expressions of Identity: Space, Performance, Politics*. London: Sage.

Ingram, G. (1997), '"Open" space as strategic queer sites', in G. Ingram, A. Bouthillette and Y. Retter (eds), *Queers in Space: Communities, Public Spaces, Sites of Resistance*. Seattle, Washington: Bay Press.

Jackson, P. (1989), *Maps of Meaning*. London: Routledge.

Jenness, V. (1992), 'Coming out: lesbian identities and the categorization problem', in K. Plummer (ed.), *Modern Homosexualities: Fragments of Lesbian and Gay Experience*. London: Routledge.

Lancaster, R. (1999), '"That we should all turn queer?": homosexual stigma in the making of manhood and the breaking of a revolution in Nicaragua', in R. Parker and P. Aggleton (eds), *Culture, Society and Sexuality: A Reader*. London: UCL Press.

Lett, J. (1983), 'Ludic and liminoid aspects of charter yacht tourism in the Caribbean', *Annals of Tourism Research*, 10: 35–56.

Le Vay, S. and Nonas, E. (1995), *City of Friends: A Portrait of the Gay and Lesbian Community in America*. Cambridge, MA: MIT Press.

Lewis, C. and Pile, S. (1996), 'Woman, body, space: Rio carnival and the politics of performance', *Gender, Place and Culture*, 3, (1): 23–41.

Maffesoli, M. (1996), *The Time of the Tribes: The Decline of Individualism in Mass Society*. London: Sage.

McIntosh, M. (1997), 'Class', in A. Medhurst and S. Munt (eds), *Lesbian and Gay Studies: A Critical Introduction*. London: Cassell.

Medhurst, A. (1997), 'Camp', in A. Medhurst and S. Munt (eds), *Lesbian and Gay Studies: A Critical Introduction*. London: Cassell.

Munt, I. (1994), 'The "Other" postmodern tourism: culture, travel, and the new middle classes', *Theory, Culture and Society*, 11: 101–23.

Phillips, R., Watt, D. and Shuttleton, D. (eds) (2000), *De-centring Sexualities: Politics and Representations beyond the Metropolis*. London: Routledge.

Savin-Williams, R. (1998), '. . . and then I became gay': Young Men's Stories. London: Routledge.

Sedgwick, E. (1990), *Epistemology of the Closet*. Berkley, CA: University of California Press.

Segal, L. (1990), *Slow Motion: Changing Masculinities – Changing Men*. London: Virago Press.

Shields, R. (1991), *Places on the Margin: Alternative Geographies of Modernity*. London: Routledge.

Shuttleton, D. (2000), 'The queer politics of gay pastoral', in R. Phillips, D. Watt and D. Shuttleton (eds), *De-centring Sexualities: Politics and Representations beyond the Metropolis*. London: Routledge.

Signorile, M. (1994), *Queer in America: Sex, the Media and the Closets of Power*. London: Abacus.

Silverman, K. (1992), *Male Subjectivity at the Margins*. London: Routledge.

Sinfield, A. (1997), 'Identity and subculture', in A. Medhurst and S. Munt (eds), *Lesbian and Gay Studies: A Critical Introduction*. London: Cassell.

Skelton, T. (1995), 'Boom, bye, bye: Jamaican ragga and gay resistance', in D. Bell and G. Valentine (eds), *Mapping Desire: Geographies of Sexualities*. London: Routledge.

Tatchell, P. (1996), 'It's just a phase: why homosexuality is doomed', in M. Simpson (ed.), *Anti-Gay*. London: Freedom Editions (Cassell).

Tresidder, R. (1999), 'Tourism and sacred landscapes', in D. Crouch (ed.), *Leisure/Tourism Geographies: Practices and Geographical Knowledge*. London: Routledge.

Turner, V. (1973), 'The centre out there: pilgrim's goal', *History of Religions*, 12 (3): 191–230.

Turner, V. (1976), 'Social dramas and ritual metaphors', in R. Schechner and M. Schuman (eds), *Ritual, Play and Performance: Readings in the Social Sciences/Theatre*. New York: Seasbury Press.

Turner, V. (1982), *From Ritual to Theatre: The Human Seriousness of Play*. New York: *Performing Arts Journal* publication.

Urry, J. (1990), *The Tourist Gaze: Leisure and Travel in Contemporary Societies*. London: Sage.

Valentine, G. (1993), 'Negotiating and managing multiple sexual identities: lesbian time–place strategies', *Transactions of British Geographers* (new series), 18: 37–248.

Weeks, J. (1971), *Coming Out: Homosexual Politics in Britain from the Nineteenth Century to the Present*. London: Quartet.

Weitman, S. (1998), 'On the elementary forms of the socioerotic life', *Theory, Culture and Society*, 15: 71–110.

Whittle, S. (ed.) (1994), *The Margins of the City: Gay Men's Urban Lives*. Aldershot: Arena.

CHAPTER 7

Gay Men's Holidays: Identity and Inhibitors

HOWARD L. HUGHES

INTRODUCTION

It is not surprising that a body such as the World Tourism Organization (WTO) – an intergovernmental agency with affiliate trade membership – should wish to encourage tourism. In the process, it has endeavoured to affirm the 'right' to tourism. Its recent Global Code of Ethics (1999), draws upon the UN Universal Declaration of Human Rights of 1948 to justify its stance. Although the 1948 Declaration does not specifically mention tourism, it does refer to other related rights such as 'freedom of movement of people'. These are referred to in the WTO Global Code of Ethics:

> The prospect of direct and personal access to the discovery and enjoyment of the planet's resources constitutes a right equally open to all the world's inhabitants ... The universal right to tourism must be regarded as the corollary of the right to rest and leisure ... guaranteed by the Universal Declaration of Human Rights 1948, Article 24 (Article 7, Global Code of Ethics, WTO, 1999).

> Tourists and visitors should benefit ... from the liberty to move within their countries and from one state to another in accordance with ... the Universal Declaration of Human Rights 1948, Article 13 (Article 8, Global Code of Ethics, WTO, 1999).

In view of this, restrictions on the movement of tourists could be regarded as an infringement of fundamental liberties and human rights. Restrictions do take many forms including external factors such as visa requirements, travel prohibitions between certain countries and currency restrictions. Adverse attitudes and dissonant cultural norms of host communities can have a less formal but equally restrictive effect on travel. Factors that are more internal to the traveller include limited incomes, poor health and social and cultural mores that do not include travel.

Restrictions may therefore influence the ability to travel at all and also the choice of destination. Travel within countries and between countries is not, for many reasons, a universal activity. In this chapter, it is suggested that there are a number of features relating to homosexuality that might influence the choice of holiday and of destination in such a way as to make the process and the outcome different from that of other people. Holiday-taking propensity is unlikely to differ from that of equivalent others, but destination choice may be more restricted. It is argued that the gay market is not an easily identifiable one, but that for many gay men the holiday does perform a vital function related to identity. Any restrictions on travel are therefore not only a limitation on a fundamental right, but also on the ability to construct that identity. The final part of the chapter discusses an analytical framework for identifying some of the key issues in holiday choice by gay men. (The discussion in this chapter is, for ease of analysis, limited to male homosexuals also referred to as gay men.)

GAY MEN AND HOLIDAY-TAKING

There is considerable interest in targeting gay men as a market segment for tourism as they are regarded as a high-income group with few dependants and with a lifestyle that is highly leisure-focused. Gay culture is widely considered to be leisure-centric. 'With more leisure and disposable income than the average person, gays have been represented as the marketing department's dream consumer' (MAPS, 1998: 5). Gays are also often characterized as being 'free thinking', and at the 'cutting edge' of life and as being individualistic and style-conscious. The propensity to go on holiday is considered to be high. Various surveys in the United States and the UK report an above-average proportion of gays as being in 'upper' social groups, earning above-average incomes and being more likely than others to have additional holidays (Clark, 1997; MAPS, 1998). It is claimed, for instance, that gay men in the United States take more overseas trips than do other US travellers (Jefferies, 1999; Wood, 1999). It is relatively uncontentious that few gay men have children and therefore discretionary incomes are likely to be higher than those of other people of a similar age and occupation. It is undoubtedly true that the financial burden of family life is not borne by most gays.

There are fundamental problems with such characterizations of gay men however. First, it is not easy to define homosexuality or being gay (see Weeks, 1992; Sinfield, 1997; Nardi and Schneider, 1998). There is a common assumption that the homosexual is defined by sexual activity. There is though a distinction between homosexual activity and homosexual orientation; the former is probably more widespread than is the latter. Some men may occasionally have same-sex sex but may not identify as gay, and they may have opposite-sex partners or spouses; others may identify as gay but not be sexually active. Sexuality is a very fluid concept and being homosexual is ultimately a self-defined category. (That is not the same as saying that a person chooses to be homosexual.)

The second problem is that the 'distinctive' characteristics of gay men are usually identified through surveys. Being homosexual is a characteristic that many people will not admit to and will conceal. The social (and legal) censure of homosexual acts means that many will choose not to be open about defining themselves as homosexual. The invisibility of the gay population creates difficulties in ascertaining the exact size and composition of the gay population. The so-called distinguishing characteristics of gay men are no more than a reflection of the readership of certain magazines and the likelihood of response to surveys. The respondents are self-selecting. The reality is that it is unwise to assume that gays are anything else but a mirror of the rest of society in terms of age, class, ethnicity and income. There are dangers in regarding the gay market as a homogeneous entity exclusively identified by sexual orientation. There are great differences within it defined by demographic, attitudinal and ideological factors (MAPS, 1998). Gays are not homogeneous in terms of employment and income, and not all gays are high-income and able to take a holiday. (The single most important reason, amongst the population as a whole, for not having a holiday is limited income.) There are many niches within the market and the distinctions are increasing so that the gay market is fragmenting making it less identifiable. It is relatively easy to segment markets by geography or demographics but not so by sexuality (MAPS, 1998).

It is unwise to assume that gay men are frequent and intensive holiday-takers as there is no clear evidence of this. Those gay men identified in self-selecting surveys may well, though, have these characteristics. They may be a segment within the overall classification of gay men which is identifiable as being 'out', young, fashion-conscious, leisure-centric, etc. It may be that such a 'sub-segment' is one at which products such as holidays are often targeted. It is not too certain, however, that gay men are a viable market segment (see Fugate, 1993; Pritchard and Morgan, 1996; Penaloza, 1996).

It also needs to be recognized that it is difficult, if not undesirable, to segment most products according to sexuality (see Field, 1995). Gay men invariably purchase the same products as anyone else and will not need to be targeted, though it is conceivable that gays may be responsive and loyal to mainstream producers who promote their products in gay media or represent gay life in advertisements. None the less there are certain products that may be reasonably targeted at the gay market – in particular those relating to leisure activity, as it is within this sphere that gays find much of their identity and wish to be with like-minded people (see below). This will be the case for bars, clubs and restaurants, and also for holidays, in the sense of destinations chosen, but also possibly in the choice of intermediary (travel agent, tour operator).

SIGNIFICANCE OF THE HOLIDAY

In the holiday market there are products being developed and targeted at the gay market (Holcomb and Luongo, 1996). There is a view that there are clearly identifiable market needs for this segment, which are not met by the more general provision of tourist products. In the UK there are a small number of specialist tour operators such as the long-established Sensations (merged with Man Around in May 1999 and relaunched itself as Respect). Mainstream operators have entered the market also, but somewhat tentatively: Going Places launched Travel Unlimited in 1998 as a call-centre booking operation. There are also a number of places that are identified as gay-friendly destinations such as Brighton, Blackpool and Manchester in the UK (see: www.gaybritain.org) and foreign destinations such as South Beach Miami, the Spanish beach towns of Sitges, Ibiza Town and Gran Canaria, the Greek island of Mykonos and the cities of New York, San Francisco, Amsterdam (The Netherlands) and Sydney (Australia).

A casual glance at the gay press and its holiday advertisements suggests that gay men are interested very largely in sun, sea, sand and sex when on holiday. There are few obvious holidays devoted to 'special-interest' tourism such as heritage, arts, sport, ethnic tourism, adventure or safari holidays (although recently, Alternative Holidays have marketed skiing holidays for gay men). There are clear sexual images in advertisements and brochures as well as information on where casual sex encounters occur. This apparent preoccupation with sex may seem no more than a reflection of the popular perception of gay life generally. Much of the 'gay scene' – the gay leisure space – appears to be directed towards the pursuit of casual sex. The popular image of promiscuity amongst homosexuals is, however, clearly a misrepresentation of the reality of the lives of most homosexual men. It is likely that the majority of gay men do not frequent the 'gay scene'. Many gay men find the 'scene' to be over-commercialized and youth-oriented, as well as a symbol of undesirable ghettoization.

Holidays for gay men are, though, rather more than 'sex-tourism' and may be more usefully interpreted in terms of their contribution to the process of establishing identity. 'The holiday ... is likely to make a very significant contribution to the creation and validation of identity for many gay men' (Hughes, 1997: 7). Being away from home gives an opportunity to be gay in a way that many people cannot experience at home or in work. The nature of society has been such that it has been difficult for gay men to be open about their sexuality. Discrimination against gays has encouraged them to find their identity in the leisure sphere.

There are a number of 'push' factors that cause gay men to construct and validate that identity away from home. These include social censure and the desires to be oneself, to relate to 'similar others' and to be anonymous. There is the push of the exclusion from 'normal' society and the consequent need for the reassurance of the open and secure company of other gay men; however, opportunities for this are limited. The gay man is, in large part, able to be himself only in gay space (Bell, 1991). In addition many gays will choose to travel in search of an anonymous environment in which to be gay. Gays may not frequent local gay space because of the fear of discovery and may choose to 'be gay' elsewhere.

The gay space acts as the 'pull' factor that meets the needs caused by these push factors. This gay space, however, is limited. The acceptance of a homosexual identity is often dependent upon the act of being 'a tourist', at least in the sense of travel. A holiday away from home is an extension of this gay man's need and desire to be away. The significance of the holiday may be even more important for gay men than it is for many others in that it provides an opportunity, over an extended and continuous period of time, to be oneself.

Gay men are likely, none the less, to have reasons for going on holiday that are similar to those of the rest of the population. Clift and Forrest (1999) not surprisingly discovered that, for gay men, rest and relaxation, comfort and good food, and sunshine were the most important factors in 'planning a holiday'. This is probably no different from the average holidaymaker but, in addition, survey

178

respondents did consider it important to socialize with gay men and to access gay culture and venues ('fairly' or 'very important' to 77 per cent and 80 per cent respectively). Opportunities to have sex were important to only a relatively low proportion.

RESPONSES OF THE TRAVEL INDUSTRY

There are undoubtedly economic activities geared towards the market segment of gay men. Apart from the activities of tour operators there are also tourist boards and visitor bureaus, which have considered this to be a market worth pursuing. The London Tourist Board (LTB) launched a major campaign in the United States in 1998, which was aimed at gays aged thirty to fifty in New York, Washington and San Francisco. It currently operates a 'pink' phone-line giving information on bars and clubs, cafés and restaurants and shops and stores. The British Tourist Authority (BTA) launched a campaign in 1999 aimed at the UK travel trade in order to raise their awareness of the potential of this market (Jefferies, 1999). It was felt that there was great potential for encouraging overseas visitors to the UK, and the BTA has published a number of brochures aimed at this gay market. In one it claims that 'Britain has a vibrant gay and lesbian culture and community just waiting to welcome you' (BTA, 1999). BTA and LTB research shows that gays are as interested in the mainstream attractions of Britain as are other travellers; they probably eat out more and visit the theatre more. They are interested in visiting a gay-friendly destination, not necessarily a gay destination and not necessarily wanting to stay in gay hotels.

These campaigns are not without their opponents however. The city of Manchester (England), through its agency Marketing Manchester, launched a promotion (1999) to establish the city as 'one of the world's gay capitals'. The particular purpose was to attract US gay visitors to the city. Reactions were not obviously homophobic but included comments such as this from the chair of the Civic Society: 'We need to be tolerant of all sorts of people but we have to get the balance right. The decision to highlight the city's gay image is misleading and . . . could alienate other visitors Manchester wants to attract' (quoted in the *Daily Telegraph*, 24 July 1999). He felt that the unique heritage of the city should have been given precedence in any tourism campaign. A prominent city councillor also expressed the view that 'the priority is to market Manchester as a family-friendly city and a place for new business. We welcome any spending tourists but gay tourism is not our priority' (quoted in the *Manchester Metro News*, 14 August 1999). In addition, not all gays welcome the idea of their gay space being promoted as part of the tourist product. Gay populations have themselves recognized that there may be adverse effects of destination popularity (Pritchard *et al.*, 1998).

Even in Amsterdam there have been problems. The city is well known for its liberal attitudes to drugs and sex and alternative lifestyles, and has a reputation for being particularly tolerant of homosexuality. The Netherlands has a more liberal approach to homosexuality than is the case with many countries and there is, ostensibly, greater toleration of gay life-styles. As a result, Amsterdam has 'one of the most sophisticated and developed lesbian and gay communities and commercial scenes of any city of its size anywhere in the world' (Binnie, 1995: 190). The city has been described as being 'second only to San Francisco in its social acceptance of homosexuality' (Catling, 1991: 151), and has been labelled the 'gay capital of Europe' (Duyves, 1995). The city is identified worldwide as a centre for gay life and is perceived as a gay-friendly place where gay lifestyles go unremarked. As a consequence, it has a strong appeal to many from outside the country and is a popular place to visit. Travel guides aimed at gay travellers invariably identify Amsterdam as an important gay destination. Nearly half of gay men from the UK in a 1996 survey had visited Amsterdam during the previous five years (Clift and Forrest, 1999) and visitors from Great Britain and Ireland make up just over 20 per cent of all gay visitors to the city (Hughes, 1998).

Despite Amsterdam's popularity, a tourist board campaign aimed at the US gay market in 1992 was not repeated, largely because of reactions amongst the tourist trade in the city. It was considered to project an undesirable image, which would alienate other visitors to the city. Gay tourism remains a 'hidden aspect of Amsterdam's tourism' (Hughes, 1998: 177).

INHIBITORS OF CHOICE

Despite the eagerness of many in tourism to capitalize on the gay market, there remain a number of practical factors that serve to inhibit gay tourism. Although participation in tourism is common in 'Western' industrialized societies there are still large proportions of their populations who are unable or unwilling to travel (Hughes, 1991). Much of this non-participation arises from 'internal' factors such as limited disposable income and social and cultural 'relevance' and, for some, travel and holidays are of little significance (Haukeland, 1990). From the above discussion, it is unlikely that these will be of great significance in the case of gay men but there may well be other, 'external', impediments to travel.

As already noted gay men may seek a destination identified as 'gay space'. Such gay-friendly places are limited and therefore destination choice is limited.

The choice of holiday destination may be constrained by the fact that in certain countries homosexual relations are illegal and in others subject to severe social censure. Amnesty International (1997) reports that homosexual acts are illegal in over 70 countries, including many Caribbean countries, many Middle Eastern countries, the countries of the Indian sub-continent and five US states. Laws relating to public decency or public order (as in China) may also be applied to demonstrations of affection. Punishments in some Islamic countries can be particularly severe. Laws are not, however, always applied, and often gay tourists are tolerated. None the less, the proscription of same-sex acts can give out signals to potential tourists.

Of course, the legality of same-sex relationships does not guarantee tolerance. Despite the legalization of homosexual acts (consenting adults in private) since 1967 in Britain, for instance, much prejudice, social disapproval and inequality of legal rights remains. The appeal of Amsterdam for two visitors from England (1996) was that 'we did something we've never done before . . . we walked down the street holding hands' (quoted in Hughes, 1998: 168). The choice of destination may well therefore be limited to those places where gays are tolerated and where it is known that hostile reaction will be minimized.

Holidays will obviously be unsatisfactory if verbal or physical abuse, social disapproval or threatening behaviour are experienced or anticipated. Such factors could result in levels of anxiety and restraint that are not experienced by heterosexual tourists. There may therefore be impediments to travel such as hostility within destinations from locals and other tourists and also from travel intermediaries such as staff of travel agencies, tour operators and hotels.

There is also some evidence of discrimination in hotel accommodation. Jones (1996) undertook a 'mystery-shopper' type of study of a number of hotels (320) in the United States. He found that in responses to enquiries for bookings 'significantly fewer requests were granted to the same-sex couple than to the opposite-sex couple' (Jones, 1996: 155). This was most evident in the smaller, bed-and-breakfast hotel. It was thought that this might be due to personal prejudice or to a fear of same-sex couples being more conspicuous. A much smaller (and non-academic) survey conducted by a national newspaper showed similar discrimination in the UK. A gay couple were refused bookings or required to sleep in separate beds by three out of ten hotels contacted in the small *ad hoc* survey (Tuck, 1998). The newspaper also referred to a Stonewall report, which indicated that 17 per cent of gay people had been made to feel unwelcome because of their sexuality when staying in a hotel.

A similar nation-wide phone survey undertaken by the internet magazine *www.queercompany.com* suggested that about 17 per cent of UK hotels outside London would refuse a booking from a gay or lesbian couple. The survey enquirers were open about employment by the magazine and it is conjectured that, as a result, responses were more favourable than would otherwise have been the case (Bustin, 2000).

There is further anecdotal evidence of gay people being given a twin room rather than a double (Clark, 1997). The manager of a Birmingham (England) hotel has stated that the hotel 'would never knowingly let a double room to two males but would ... offer them a room with twin beds'. The policy was introduced after complaints from other guests in the past (Skinner, 1995). An obvious explanation for much of this is prejudice, though there is also some fuzziness in the law as it relates to men. The (UK) *Sexual Offences Act 1967* which legalized sexual acts between (adult) men did so only if they were 'in private'. It is arguable that a hotel is a public place. It is not altogether surprising that gays seek out gay-friendly accommodation and tour operators, as well as gay-friendly destinations.

It is common for persons (gay or straight) who are HIV-positive to be refused long-stay visas or immigration status in many countries of the world, but even visits for holiday purposes may be difficult. Any HIV-positive person wishing to holiday in the United States, for instance, is likely to be denied entry (Alcorn, 1999). Any HIV person, gay or straight, who wishes to holiday in the United States therefore faces a problem. Being open about status to immigration officials runs the risk of entry being denied. Not disclosing status may be inadvisable, as many HIV-positive people will be taking medication, which may be identified at immigration. An alternative is to send on medication to a 'safe address' (Alcorn, 1999). An added problem for an HIV-positive person is that travel insurance usually excludes claims arising from HIV infection (although some insurance companies will insure HIV travellers, see Scholey, Chapter 11 this volume).

Much of the imagery of holidays is (understandably) heterosexual and often family-oriented, which in itself may reduce the willingness of gays to use the services of the major inclusive tour operators. The difficulties associated with being openly gay are not removed by being on holiday but by being on holiday with similar others and in gay-friendly locations. Travelling and staying with heterosexuals may not be popular.

A number of studies, not concerned with gay men specifically, have identified similar inhibitors to destination choice and also to holiday or leisure participation. A study of the Afro-Caribbean community in the UK suggested that their holiday profile differed considerably from that of the white population (Stephenson, 1998). Travel, for this community, has overtones of exploitation in the transatlantic slave system. It is also associated with economic necessity – the migration to industrial societies – and is regarded as having been a mechanism for oppressing the Afro-Caribbean community. The holiday was regarded as a Western white activity, and for the Afro-Caribbean community, travel was most often visits to friends and relatives in the Caribbean. There was evidence too that domestic tourism based on the countryside was not undertaken often. Again it was associated with a white concept of ruralness and heritage.

Travel was also inhibited by perceptions of rejection and exclusion. There was a fear that presence in rural areas would be conspicuous and would arouse antagonism. At the least, the prospect of being the object of the residents' and other tourists' 'gaze' was sufficient to confine leisure activities to familiar urban areas. Travel to many parts of Europe was also considered undesirable in view of perceived strong racist feelings in some countries. There was a fear too of harassment at borders by customs and immigration officials.

Disadvantaged families living in the north of England also felt uncomfortable and conspicuous when on holiday (Smith and Hughes, 1999). Even though they recognized a number of particularly beneficial outcomes of the holiday, there were a number of aspects that made them 'uncomfortable'. They were not familiar with the 'rituals' and they often felt that their clothes and travel cases and bags made them conspicuous. Some also felt self-conscious about the fact that they were receiving subsidized holidays and this was obvious to guesthouse or caravan owners.

These experiences may be analogous with the situation of gay men. Holidays are something that are associated with 'others' – at least in terms of images and marketing strategies – and presence in a place may give rise to adverse reactions from others. 'All tourists transform the space they occupy, but in the case of gay tourists, transformation is the consequence of a group of people who are marginalised in society. The transformation thus has the potential for alienating other tourists' (Hughes, 1998: 164). Knowledge of the adverse tourist and locals' gaze may be sufficient to limit destination choice considerably.

Destination choice may therefore be a much more constrained process than it is for heterosexual tourists, and there may be a significant number of inhibitors in destination choice. Within destinations there may be further inhibitors which restrict activity in terms of behaviour and in terms of places visited. The holiday may not be the liberating experience that was expected in that many of the restraints experienced at home may be equally evident on holiday. These

Table 7.1 Types of risk associated with international travel. *Source:* based on Sömmez and Graefe, 1998.

- *Equipment and functional*: mechanical, equipment, organizational problems (transport, accommodation, attractions)
- *Financial*: trip will not provide value for money
- *Health*: becoming sick
- *Physical*: physical danger or injury (accidents)
- *Political*: becoming involved in political turmoil
- *Psychological*: trip will not reflect the individual's personality or self-image (disappointment)
- *Satisfaction*: trip will not provide personal satisfaction or self-actualization (dissatisfaction)
- *Social*: trip will affect others' opinion of individual (disapproval of destination or activities)
- *Terrorism*: being involved in terrorist act
- *Time*: trip takes too much time or wastes time

---

experiences (actual or anticipated) feed into the destination choice process. Anticipation of such experiences will not only restrict behaviour whilst on holiday but will restrict destination choice.

Even though the gay man may find fulfilment in the holiday and adverse experiences do not occur, there is still the irreducible fact of limited choice. There remain constraints in terms of places that may be chosen for holiday purposes. The awareness of limited choice may confirm a perception of hetero-hegemony and reduce self-esteem.

A FRAMEWORK FOR ANALYSIS

Destination choice can be analysed in a number of ways. It is a complex process into which risk-avoidance may enter. Some general studies have focused on risk-avoidance as a key element in destination choice. By its very nature travel involves risk as invariably it is an untried product and even return trips to places occur under 'new' circumstances. Different people have different reactions to risk, and undoubtedly some places are perceived to be more risky than others. Risk can be categorized into several types (see Table 7.1). Perceptions of these risks and of personal safety can influence destination image and choice. Risk-avoidance may be a particularly relevant issue in gay men's holiday choice. The risks in Table 7.1 are generally applicable, and it may be that risks to gay men can be encompassed within these. Some risks are not explicit in Table 7.1 however: gay men may face a greater 'physical risk' than other travellers given the ever-present possibility and fear of violent attack (and perhaps sexual assault). Being a victim of 'crimes' such as theft, mugging and assault is not explicit either (Mawby, 2000). Minority groups (ethnic and sexual) are frequently the objects of physical and verbal abuse. In addition, gay space is (in urban areas in particular) close to or within marginal, run-down areas. Typically, gay urban spaces and gay cruising areas have arisen outside mainstream develop-ments and in places which are isolated and where 'deviant' and criminal behaviours are more common and likely. The possibility of physical attack is greater in such places and adds to the risks related to personal safety.

The 'satisfaction' risk could be amended or added to by reference to a 'discomfort' risk. This would include the possibility of being subject to verbal abuse and being the object of anti-social or threatening behaviour. Even if these do not actually occur, there is discomfort in feeling that they *may* occur in social situations. The desire to avoid the risk of being unaccepted, censured or threatened may be highly significant in destination choice. Inhibitors may restrict the opportunities for personal freedom and may detract from the level of enjoyment.

Studies suggest that considerations of risk and safety have a greater influence on avoidance of places than on positive choice (Sönmez and Graefe, 1998; Mawby, 2000). Tourists avoid and discard unsafe and risky places from consider-ation, but do not necessarily choose places because they are safe or low-risk. Some travellers, however, see uncertainty and risk as an attractive aspect of their travel decisions and experiences (Roehl and Fesenmaier, 1992). Risk does not inevitably lead to a place being avoided, as a certain amount of risk may add to enjoyment and risky places may well be ones with attributes which are particularly attractive (and vice versa) (Carter, 1998).

A convenient framework for analysing destination choice, into which risk-avoidance can be incorporated, is that of 'tourism opportunity sets'. Choice can be explained as the outcome of the interaction between destination attributes and images, the tourist's motives and values, and time and income constraints. Um and Crompton (1990; 1992) categorize beliefs about a destination into facilitators (beliefs about a destination that help satisfy motives for travel) and inhibitors (beliefs that are not harmonious with motives). The choice decision is made initially from within an 'awareness set' or 'perceived set' of desti-nations, all of which could be considered (Stabler, 1991). This is restricted to a 'consideration set' or 'evoked set' that is actually considered, though there may also be a more manageable 'decision set' of destinations from which the final choice is made. Um and Crompton (1992: 24) suggest that facilitators are important in the early stages of the choice process but that 'at the final stage it is inhibitors which prevail'. Initially, the positive attributes of a destination guide the determination of the evoked set, but there is a strong negative influence that acts to discard destinations at the decision or choice stage. Destinations discarded from the awareness set, to leave the evoked set, are categorized as being in the 'inept set'. A consideration of why such places are avoided may add to understanding of how destinations are chosen (Lawson and Thyne, 2000).

Studies put the numbers of destinations in evoked sets at about four and lower numbers in inept sets (Woodside and Lysonski, 1989; Crompton *et al.*, 1999). For gay men, the number of destinations in the inept set is likely to be high. The number in the evoked set may well be similar to that considered by general tourists, but the actual destinations considered will differ.

Destination-avoidance associated with risk-minimization may be particularly significant issues in the gay men's holiday choice process. Behaviour modification may be an equally significant issue: gay men may not only avoid certain destinations, but may also continue to be restricted in their 'out-ness' when on holiday to minimize risk. This does not necessarily detract from the significance of the vacation for gay men. It has an important role to play in constructing and confirming identity. Despite the inhibitors, a substantial number of 'desirable' destinations may be left for consideration. The overall holiday experience may offer considerable satisfaction to gay men and the fulfilment of their tourist motivations. These and related propositions will only be confirmed or rejected through further research.

CONCLUSION

There is a widespread view that gay men are more likely to go on holiday, have more holidays and travel further than the general population. They are regarded as being high-income earners with few family commitments, and they are therefore considered to be a particularly attractive market to target. These conclusions, however, are generally arrived at on the basis of surveys that were not completed by representative samples. Because of the response to homosexuality in most societies, the population's size and characteristics are unknown. Sexuality is a very imprecise concept and there is no clear agreement about what constitutes homosexuality. Those who complete surveys are unlikely to be representative of the homosexual population, however defined, though they may well be high-earning, leisure-centric individuals.

Despite the lack of knowledge about this market segment, there are holidays targeted at a 'gay market'. Invariably the products focus on a few recognizably gay-friendly destinations and often have images of sexual activity associated with them (although this is not noticeably the case in tourist-board campaigns). The reasons why gay men go on holiday are fundamentally no different from those of the rest of the population. Holidaymakers seek escape, change and freedom, and holiday-taking is regarded as part of the 'good life' to which all aspire. The holiday has more significance, however, for the gay man in as much as it is a means of confirming identity. It is difficult in many societies for gay men to be open and, as a consequence, many find it necessary to be away from home, usually in some form of leisure space, in order to be themselves. The holiday can enable the gay man to do this over a concentrated period of time.

Despite the apparent high levels of holiday-taking and the significance of the holiday, there are a number of factors that are likely to inhibit choice of holiday destination and holiday experiences. Undoubtedly destination choice and holiday experiences for many gay men may be entirely satisfactory, but some societies are less tolerant of homosexuality than are others and there remain many where homosexual activity is illegal. Social disapproval is widespread. The fear of adverse reactions may influence destination choice as well as influence behaviour at the destination. The escape and freedom that a gay man may seek from a holiday may prove unattainable.

There is increasing recognition within tourism studies of the diversity of tourism markets, motivations and desired experiences. This exploration of the gay men's market confirms the desirability of approaching consumer behaviour in a less uniform way. Risk-avoidance will have a particular role in destination choice by gay men and can be incorporated into 'choice-sets', a well-established concept for analysing the destination choice process. From such an approach, perceptions and the nature of risk and inhibitors can be established, and the destinations that are discarded into the inept set and those left for consideration in the evoked set can be determined.

The tourist industry is conscious of the potential rewards to be derived from meeting the needs of niche markets, and there are tour operators and hotels targeting the gay market, though there is some reluctance on the part of destinations to do this. The discussion in this chapter suggests the need for the tourist industry to offer more reassurance to the potential holidaymaker. Currently, gay tourists tend to reduce risk by choosing destinations and staying in accommodation where there are other gay people and where host societies are gay-friendly. Homophobia is not an issue that the tourism industry can tackle on its own, and is clearly an issue that is embedded within many societies. The travel industry could, however, be encouraged to resist and challenge the more extreme reactions to destination-marketing targeted at gays. Tour operators and accommodation-providers could also ensure that their employees are sensitive to the needs of gay tourists. If there are significant barriers to travel faced by gay men, these are a threat to the ability of the tourist industry to develop an allegedly lucrative market.

The issue of barriers does, though, go beyond the exploitation of markets. Barriers are further instances of social censure, adding to the low self-esteem of the homosexual and restricting the ability to construct a full and meaningful identity. As noted at the beginning of this chapter, such barriers have significance at a fundamental level of human rights, in so far as they relate to the free movement of peoples and the pursuit of leisure activities.

NOTE

An earlier version of this chapter was presented at the Tourism 2000 conference at Sheffield Hallam University (England), in September 2000, and was published in the proceedings. See M. Robertson, P. Long, N. Evans, R. Sharpley and J. Swarbrooke (eds), *Reflections on International Tourism: motivations, behaviour and tourist types* (Sunderland: Business Education Publishers 2000, pp. 221–30)

REFERENCES

Alcorn, K. (ed.) (1999) (22nd edn), *AIDS Reference Manual*. London: NAM Publications.
Amnesty International, UK (1997), *Breaking the Silence: Human Rights Violations Based on Sexual Orientation*. London: Amnesty International, UK.
Bell, D. (1991), 'Insignificant others: lesbian and gay geographies', *Area*, 23: 323–9.
Binnie, J. (1995), 'Trading places, consumption, sexuality and the production of queer space', in D. Bell and G. Valentine (eds), *Mapping Desire: Geographies of Sexualities*. London: Routledge.
British Tourist Authority (BTA) (1999), *Britain: You Don't Know the Half of It*. London: BTA.
Bustin, S. (2000), Director, *www.queercompany.com*, personal communication.
Carter, S. (1998), 'Tourists' and travellers' social construction of Africa and Asia as risky locations', *Tourism Management*, 19 (4): 349–58.
Catling, C. (ed.) (1991), *Insight Guide: The Netherlands*. London: APA Publications.
Clark, S. (1997), 'Glad to be gay?', *Caterer and Hotelkeeper*, (5 June): 62–3.
Clift, S. and Forrest, S. (1999), 'Gay men and tourism: destinations and holiday motivations', *Tourism Management*, 20 (5): 615–25.

Crompton, J., Botha, C. and Kim, S. (1999), 'Testing selected choice propositions', *Annals of Tourism Research*, 26 (1): 210–13.

Duyves, M. (1995), 'Framing preferences, framing differences: inventing Amsterdam as a gay capital', in R. Parker and J. Gagnon (eds), *Conceiving Sexuality: Approaches to Sex Research in a Postmodern World*. London: Routledge.

Field, N. (1995), *Over the Rainbow: Money, Class and Homophobia*. London: Pluto Press.

Fugate, D. (1993), 'Evaluating the US male homosexual and lesbian population as a viable target market segment', *Journal of Consumer Marketing*, 10 (4): 46–57.

Haukeland, J. (1990), 'Non-travellers: the flip side of motivation', *Annals of Tourism Research*, 17 (2): 172–84.

Holcomb, B. and Luongo, M. (1996), 'Gay tourism in the United States', *Annals of Tourism Research*, 23 (3): 711–13.

Hughes, H. (1991), 'Holidays and the economically disadvantaged', *Tourism Management*, 12 (3): 193–6.

Hughes H. (1997), 'Holidays and homosexual identity', *Tourism Management*, 18 (4): 3–7.

Hughes, H. (1998), 'Sexuality, tourism and space: the case of gay visitors to Amsterdam', in D. Tyler, Y. Guerrier and M. Robertson (eds), *Managing Tourism in Cities*. Chichester: Wiley.

Jefferies, T. (1999), 'Trade told to target overseas gay market', *Travel Weekly* (1 November): 28.

Jones, D. (1996), 'Discrimination against same-sex couples in hotel reservation policies', in D. Wardlow (ed.), *Gays, Lesbians and Consumer Behavior: Theory, Practice and Research Issues in Marketing*. New York: Harrington Park Press.

Lawson, R. and Thyne, M. (2000), 'Destination avoidance', in M. Robinson, P. Long, N. Evans, R. Sharpley and J. Swarbrooke (eds), *Reflections on International Tourism: Motivations, Behaviour and Tourist Types*. Sunderland: Business Education Publishers.

MAPS (1998), *The Pink Pound 1998: Strategic Market Report*. London: Market Assessment Publications.

Mawby, R. (2000), 'Tourists' perceptions of security: the risk–fear paradox', *Tourism Economics*, 6 (2): 109–21.

Nardi, P. and Schneider, B (eds) (1998), *Social Perspectives in Lesbian and Gay Studies: A Reader*. London: Routledge.

Penaloza, L. (1996), 'We're here, we're queer and we're going shopping! A critical perspective on the accommodation of gays and lesbians in the US marketplace', in D. Wardlow (ed.), *Gays, Lesbians and Consumer Behavior: Theory, Practice and Research Issues in Marketing*. New York: Harrington Park Press.

Pritchard, A. and Morgan, N. (1996), 'The gay consumer: a meaningful market segment?', *Journal of Targeting, Measurement and Analysis for Marketing*, 6 (1): 9–20.

Pritchard, A., Morgan, N., Sedgley, D. and Jenkins, A. (1998), 'Reaching out to the gay market: opportunities and threats in an emerging market segment', *Tourism Management*, 19 (3): 273–82.

Roehl, W. and Fesenmaier, D. (1992), 'Risk perceptions and pleasure travel: an exploratory analysis', *Journal of Travel Research*, 30 (4): 17–26.

Sinfield, A. (1997), 'Identity and subculture', in A. Medhurst and S. Munt (eds), *Lesbian and Gay Studies: A Critical Introduction*. London: Cassell.

Skinner, T. (1995), 'Gay couple denied room in top hotel', *Pink Paper* (24 November): 6.

Smith, V. and Hughes, H. (1999), 'Disadvantaged families and the meaning of the holiday', *International Journal of Tourism Research*, 1 (1): 123–33.

Sönmez, S. and Graefe, A. (1998), 'Determining future travel behaviour from past travel experience and perceptions of risk and safety', *Journal of Travel Research*, 37 (2): 171–7.

Stabler, M. (1991), 'Modelling the tourism industry: a new approach', in T. Sinclair and M. Stabler (eds), *The Tourism Industry: An International Analysis*. Wallingford: CAB International.

Stephenson, M. (1998), 'The Perceptions of Manchester's Afro-Caribbean Community Concerning Tourism Access and Participation', unpublished PhD thesis, Department of Hospitality and Tourism Management, Manchester Metropolitan University.

Tuck, A. (1998), 'Book a double room? Not if you're gay, sir', *Independent on Sunday* (8 February): 5.

Um, S. and Crompton, J. (1990), 'Attitude determinants in tourism destination choice', *Annals of Tourism Research*, 17 (3): 432–48.

Um, S. and Crompton, J. (1992), 'The role of perceived inhibitors and facilitators in pleasure travel destination decisions', *Journal of Travel Research*, 30 (3): 18–25.

Weeks, J. (1992), 'The body and sexuality', in R. Bocock and K. Thompson (eds), *Social and Cultural Forms of Modernity*. Cambridge: Polity Press in association with the Open University.

Wood, L. (1999), 'Think pink! Attracting the pink pound', *Insights* (January): A107–10.

Woodside, A. and Lysonski, S. (1989), 'A general model of traveler destination choice', *Journal of Travel Research*, 27 (4): 8–14.

World Tourism Organization (WTO) (1999), *Global Code of Ethics for Tourism*. (Adopted by the General Assembly of the World Tourism Organization at Santiago, Chile, 1 October 1999), Madrid: World Tourism Organization (see: *www.world-tourism.org*).

WEBSITES

Gay Britain Network (for information about UK gay travel companies): *www.gaybritain.co.uk*

Respect Holidays for gay men: *www.respect-holidays.co.uk*

World Tourism Organization (WTO) (Global Code of Ethics): *www.world-tourism.org*

CHAPTER 8

Trouble in Paradise: Homophobia and Resistance to Gay Tourism

PHILIP WANT

INTRODUCTION

The Paradise Island of tourism brochures is an imaginary place of escape from the real world to an earthly heaven. It is a place, originating from the biblical Garden of Eden or the Elysian fields of Greek mythology, where problems are forgotten, everything is possible and we can find and be our true selves. In such a world mosquitoes and poverty do not exist and the sun always shines. However, paradise like heaven is reserved for a particular type of person, and though the travel industry markets holidays as areas of '*communitas*' where social and other differences are absent, at the same time it promotes sexual, racial and national stereotypes.

This chapter is about the ways in which the sexualization and segregation of gay tourists has led to resistances and reactions which reflect an underlying homophobia. It will begin by discussing the growth of gay tourism and the commodification of a whole range of products that are now on offer to gay men and lesbian women. The role of the gay consumer is thought by many to be positive, and given that taking holidays is thought of as a necessary component of modern life, it would appear to include elements of citizenship and human rights. However, unlike many other products targeted at this specific group, tourism, because of the direct contact between different nationalities with different cultures and values, has a far greater potential for conflict. In consequence, gay tourism rather than promoting legitimate rights has, in some destinations, resulted in protest, harassment, violence and denial of access. These incidents can be viewed within the framework of openly gay and lesbian tourists attempting to find and create tourism space in which they can define and express their own sexual identities.

This chapter will discuss ways in which the history, legislation, culture and religion of a country may impact on the negative treatment of gay and lesbian tourists. It will mainly argue, however, that many of the problems lesbians and gay tourists may face stem from the power of mainstream tourism industries, in conjunction with local elites, to exclude gay and lesbian tourists, who are consequently marginalized and segregated. This is achieved by the 'hetrosexuali-zation' of some destinations and an emphasis on gay tourists as being motivated solely by sexual contact. Within this perspective, what appears to be a growth of gay consumerism and a growing globalization of open (Western) minority sexual identities, in practice ensures segregation and hostility and privileges some consumers (tourists) over others. The final part of the chapter will reflect on the links between political economy, sexuality and the contest for tourism space. Despite its emphasis on the selling of dreams and having a good time, the private-sector tourism industry is a highly political organization which, in order to gain short-term profit for its investors will represent and reflect the views and prejudices held by many in the tourism-generating countries.

In its conclusion, however, this chapter will detail how some public-sector tourism authorities in Europe have recently promoted major urban cities as gay destinations with an emphasis on a shared identity, gay-friendly environments and conventional tourism attractions. This could serve as an example to private industry and help to create tourism environments that encompass different types of sexual orientations without prejudice and fear.

THE EMERGENCE AND GROWTH OF GAY TOURISM

Gay men and lesbians have been described as 'natural' travellers (Van Gelder and Brandt, 1992). This is in part due to their marginalization 'within a dom inated heterosexual milieu' (Holcomb and Luongo, 1996: 712), which means that the 'outside perspective of the traveller is a second skin to us' (Van Gelder and Brandt, 1992: 190). The idea of escape from moral and legal constraints imposed upon gays and lesbians within their own countries is not new. Aldrich's (1993) study of male homosexual travel to the southern Mediterranean in the late eighteenth and early nineteenth centuries notes how it was: 'The social con-ditions, the leniency of the law codes and the attitudes of the local people, which made it possible to find native partners or have affairs with others from northern countries similarly drawn to the area' (Aldrich, 1993: 217). The desire to travel, although restricted to those who were wealthy and mostly male, later began to spread to exotic destinations such as Tangiers and, with the growth of gay urban subcultures, to European cities such as Paris and Berlin.

The first developments of tourism being marketed exclusively to gay men and lesbians were a result of the emergence of politicized lesbian and gay communities in the United States and Europe. In 1964 One World Travel Service offered 'gay' tours to Europe and the Orient to readers of *One*, a magazine published by the Mattachine Society, which was America's first gay rights organization. In the UK, the earliest record was in 1973 when the Campaign for Homosexual Equality set up a travel service exclusively for its own members. Later, as one commentator noted:

> Concurrent with the gay liberation of the 70s, homosexuality, it seemed could be realised in the liberated zones at the centres of the civilised world. It was possible to travel to them, try to live one's life in the ghetto communities or at least go there for a weekend. Whatever was missing could be made up on holidays to Ibiza, Mykonos and Haiti. The wish for a place to be became the wish for change, escapism from the world turned into gay tourism (Beech, 1997: 150)

Today tourism products are marketed via the gay media and sold through a variety of gay-owned or gay-friendly tour operators and travel agents to the community as a whole. The size of the American market was estimated by the International Gay and Lesbian Travel Association in 1999, to be worth $17 billion a year, or just over 10 per cent of all US travel revenue (IGLTA, 1999). In the UK, a recent report on the gay travel market estimated that in 1999, 1.3 million gay men and lesbian women took holidays for a period of seven days or longer (Mintel, 2000).

Following the growth of politicized lesbian and gay communities came an ever-increasing commodification of a whole range of products and services aimed at the gay and lesbian consumer. Weeks (1985: 24) argues that it is possible 'to see clear points of articulation in the structure of capitalism and changes in sexual life' (what he refers to as the unintended consequence of capitalist growth). These new commercial opportunities are supported by marketing concepts such as the 'pink pound', whereby gay men, and to some extent lesbians, are perceived as high earners and more likely to buy leisure and tourism activities. This role of the gay consumer, it can be argued, is positive in that it creates and promotes a gay identity, develops separate markets and can result in change through actions such as boycotts.

It has also been noted by some commentators how this development of queer capitalism provides for a social status denied in other areas of life, such as partnership and employment rights. As Evans has noted: 'for many lesbians and gay men commitment to their sexual citizenship is chiefly expressed through their "out" participation in commercial "private" territories' (Evans, 1993: 63). Based on Veblan's notion of the status associated with leisure activities this would appear to include the right to consume tourism products. Urry has noted that 'being able to go on holiday, to be obviously not at work, is presumed to be a characteristic of modern citizenship which has become embedded into people's thinking about health and well being' (Urry, 1990: 24). Hughes suggests that an inability to go on holiday and engage in other leisure activities is an inability 'to participate in the commonly accepted life style of the community' (Hughes, 1991: 193).

RESISTANCE TO GAY AND LESBIAN TOURISM

However, unlike many other products targeted at this specific group, gay tourism, while promoting legitimate rights, has also created conflict from those opposed to it. A consequence of its growth has been an increased incidence of protests, harassment, violent acts and denial of access.

In 1998 a cruise ship carrying 900 gay men was refused permission to dock in the Cayman Islands. As reported by the BBC (1998a):

The government of the British territory of the Cayman Islands in the Caribbean has refused permission for a cruise liner carrying hundreds of homosexual holiday makers to dock there. The authorities claimed that there was no guarantee that, as they put it, the group would uphold appropriate standards of behaviour. . . . In a letter explaining the decision of the authorities, the tourism minister said landing rights were being denied because of what he called careful research and prior experience.

In another incident in the Bahamas in 1998, protesters met a lesbian-chartered ship as it docked (BBC, 1998b):

Hundreds of people in the Bahamas have staged a protest after a cruise ship carrying lesbian holidaymakers docked at the capital, Nassau. The demonstrators from a group called Save the Bahamas screamed and chanted as the women came ashore. Waving placards and chanting 'No gay ships', the protesters greeted the arrival of the cruise liner *SS Seabreeze*, which had sailed from Miami with about 800 mainly female passengers on board.

A further instance of protest over gay tourism occurred later that year in Costa Rica. As Soriano (1998) reported in the *Tico Times*:

> ... organizers of Costa Rica's second annual Gay and Lesbian 'Festival' cancelled [a] 20-person tour to the Pacific beach area of Quepos/Manuel Antonio, fearing physical and verbal attacks on their clients. Festival supporters received a series of threats following public objections to the event by Catholic Church leaders and President Miguel Angel Rodriguez ... Gay-rights groups and the event's organizers, Tiquicia Travel, said the statements fuelled an ugly anti-gay uprising in Quepos, which quickly spread out of control and would have put the tourists in danger.

Concerns in government circles about the prospect of Costa Rica becoming a popular destination with lesbian and gay tourists have continued to be expressed since:

> Any doubts about the government's attitude toward gay tourists were dispelled this week by new tourism chief Eduardo León-Páez, who, lumping them together with tourists who come here looking for sex, said they are definitely not welcome. 'Costa Rica's legislation does not prohibit [this type of tourism]. There's nothing we can legally do to stop it. But we certainly don't want to encourage it,' said León-Páez, in reference to gays and lesbians who come to Costa Rica as ordinary tourists (Escofet, 1999).

Other parts of the world where controversy has arisen over lesbian and gay tourism include Vanuatu (formerly the New Hebrides). An article in the *Vanuatu Weekly*, headed 'The tourist dollar that's being questioned', noted that, had the Council Secretary known that a group of 40 women tourists staying on the island were lesbian, they would have refused approval for their visit (*Vanuatu Weekly*, 1998).

In the summer of 1999, concern about gay tourism emerged in New Zealand. *PlanetOut News* (1999) reported the background to the story:

> The city of Queenstown is far from unanimous in backing initial moves to become a tourist destination for gays and lesbians. That image is something that Wellington's Gay Link Travel has been developing for three years and now

hope to capitalize on with a week-long Ski Gay Queenstown event next month and a major sports event, the Rainbow Festival, next year. Local ski operators are coming around and the Heritage Hotel has declared itself gay-friendly.

Unfortunately, however, Queenstown City Council was not happy with the developments, and a local councillor, Chris Blackford, was quoted as saying, 'while everyone is welcome to Queenstown, sexuality should not be "promoted" and residents didn't want their children "exposed to that sort of behaviour"'.

In September 2000 a group of homosexual tourists was banned by Turkish police from visiting the ancient site of Ephesus (Morris, 2000). As reported by the BBC (2000a):

The 800 tourists – from the United States, Britain, France and The Netherlands – arrived in the port of Kusadasi aboard a cruise liner. They say a number of their buses were prevented by the police from leaving the port and others were turned back from the ancient site itself. Many passengers were ordered to return to the ship.

Another controversy surrounding gay tourism arose later in the same month in Peru. The rainbow flag, an important symbol for the ancient South American Inca people, can still be seen flying from homes, bars, shops and other public buildings in the popular tourist destination of Cuzco, close to the Inca fortress of Machu Picchu. Some residents became concerned, however, over their flag 'being mistaken as a tribute to gay pride', while others have welcomed this association. According to a report from the BBC (2000b):

Bar and shop owners have seen their businesses badly hit – some heterosexuals think that establishments flying the rainbow flag cater only for homosexuals. Meanwhile, other shop owners are making huge profits by selling multicoloured souvenirs to unsuspecting tourists and taking pride in Cuzco's appeal as a 'gay city'.

Also in September, further protest erupted over lesbian tourism on the Greek island of Lesbos. As Anderson (2000) explained:

. . . a couple of weeks ago . . . a saucy flyer for a lesbian holiday package sent the local mayor, Polydoros Abatzis, to court to try to block the tour. The fuss stems from a few phrases: 'erotic dancing', 'sexy room service' and 'wet pussy pool party', words that tour organiser Kim Lucas says were never meant to be seen outside the UK. 'The language used in the ad was tongue-in-cheek', she says. 'Unfortunately, it was translated literally.'

The controversy generated a great deal of media publicity, but eventually, Mr Abatzis withdrew his action 'mollified by assurances that the flyers would be kept under wraps and the girls would behave'.

The most recent case of opposition to gay tourism arose early in 2001 in Cape Town, South Africa. As reported by Macgregor (2001) in the *Independent*:

> A campaign aimed at attracting homosexual tourists to Cape Town – billed as an international holiday destination for gays – has sparked a backlash among religious groups. Thousands of Christians will gather at Newlands rugby ground in South Africa's gay capital on Wednesday, Human Rights Day, to pray for a sin-free city and an end to this official promotion of a town already ranked fifth in the world as a venue for gay travellers.

In addition to resistance to gay tourism arising in destinations, tour companies themselves can operate explicit exclusionary policies towards gay men and lesbian women. In February 1999 Sandals Resorts specifically excluded couples of the same sex from staying at their resorts. A spokeswomen for ZFL Public Relations Ltd, the company which handles Sandals publicity, confirmed that the policy of the hotel chain is to accept bookings from straight couples only. As she stated: 'The original concept was to build resorts only for straight couples. That concept remains in place' (*Pink Paper*, 1999a). Recently, however, Sandals has had its television advertisements banned in Britain 'for failing to make clear that its resorts are not open to gay and lesbian couples' (Reuters, 2001).

Reluctance among British hoteliers to book gay couples was also revealed by a survey undertaken in 1998 for the *Independent*. It found that '30 per cent of hotels either refused bookings by a gay couple or required them to sleep in separate beds' (Quest, 1998).

In addition, companies that market travel, holidays and leisure events to the gay community have become targets of those opposed to homosexuality. The position adopted by American Airlines, for example, in marketing to lesbian women and gay men, sponsoring lesbian and gay events, and offering partner benefits to lesbian and gay employees (Human Rights Campaign, 1999), has resulted in criticism from right-wing organizations. Americans for Truth have criticized American Airlines for 'becoming America's homosexual airline at the risk of offending and alienating millions of American families and loyal customers' (see: *www.americansfortruth.com*). The 'Gay Days' at Disney World have also brought criticism and attempts at boycotts from the American Family Association (AFA). Chaney (2001), an officer of AFA, explained the background and purpose of the Disney boycott:

'Gay Day' began in 1990 in the Magic Kingdom when the homosexual community was encouraged to visit the park on a given day and 'Wear Red and Be Seen' while visiting. It has evolved into a week-long gathering of over 130,000 attendees from around the world. . . . If concerned Christians will refuse to spend their hard-earned 'greenbacks' with Disney, our hope is that the company will eventually get the message that doing such things as courting the favor of the homosexual community is not good business.

The issues of gay-friendliness, acceptance and safety are of prime importance for gay and lesbian travellers, and are of key significance in the marketing of many lesbian and gay tourism products (see Stuber, Chapter 4, and Luongo and Roth, Chapter 5, this volume, for a fuller discussion of marketing issues). This is reflected in the phrase 'gay-friendly', which often appears in gay tour operators' publicity and websites. The gay-friendly character could be due to a large resident gay community, a general liberal attitude to homosexuality, or both – as exists in Scandinavia and The Netherlands. For many southern Mediterranean resorts such as Tangiers, Sitges or Mykonos, the liberal attitude can be partly based on their historic appeal to artistic communities, which included and attracted lesbian and gay men (Want 1998/9). The UK gay travel company Sensations offered ratings of destinations based on criteria such as ambience, location and proximity to existing gay facilities. Even so, many of those affected by the various conflicts described above were booked with gay travel companies and it is clear that 'the geography of gay friendliness or hostility is extremely complex' (Pritchard *et al.*, 1998: 272). Gran Canaria is described in gay travel brochures as the most popular gay destination in Europe, but there too, gay men have experienced harassment. In 1989, for example, the British Foreign Office demanded an explanation from the Spanish government after more than 100 mainly British and German gay tourists were arrested and 'herded into urine-flooded cells and beaten around the head and spine with wooden police batons' (*Capital Gay*, 1989).

Anti-homosexual legislation and attitudes in tourist destinations

It is clear that a country's legislation can be an indicator (though not always) of the local climate towards lesbian and gay tourists. In many parts of the world, there are penalties for homosexual behaviour ranging from fines all the way to the death sentence (see the website of the International Lesbian and Gay Association (IGLA) for a global survey). As one Australian commentator noted:

What could be more romantic than a tropical holiday with a loved one? Sipping cocktails and watching a magnificent sunset on a deserted beach and then doing what comes naturally to all of us. It's at this stage – just when it all becomes interesting – that you should remember – that in many of the tropical islands you are about to commit a very criminal offence that could have you in jail for a number of years (Baird, 1999: 19).

In the Caribbean, many British territories have until recently retained 100-year-old laws inherited from the British, which criminalize homosexual inter-course (the situation is very different in former French and Dutch Caribbean islands, see Bedford and Rauch, 2000). In January 2001, however, Britain ordered its five Caribbean territories (Anguilla, the Cayman Islands, Montserrat, the Turks and Caicos Islands, and the Virgin Islands) to repeal their anti-gay legislation and so legalize homosexuality. As reported, with deep misgivings, by the American Family Association:

British officials have said the government's demand is based upon international treaties on human rights, which have been interpreted in such a way as to make homosexuality a protected class – on the same level as race, nationality and gender. One homosexual news source said the sodomy laws violate, among other treaties, the European Convention on Human Rights and the International Convention on Civil and Political Rights. 'We simply can't be seen to have territories with laws that violate these agreements', Anguilla's deputy British Governor Roger Cousins told the Associated Press (American Family Associa-tion, 2001).

In addition to legislation, local people and other tourists 'have the potential to create barriers by directing negative labels and manifesting stereotypes that are influenced by popular mass representations' (Morgan and Pritchard, 1999: 118). Some of the conflicts have arisen in the Caribbean area, noted for its negative attitude to homosexuality, and where some islands can be described as socially conservative and deeply religious. Much of the opposition is voiced by religious leaders and politicians. In response to the gay tourist ban and the surrounding publicity, the Cayman Islands community affairs minister stated that 'the islands have a mandate from God to criminalize gay sex' (*Pink Paper*, 1999b). The

Guardian reported religious leaders and local politicians as saying that 'the disagreement over homosexuality reveals a widening cultural rift between what they condemned as an increasingly atheist Britain and its faraway Caribbean possessions' (*Guardian*, 2001: 7).

Opposition to homosexuals is not targeted specifically at any one ethnic group, and controversies surrounding gay tourists both reflect and affect the difficult circumstances of local gay men and lesbian women in some tourist destinations. As Adam *et al.* (1999: 352) have noted: 'there are fundamental differences in the functioning of civil society and consequently in the space for gays and lesbians to organise, according to characteristics of national political cultures and values.' J-Flag, a gay organization based in Jamaica, has attempted, through its website, to publicize the problems, noting that Amnesty International has documented the country as 'killing citizens because of their sexual orientation' (J-Flag, 1999). A petition was recently put out on the Internet asking for support from around the world against what it sees as a growing number of violent hate crimes on the island and increasing homophobia against lesbian and gay tourists:

> Jamaica's internationally known homophobia will alienate it from more progressive nations that have no sanctions against sexual practices between practising adults. Jamaica will also come under increasing pressure from international gay and lesbian organisations such as the International Gay and Lesbian Travel Association which has stated that the organisation strongly condemns Jamaican authorities for failing to ensure the safety, welfare and comfort of lesbians and gays living on and visiting the island. This island nation appears to be a leader in the region's emerging homophobia that has already shown its ugly face in the Cayman Islands and Costa Rica. That is a tragedy (Q Announce News, 1999).

Whilst it is clear that a destination's legislation and religion can lead to negative reactions to non-heterosexual tourists, there are other causes. Despite what would appear to be a growing globalization of open (Western) minority sexual identities, it is apparent from the cases described above that these identities are sometimes in conflict with local cultures. Some of the destinations so far mentioned are ex-colonial small island states, which have plenty of sun, sea and sand but very little else, and have been forced after independence to adopt tourism as a major development strategy. Due to the large amounts of investment needed, much of the industry is owned and controlled by the tourism-generating countries to the extent that it is estimated by some tourism commentators that 75 cents out of every US dollar spent by tourists goes back to the tourism-generating countries. This has created a dependency on the industry, much resentment and accusations of neo-colonialism. As one commentator notes:

> The travel industry in the Caribbean may well represent the latest development in the historical evolution of the neo-colonial context of the West Indian socioeconomic experience. Through tourism, developed metropolitan centres in collaboration with West Indian elites have delivered the Caribbean archipel-ago to another region of monoculture. As an industry based on the appropria-tion of West Indian human and natural resources for the ephemeral pleasure of foreigners, tourism offers . . . less opportunity and less immediate likelihood of modifying the basic constellation of dependent relationships established first in the 16th century (Perez, 1975: 1).

In addition to this, the obvious disparities in wealth have resulted in 'the welcome to tourists becoming ambivalent and tourism becoming a political, as well as a social, economic and moral issue' (Harrison, 1992: 119). Within this neo-imperialist framework, there is the issue of contamination from the West and from the tourists who originate from there. This could be based on moral issues such as homosexuality and AIDS. This concept of the 'outsider' aspect of homosexuality is described on the Jamaican gay organization J-Flag website in the following terms:

> Among the many myths created about Africa, the myth that homosexuality is absent or incidental is one of the oldest and most enduring. Historians, anthropologists and many contemporary Africans alike have denied or over-looked African same-sex patterns or claimed that Europeans introduced such patterns. In fact same-sex love was and is widespread in Africa. The African issue that homosexuality is a European imperialist import is a lie. The actual European imperialist import is the homophobic tradition of British law (J-Flag, 2001).

The issue is not just African. Jowitt (1999) reflects on similar issues in Vanuatu, in the Pacific, where the visit of a group of 40 Australian lesbian tourists caused a furore. She notes how, despite homosexuality being part of the island's custom, the position of the local government is that same-sex behaviour did not feature in Vanuatu's past and that the lesbians were perceived as a danger to Vanuatu's culture since it 'contradicts traditional beliefs and custom values'. Changes brought about by post-colonialism and a newfound Christianity have resulted in homosexuality being seen as a Western concept and though legal, being frowned upon.

THE GAYING AND DE-GAYING OF TOURIST SPACE

The conflicts caused by gay tourism can be viewed within the framework of visible lesbian and gay tourists attempting to find and create holiday space in which they can exercise their rights as consumers. However, in many areas, 'violence regulates access to public spaces and restricts the ability of gays and lesbians to exercise full citizenship' (Allison, 1999). Valentine and Bell (1995) have noted that lesbians and gay men have a whole variety of spatial expressions 'which have created distinct social, political and cultural landscapes'. Most of these spaces are urban areas such as Soho in London, the Marais in Paris or the Castro district in San Francisco, but can equally be tourism destinations such as Cherry Grove/The Pines on Fire Island or the Yumbo Centre in Gran Canaria, or one of the many lesbian and gay beaches dotted around the world. These clearly provide areas in which sexual minorities can feel safe, and have a feeling of community and territory. This would appear to be an important motivating factor for gay tourists, given the nature of the tourism product with its emphasis on relaxation, escape and social interaction. The majority of lesbians and gays work and live in a predominantly heterosexual environment and holidays in gay environments 'offer the chance to be oneself and to enjoy the possibilities which gay social settings can offer' (Holcomb and Luongo, 1996: 712).

Despite the benefits that gay tourist spaces may provide to some gay tourists, they will always be contested and under threat because 'the hetorising of space is a performative act naturalised through repetition and control and is fundamental to heterosexuals' ability to reproduce their hegemony' (Valentine and Bell, 1995: 17). This can take the form of violent acts, harassment and verbal abuse, as we have seen, but another, subtler threat to such space is the phenomenon of 'de-gaying'. The use of gay extravagance in some destinations such as Mykonos and Ibiza has become a selling point and has resulted in an increased number of non-gay visitors. This appears to have pleased the local populations, whose famed tolerance, 'as much a by-product of the liberal orthodox tradition as a thirst for money and development', has run out (Smith, 1995: 10). A consequence of this, according to one gay tourist, is that 'we have become like the quaint spelling mistakes in taverna menus and all the clubs are now gay clubs for heterosexuals' (ibid.).

Pritchard *et al.* (1998) have also shown how Manchester's Gay Village has become a tourist attraction for visitors to the city. The authors suggest that while this may signal a more liberal approach to gay spaces, it could also be the case that 'the challenge posed by degaying is as much a threat to gay space . . . as any posed by state legislation or civilian disapproval or aggression' (Pritchard *et al.*, 1998: 282). Not all agree, however. One gay Manchester club owner noted how 99 per cent of straight people come for the right reasons and go home with a more tolerant understanding of gay people: 'That's something we should be proud of. I don't ever want to go back to running a gay ghetto' (Aitkenhead, 1995: 7).

The gay community itself may be the cause for the de-gaying of certain attractions. The decline in the political focus and greater emphasis on the carnivalesque element now associated with many of world's pride events has ensured that they become major tourist attractions. Sydney's annual gay Mardi Gras is attended by 600,000 spectators, shown live on national television, and has been recently recognized as 'Australia's largest tourist event' (Luongo, 2000: 110). However, there is an irony in this, since: 'tourism paradoxically makes a commodity of the events held to claim a sense of homosexual community and in doing so legitimises and makes safe any challenge to mainstream society' (Ryan, 2000: 25).

THE ROLE OF MAINSTREAM TOURISM INDUSTRIES

While acknowledging the impact of the various issues mentioned above, the remainder of this chapter will argue that the marginalization of the gay market segment by mainstream tourism industries is an important factor accounting for some of the conflict that has arisen in relation to gay tourism. As Wilson noted:

Tourism as with all leisure phenomena is part of the struggle for space and time in which social groups are continuously engaged, a struggle in which the dominant group seeks to legitimise, through statute and administrative fiat, its understanding of the appropriate use of space and time and the subordinate groups to resist this control through individual action and collective action (Wilson, 1988: 12).

And as Papson (1981: 177) has noted:

Tourism depends on preconceived definitions of place and people. These definitions are created by the marketing arm . . . of private enterprise in order to induce the tourist to visit a specific area ... it not only redefines social reality but also recreates it to fit these definitions. This process is both interactive and dialectical. To the extent that this process takes place, the category of everyday life is annihilated.

Despite the demographic changes taking place in many Western tourism-generating societies with regards to marriage, ethnicity and sexuality, it is apparent that almost all mainstream holiday products are 'very much a reflection of heterosexual society, especially couples and families' (Hughes, 1997: 6). The imagery used in travel brochures is a clear reflection of this, with its emphasis on key ideological concepts 'which includes the representation of men as power and ownership and women as passive, available and being owned' (Kinnaird and Hall, 1994: 12). This is not just an issue affecting lesbian women and gay men. Stephenson's study of tourism access and participation by Manchester's Afro-Caribbean community show how it is limited partly by the lack of multicultural images used in promotion and 'that when ethnic others are shown, they form part of the product on offer and are denied the status of tourism consumer' (Stephenson, 1997: 79). Despite promoting many gay-friendly destinations such as Mykonos, Ibiza or Sitges to their customers, mainstream tour operators include little or no reference in their brochures to different sexualities. The Australian airline Quantas promotes Sydney's Mardi Gras as ' the city's wildest, brightest and most fabulous festival', without ever mentioning the words 'lesbian' or 'gay', noting only that 'some tourists may get a surprise' (Q Announce, 1999).

Many of the sexual images associated with third world tourist destinations are based on historical and to some extent colonial constructs. Captain Cook's journals, which describe sexual relationships between his sailors and the Poly-nesian women, for example, can be seen as the beginning of the sexualization of the Pacific as a sexual paradise. Such a portrayal of the area 'is linked with the expansion of sex tourism in the region by Americans and Europeans' (Gatter, 2000). Sanchez Taylor (2000: 49) notes how, in the Caribbean, tourism is partly responsible for the sexualization of women. She also refers to the racist-sexualized stereotype given to black men such as defined by 'large dicks and sexual stamina', which she notes 'is a subjective identity directly related to the historical and cultural ideology used by colonial white males to construct black male identity'. As a result, local men are perceived as being sexually attractive to female tourists, with an emphasis on masculinity that is not available in the tourism-generating countries. As one local noted: 'because all the white men in those places like New York and London are homosexuals, you women have come down to Jamaica to find some real men, to find real sex' (Skelton, 1995:

267). This emphasis on the availability and sexualization of masculinity and femininity and its promotion by commercial and media imagery will ensure that 'the tourist industry will continue to provide a framework which permits (even encourages) sex tourism' (Sanchez Taylor, 2000: 51). As if to confirm this, the tourism director for Trinidad and Tobago noted in a newspaper article headed: 'Area capitalises on "sexy" image' that 'the product was not all sex but it's part of the reason for choosing the Caribbean, it's one of our assets and we should not hide it' (*Travel Trade Gazette*, 1998).

Despite the use of the sexual 'other' to market certain destinations, it is applied only to heterosexuals, and 'gay tourism' is perceived by the mainstream tourism industry and by many tourism commentators under the negative heading of 'sex tourism'. While acknowledging that tourists are motivated to travel by the sexualized fantasies associated with romance and the exotic, the issue of sex and tourism is still considered 'one of the most emotive and sensationalised issues in the study of tourism' (Kinnaird and Hall, 1994: 142). A generally accepted definition of 'sex tourism' is leisure travel 'to consummate commercial sexual relations' (Opperman, 1999: 251) and is usually associated with paedophilia and prostitution. More recently, some tourism commentators have attempted to widen this perspective to include: 'Notions of how the interconnectedness between travel and sex can be positively valued as reflections of human autonomy and freedom to pursue uncommitted sexual encounters in novel environments purely for pleasure and excitement' (Clift and Carter, 2000: 281). Such views are rare, however, and in tourism texts, sex tourism has tended to be characterized as a form of deviance. In defence of the anti-gay tourist protests in Costa Rica, the executive tourism director told a group of gay tourism businesses that 'the island cannot give any support to gay tourism because it sees it as a form of sex tourism' (Espinoza, 1998). In the Cayman Islands, the tourism minister, responding to the exclusion of the gay cruise ship, noted 'that careful research and prior experience has led us to believe that we cannot count on this group to uphold the standards of behaviour expected of visitors to the island' (*Gay Lesbian Travel and Vacation News*, 1999). In Vanuatu, the local paper reported that the local police would conduct investigations to see whether the lesbian tourists would 'engage in activities on the island which could be classified as indecent' (*Vanuatu Weekly*, 1998).

GAY MEN'S MOTIVATIONS FOR TRAVEL

There can be little doubt that sexual contact was and still is an important motivating factor for gay male tourists, given the legal and moral censures that existed, or still exist to some extent, in the tourism-generating countries. In addition, the history of gay tourism would appear to be based on inequalities of wealth resulting not so much in prostitution as in the 'reciprocal advantages which could be procured by sexual liaisons' (Aldrich, 1993: 182). In explaining the motivation of writers such as Joe Orton and other frequent gay visitors to Tangier, Boone (1995: 99) notes: 'for over a century numerous gay men have journeyed to N. Africa to discover what they already suspected: a colonised Third World in which the availability of casual sex is based on an economics of boys'. Today, given the homoerotic imagery used in many gay male tourism brochures by companies such as Throb Holidays (1998: 10): 'you can take part in one big mother of a party with hot leather, hot bars and hot guys' – sex is clearly a major motivating factor when purchasing these specific products.

There is much research concerned with the motivating factors associated with segmented markets such as the elderly or young singles, but very little work has been undertaken concerning the gay travel market, despite it being generally accepted as a rapidly growing and profitable sector (the main exception being the work of Clift and Forrest, 1998; 1999a; 1999b). Part of the reason may be the difficulties associated with researching gay and lesbian consumers. Consequently, businesses that want to target this particular sector are restricted by 'a lack of accurate information on gay demographics, attitudes and purchasing behaviour' (Fugate, 1993). While undertaking consultancy work at the London Lesbian and Gay Pride Festival in 1997, the author was able to distribute a questionnaire concerning motivating factors for gay men when purchasing travel products. In total, 1507 short questionnaires mainly concerned with demographics were completed on the day by a team of 25 paid interviewers. Among these respondents, 1034 agreed to take part in further research and provided names and addresses. A month later, a more extensive questionnaire was posted out, and of the 480 returned, 393 identified themselves as gay. Good food and good accommodation were seen as the most important factors when choosing where to go on holiday, followed by good weather, price and avoiding children and families. Sexual contact was considered very important by only 7 per cent, important by 12 per cent, as somewhat important by 22 per cent and by half as not important at all. This research suggested that canvassing a wider spectrum of respondents (as distinct from those who purchase gay tourism products) produces quite different findings. In addition, less than 1 per cent of the respondents had used the services of a gay travel agency or tour operator.

The findings would appear to show that only a minority of gay men regard sex as a primary motivating factor for travel, and issues such as partnership status, wealth, special interests, quality of attraction and price appear to play a far more important role for the majority of men researched. These findings are in line with those reported by Clift and Forrest on gay tourism, which reveal that 'the principal issues which structure holiday decision-making and experiences are largely common to gay and straight tourists, although the relative significance of each dimension may vary from group to group and by destination' (Clift and Forrest, 1999b: 622).

PUBLIC-SECTOR PROMOTION OF GAY TOURISM

Despite the general exclusion of gay tourism by the mainstream tour operators, there have been recent challenges to the dominant discourses in tourism that have come mainly from public-sector tourism authorities. In 1998, the British Tourism Authority became one of the first European state tourism organizations to undertake marketing to a lesbian and gay market. Initially, it was aimed at the American market with plans to extend into the German and Australian gay markets in future. Sandra Elliot, the Director of Marketing, explained why they and not the private sector were marketing tourism to the gay men and lesbian women: 'they [the private sector] are hesitant to get involved possibly because they fear a backlash from their current customers' (De Los Reyes, 2000: 67). The motive behind the campaign, however, is clearly economic: 'they [the gay tourists] represent good business for Britain and that is the only reason we are involved with it. There has been criticism by some bodies, which did not think it appropriate to use public money to promote the gay community, but because much of it happens overseas it is less visible.' Chris Smith, Secretary of State for Culture, Media and Sport at the time was due to speak at a Gay Tourism Conference held in London (Forum Hotel, January 1998), to promote the campaign, but cancelled at the last minute. His office stated that this was due to other commitments, but those attending suspected it was because of the amount of pre-publicity about his attendance, especially in the tabloid press.

Within the UK, public-sector tourist authorities from both Manchester and Brighton (both with large gay communities), market the appeal of their cities to gay men both in the UK and overseas. The biggest change with regards to this marketing is the imagery and literature used in the promotional material, which resembles conventional brochures, except the focus is on same-sex couples and groups. London is described in the BTA brochure as: 'the gay capital of Europe – bold, assured, smart and proud. It's called the coolest spot on the planet, due in no small part to the gay and lesbian community' (BTA brochure, 1998: 9).

The Netherlands Board of Tourism has also received praise for its progressive approach to tourism marketing targeting gay and lesbian travellers. *PlanetOut News* (2001) reported that in March 2001 the Board:

> ... was honoured ... with the Global Leadership Award at the 2nd International Conference on Gay and Lesbian Tourism in Washington, DC. The NBT was one of the first tourist boards to appeal specifically to gay and lesbian travellers when it launched an advertising campaign aimed at the market in 1992. Since then, the board has continued to court GLBT tourists, most recently hosting the 1998 Gay Games in Amsterdam.

Ironically, however, while this award may be justly deserved, one can search in vain on the Board's website to find any details of gay and lesbian life in Holland or information for gay and lesbian tourists. Even more remarkably, their list of ten reasons to visit Amsterdam places the Red Light District third, but makes no mention of the vibrant Amsterdam gay scene (see *www.goholland.com*).

There have been some signs recently of mainstream tour operators in the UK beginning to consider targeting the gay travel market. The lead has been taken by Thomas Cook:

> Thomas Cook, one of Britain's oldest travel companies, is to enter the gay and lesbian market. The move represents a dramatic new initiative in the package holiday sector, which is best known for staid family vacations. The company, founded by a temperance campaigner in 1841, has opened negotiations with operators providing leisure facilities in destinations all over the world, as well as in established gay holiday locations such as Sydney and Lesbos. Operators will be vetted to ensure owners of hotels, villas, ski chalets and cruise ships offer gays as warm a welcome as heterosexuals (Summerskill, 2001: 7).

The prime motivation, of course, is a financial one, and Thomas Cook are keen to 'tap into' a lucrative potential market:

> 'We've identified a market of two million [lesbian and gay holidaymakers] in Britain', said Mike Beaumont, Thomas Cook's commercial director. 'Main-

stream retailers like ourselves have simply not done enough in the past to tap into this area. We intend to rectify that' (ibid.: 7).

Whether this venture will turn out to be a commercial success remains to be seen.

CONCLUSION

It is apparent that with the growth, visibility and spending power of the lesbian and gay community more products are being marketed exclusively to what is now recognized as a distinct market segment. Despite lesbians and gay men having always travelled, it is only in the last decade, with an increasing emphasis on openness and visibility, that there is now an organized tourism sector catering to this particular market. However, tourism would appear to differ from other products in that it entails travelling in order to consume the product. This could be to a destination not tolerant towards homosexuality, which can result in conflict. While acknowledging political, social, historical, cultural or religious reasons in the destination, this chapter has attempted to show that such conflicts are in part due to the marginalization of gay tourism by the private-sector mainstream tourism industry. This has resulted in the segregation and sexualization of this particular sector, which is labelled as deviant, and has resulted in opposition from the resident population and from other tourists. The tourism product is today recognized as an important component of modern life, which provides status and entails issues of human rights with regards to travel without restrictions. In some destinations, lesbian and gay tourists have experienced opposition and restrictions in exercising such rights.

The notion of the tourism industry as being concerned only with pleasure and a good time, and as being politically neutral, is like many other aspects of this industry, a myth. Its power lies in the way it can market destinations as fantasy islands, which incorporate particular ideological constructions of gender, ethnicity and sexuality. This power to promote such ideologies will define who is admissible, and has led to many of the troubles.

Despite all of this, there have been recent examples of the promotion of gay tourism (albeit for economic reasons) by some public-sector authorities. Here the marketing focus is concerned with sexual identity and gay-friendly destinations and should serve as an example to the private sector. Finally, the politics of homosexuality, since the late 1960s, has resulted in important questions being raised concerning sexuality. This includes discussions around areas such as identity, space and citizenship, and these need to be incorporated into our understanding of the similarities and differences between lesbian/gay and hetero-sexual tourists. If the travel industry, both gay and straight, is to become more representative, it needs to diversify its product by taking on board these concerns and issues. Perhaps only then can we begin to accept that all people, regardless of sexual orientation, have the freedom and right to travel without fear of prejudices and restrictions.

REFERENCES

Adam, B., Duyvendak, J. and Krouwel, A. (1999), *The Global Emergence of Gay and Lesbian Politics*. Philadelphia, OH: Temple University Press.

Aitkenhead, D. (1995), 'Drug gangs take the gay out of Gaychester', *Independent On Sunday* (22 February): 7.

Aldrich, R. (1993), *The Seduction of the Mediterranean. Writing, Art and Homosexual Fantasy*. London: Routledge.

Alexander, J. (1994), 'Not just (any) body can be a citizen: the politics of law, sexuality and postcoloniality in Trinidad and Tobago and the Bahamas', *Feminist Review*, 48: 5–26.

Allison. T, (1999), 'Good gay citizen', paper presented at the International Association for the Study of Sexuality, Culture and Society Conference, Manchester Metropolitan University.

American Family Association (2001), 'Britain forces Caribbean territories to accept homosexuality', *American Family Association Journal*, January (see *www.afa.org*).

Americans for Truth Pressroom (1999), 'Pro-family groups educate shareholders on American Airlines continued funding of homosexual groups', 19 May (*www.americansfortruth.com*).

Anderson, A. (2000), 'Lesbos falls out of love with lesbian tourists', *Independent*, 17 September (see *www.independent.co.uk*).

Q *Announce* News (1999), 'Concern for Jamaica's homophobia and tourism market', Q *Announce News*, 10 February.

BBC (1998a), 'Despatches', 7 January (see *www.news.bbc.co.uk*).

BBC (1998b), '"No gay ships" shout Bahama protesters', BBC News Online, 14 April (see *www.news.bbc.co.uk*).

BBC (2000a), 'Turkey bans homosexuals from ancient site', BBC News Online, 7 September (see *www.news.bbc.co.uk*).

BBC (2000b), 'Inca concerns over "gay" flag', BBC News Online, 29 September (see *www.news.bbc.co.uk*).

Baird, M. (1999), 'Where are we now?' in *Sydney Gay and Lesbian Festival Guide*. Erskinville: Sydney Gay and Lesbian Mardi Gras.

Bedford, B. and Rauch, R. (eds) (2000) (29th edn), *Spartacus International Gay Guide: 2000–2001*. Berlin: Bruno Gmünder Verlag.

Beech, H. (1997), *When Men Meet Homosexuality and Modernity*. Cambridge: Polity Press.

Boone, J. (1995), 'Vacation cruise or the homoerotics of orientalism', *Publications of the Modern Language Association*, 110 (1): 89–107.

British Tourist Authority (1998), *Britain, You Don't Know the Half Of It!* London: British Tourist Authority.

Capital Gay (1989), 'Holiday ends in night of terror', 26 May: 1.

Capital Gay (1992), 'Sex on beach man faces 20 years in Bahamas prison', 1 May: 4.

Chaney, P. (2001), 'Not exactly what Walt intended', *American Family Association Journal*, January (see *www.afa.org*).

Clift, S. and Carter, S. (eds) (2000), *Tourism and Sex: Culture, Commerce and Coercion.* London: Continuum.

Clift, S. and Forrest, S. (1998), *Gay Men, Travel and HIV Risk.* Canterbury: Centre for Health Education and Research, Canterbury Christ Church College.

Clift, S. and Forrest, S. (1999a), 'Factors associated with the sexual behaviour and risk of gay men on holiday', *AIDSCare*, 11 (3): 281–95.

Clift, S. and Forrest, S. (1999b), 'Gay men and tourism: destinations and holiday motivation', *Tourism Management*, 20: 615–25.

Clift, S. and Wilkins, J. (1995), 'Travel, sexual behaviour and gay men', in P. Aggleton, P. Davies and G. Hart (eds), *AIDS: Sexuality, Safety and Risk.* London: Taylor & Francis.

CNET News Release (1999), 'Gay rights travel flap snares Microsoft, Yahoo', 4 February (see *www.cnetnews.com*).

Community Marketing Inc. (1999), *A Place For Us: 5th Annual Gay and Lesbian Travel Survey.* San Francisco, CA: Community Marketing.

Cox, M. (1996), 'Gay tourism: globalisation, consumption and identity', paper presented at Geography Department Seminar, University College London, 27 November.

De Los Reyes, R. (2000), 'The UK Public Sector is Targeting the Gay Scene; Are They Using an Effective Approach?' BA Hons dissertation, South Bank University, London.

Economist (1992), ' "Howls" an American survey,' December: 27.

Escofet, G. (1999), 'Gay tourism gets rebuff', *Tico Times*, 9 April (see *www.ticotimes.net*).

Espinoza, M. (1998), 'More opposition to gay tourism', *Tico Times*, 4 October (see *www.ticotimes.net*).

Evans, D. T. (1993), *Sexual Citizenship: The Material Construction of Sexualities.* London: Routledge.

Fugate, D. L. (1993), 'Evaluating the US male homosexual and lesbian population as a viable target market', *Journal of Consumer Marketing*, 10 (4): 46–57.

Gatter, P. (2000), 'Global theories and sexuality', Sexual Identities and Changing Values Workshop, South Bank University, 24 March.

Gay Lesbian Travel and Vacation News (1999), 'International gay and lesbian association', 12 March.

Guardian (2001), 'Britain scraps islands anti-gay laws', 6 January: 7.

Hall, C. M. (1996), *Tourism and Politics: Policy, Power and Place.* Chichester: Wiley.

Harrison, D. (1992), *Tourism and the Less-developed Countries.* London: Belhaven Press.

Haulot, A. (1981), 'Social tourism: current dimensions and future developments', *Tourism Management*, 2: 207–12.

Holcomb B. and Luongo, M. (1996), 'Gay tourism in the United States', *Annals of Tourism Research*, 23 (2): 711–13.

Hughes, H. (1991), 'Holidays and the economically disadvantaged', *Tourism Management*, 12: 193–6.

Hughes, H. (1997), 'Holidays and homosexual identity', *Tourism Management*, 18 (1): 3–7.

Human Rights Campaign (1999), 'Action alert: support American Airlines', 26 April (see *www.hrc.org*).

Human Rights Campaign (1999), 'HRC applauds American Airlines for offering domestic partner benefits to lesbian and gay employees worldwide', 5 August (see *www.hrc.org*).

IGLTA (1999) (see *www.iglta.org*).

J-Flag. (1999), 'Hate crime petition for Jamaica', 3 July (see *http://village.fortunecity.com/garland/704/*).

J-Flag. (2001), 'Jamaica Forum of Lesbians, All-Sexuals and Gays', 8 January (see *http://village.fortunecity.com/garland/704/*).

Jowitt, A. (1999), 'Reconstructing custom: the politics of homophobia in Vanuata', paper presented at The International Association for the Study of Sexuality, Culture and Society Conference, Manchester Metropolitan University, July.

Kinnaird, V. and Hall, D. (1994), *Tourism: A Gender Analysis*. Chichester: Wiley.

Kinnaird,V. and Hall, D. (1996), 'Understanding tourism processes: a gender-aware framework', *Tourism Management*, 17 (2): 95–102.

Krippendorf, J. (1987), *The Holiday Makers: Understanding the Impact of Leisure and Tourism*. London: Heinemann.

Luongo, M. (2000), 'Gay tourists in New York City', in S. Clift and S. Carter (eds), *Tourism and Sex: Culture, Commerce and Coercion*. London: Continuum.

Macgregor, K. (2001), 'Faiths unite to fight gay invasion of Cape Town', *Independent*, 18 March (see *www.independent.co.uk*).

Mintel (2000), *The Gay Holiday Market*. Market Intelligence Report UK, London: Mintel Publishers.

Morgan, N. and Pritchard, A. (1999), *Tourism Promotion and Power: Creating Images, Creating Identities*. Chichester: Wiley.

Morris, C. (2000), 'Turkish police block gay tour from Roman ruins', *Guardian*, 8 September (see *www.guardian.co.uk*).

Northmore, D. (1998), 'So where are you off to?', *Pink Paper*, 17 July: 11.

Opperman, M. (1999), 'Sex tourism', *Annals of Tourism Research*, 26 (2): 251–304.

Papson, S. (1981), 'Spuriousness and tourism politics of two Canadian provincial governments', *Annals of Tourism Research*, 8 (2): 220–35.

Perez, L. A. (1975), 'Underdevelopment and dependency: tourism in the West Indies', Center for inter-American studies, University of El-Paso. Quoted in C. M. Hall (ed.), *Tourism and Politics: Policy, Power and Place*. Chichester: Wiley.

Pink Paper (1999a), 'Gay ban at Caribbean hotel', 23 April: 4.

Pink Paper (1999b), 'Cayman islands still defiant on discrimination demands', 23 April: 4.

PlanetOut News (1999), 'Updates from New Zealand', 9 August (see *www.planetout.com*).

PlanetOut News (2001), 'Netherlands wins gay tourism award', 1 March (see *www.planetout.com*).

Pritchard, A., Morgan, N. and Sedgely, D. (1998), 'Reaching out to the gay tourist: opportunities and threats in an emerging market segment', *Tourism Management*, 19 (3): 272–82.

Quest, R. (1998), 'Gay travel boom', BBC News Online, 2 August (see *www.bbc.co.uk*).

Reuters (2001), 'UK bans TV ads for straights-only resort', 5 July (see Human Rights Campaign website: *www.hrc.org*).

Ryan, C. (2000), 'Sex tourism: paradigms of confusion', in S. Clift and S. Carter (eds), *Tourism and Sex: Culture, Commerce and Coercion*. London: Continuum.

Sanchez Taylor, J. (2000), 'Tourism and embodied commodities: sex tourism in the

Caribbean', in S. Clift and S. Carter (eds), *Tourism and Sex: Culture, Commerce and Coercion*. London: Continuum.

Skelton, T. (1995), 'Boom, bye, bye: Jamaica ragga and gay resistance', in G. Valentine and D. Bell (eds), *Mapping Desire: Geographies of Sexualities*. London: Routledge.

Smith, H. (1995), 'Greek myth', *Guardian Weekend Travel*, 7 January: 10.

Soriano, G. (1998), 'Gay tour cancelled after protest', *Tico Times*, 28 August (see: *www.ticotimes.net*).

Stephenson, M. (1997), *Tourism, Race and Ethnicity: The Perceptions of Manchester's Afro-Caribbean Community Concerning Tourism Access and Participation*. Unpublished PhD, Manchester Metropolitan University.

Summerskill, B. (2001), 'Package holiday giant dares to think pink', *Observer*, 25 March: 7.

Throb Holidays (1998), *Summer Sun Brochure*. London.

Travel Trade Gazette (1998), 'Area capitalises on sexy image', 1 July: 6.

Urry, J. (1990), *The Tourist Gaze: Leisure and Travel in Contemporary Societies*, London: Sage.

Valentine, G. and Bell, D. (eds) (1995), *Mapping Desire: Geographies of Sexualities*. London: Routledge.

Van Gelder, L. and Brandt, P. R. (1992), *Are You Two Together? A Gay and Lesbian Travel Guide to Europe*. London: Virago.

Vanuatu Weekly (1998), 'The tourist dollar that's being questioned', 22 August: 1.

Want, P. (1998/9), 'Gay times', *Tourism Concern*, winter: 14–15.

Weeks, J. (1985), *Sexuality and its Discontents, Meanings, Myths and Modern Sexualities*. London: Routledge.

Wilson, J. (1988), *Politics and Leisure*. Boston: Unwin Hyman.

World Tourism Organization (1999), *Global Code of Ethics for Tourism*. Lisbon (see: *www.world-tourism.org*).

WEBSITES

British Tourist Authority website: *www.visitbritain.com*

British Tourist Authority website for lesbian and gay visitors: *www.gaybritain.org*

Gay Amsterdam website: *www.gayamsterdam.com*

International Lesbian and Gay Association (information on anti-gay law around the world): *www.ilga.org*

Netherlands Board of Tourism website: *www.goholland.com*

PlanetOut News (reporting on lesbian and gay issues): *www.planetout.com*

World Tourism Organization: *www.world-tourism.org*

CHAPTER 9

Better Living Through Circuitry: Lesbians and Circuit Parties

CLAUDIA MILLER

INTRODUCTION

The Circuit is a series of gay dance parties that are held in North America. A circuit party gives us the chance to escape the pressures of our day-to-day existence and to enter the altered world where friendship, dancing, love, spirituality and self expression are celebrated. When The Circuit comes to town, that town becomes an instant gay ghetto full of men. Groups travelling from all across the country enjoy the festivities, sightsee and engage in different events from skiing to river-rafting, all scheduled around large dance events. This trend is now expanding to international destinations as well (*Circuit Noize Magazine*, North America's premier guide to the Gay Party Circuit, at *www.Circuitnoize.com*).

Lesbians began creating their own unofficial version of a 'circuit' over 25 years ago with the Michigan Womyn's Music Festival and other annual music gatherings that followed across the country. Mostly grassroots/separatist events, these festivals were held in remote locations and without the benefit of corporate sponsors, focusing on politics instead of profits. But in the past few years, lesbians have been coming out of the woods and demanding different types of events, which mirror the typically known gay male circuit parties. Across North America, lesbians are attending popular male circuit events in growing numbers, changing and diversifying existing lesbian events to mirror circuit-party structures and creating totally new upscale lesbian circuit destinations.

The reasons for this shift in demand are manifold. Some are based in the changing face of the lesbian community. 'There's definitely a delineation between the modern lesbian and an old-school lesbian', notes Mariah Hanson (personal communication, February 2001), co-founder of one of the largest party weekends for lesbians, the Dinah Shore Weekend in Palm Springs: 'Modern lesbians come in all shapes and sizes and ideologies. But there's a different sensibility, between feeling like we need to be empowered only within our community and a feeling that we've broken through ceilings, are part of society and are comfortable with that.'

Many younger women are defining their own identities and are refusing to follow a set pattern of actions or behaviours in order to be considered a 'true lesbian'. Lark Bennett (pc, February 2001), former Director of Development at CARE Resource who organized Women's White Party Week Miami in 1999, explains: 'It's not a political hot potato anymore. If you like to dance, dance. It doesn't mean you're selling out being a lesbian, and you can't be political and go to a march tomorrow. It just means that you want to dance today.'

Also, many lesbians want to move away from the separatism found at traditional women's festivals. 'Michigan Music Festival started at a time when the whole idea of "chic" or "mainstream" or even the "modern lesbian" hadn't even been born yet', says Hanson: 'So there was a different sense of lesbian community centered around women's music that was very women-identified. Their event is separatist, for instance. Our events are women-identified as well, however, we don't tell women that they can't bring their male friends.'

And beyond the psychological and sociological impetus, the move to more upscale events boils down simply to money: women are finding themselves with more of it. The incomes of women have been gradually increasing across the board, and the inequities between men and women's salaries, although still prevalent, are smaller in degrees. Lesbians have been aggressively pinpointed in the past years as a lucrative target market for advertising dollars by major corporations. A quick search on the Commercial Closet website (*www.commercialcloset.com*), a non-profit-making project that charts evolving worldwide portrayals of the gay community in mainstream advertising, reveals over 98 lesbian-themed ads from corporations like American Express, Bud Light, Johnnie Walker, Donna Karan, Levi's, MAC Cosmetics and more.

Subaru was one of the first companies to court the lesbian market (Palmer, 2000). Starting in 1997 they offered several campaigns including a television commercial with Martina Navratilova, and a print campaign featuring vanity licence plates like 'XENA LVR' (a reference to a woman's adventure show) and 'PTOWNIE'. During the 2000 US gymnastics championships, John Hancock

Financial Services ran a TV spot showing a female couple in an airport with their newly adopted Chinese baby in tow. Though some dialogue was edited after initial airings, the ad was clearly portraying a lesbian couple and ran again during the Olympics and the World Series.

Bennett notes: 'Bottom line, business is business and the lesbian market has been growing steadily, especially in the past ten years. You've really seen the impact of the market – the demographics don't lie, and corporate America can't afford to alienate anyone who brings in a market share.' A recent research report by the New York City ad agency Young & Rubicam called *The Single Female Consumer* found that single women (a group that the lesbian, whether in a relationship or not, is unceremoniously lumped into) are now the strongest consumer block, numbering over 30 million. The report says: 'Women living alone increasingly comprise the strongest consumer block in much the same way that yuppies did in the 1980s.' The study also notes that single professional women show three basic characteristics: first, they are brand-loyal; second, they influence their friends in buying decisions; and third, they are very information-oriented (Young & Rubicam, 2000).

'You see it every generation. More women that not only want to go to these events but who have the financial capability', says Bennett:

You're seeing women who have the opportunity to travel for business and for leisure, and they want to have a travel destination with entertainment attached to it, not having to search out activities once they get there. So you see women, even internationally, who, for the right party, will get on that plane. But you better damn well not disappoint them when they get there.

TRAVELLING THE GAY MALE PARTY CIRCUIT

Noticing the rise in women's attendance over the past four years, many male-dominated circuit party weekends have started including women's events in their schedules. In 1999 the Miami White Party Week produced by the Miami-based non-profit AIDS organization CARE Resource, created Women's White Party Week in co-ordination with their regular programme of activities. Spearheaded by the then Director of Development, Lark Bennett, and the Corporate Sponsorship Manager, Clara Eshkenazi, Women's White Party Week included two dance parties and a concert with Eartha Kitt. These events were organized in conjunction with three local women's promoters: Alison Burgos, Yesi Leon and Mary D.

Bennett explains the creation of these events:

After fifteen years of White Party Week, a very successful event where 15,000 people came from all over the world, I saw in 1997 a burgeoning trend of women, gay women, who were coming to support events for the entire week. I thought, wouldn't it be fantastic if they had their own events that could be a part of this week?

In response to the marketing of the Women's White Party Week, both nationally and internationally, Bennett estimates that approximately 4000 women attended events that week. This included a record number of women who attended the actual White Party at the Vizcaya Mansion. She recalls: 'To look out over that party, as I'd done before, and see all these women dressed up in the finest, incredible, outrageous outfits, who paid $150 to go to that party and showcase just like the men. I'll never forget it.'

Both Eshkenazi and Bennett left CARE Resource on the heels of their 1999 success. During the 2000 White Party Week, women were again included, but on a smaller scale. CARE Resource tapped Burgos and Leon to work as a team to create a single lesbian event, Cirque Blanc. This extremely successful party drew approximately a thousand women to the rooftop of the Sony Building on Lincoln Road in South Beach. Ruth Hamilton, current Director of Development for CARE Resource, reports that women's participation in all of the week's events was significant and that the organization plans to include women's parties in future years.

In addition, other long-standing circuit party weekends have seen the same rise in women's attendance. The Black and Blue Festival in Montreal has been holding lesbian-specific events for the past five years as part of their week-long festival each October. According to Robert Vezina (pc, April 2001), Founding President of Bad Boy Club Montreal (BBCM), the producers of the festival, in 2000 there were four events for women. In addition, 25–30 per cent of the attendees at the main event, the Black and Blue Party at the Olympic Stadium, were women, a mix of straight and gay, who paid US$65 per ticket. The festival has been going for ten years as a benefit for the BBCM Foundation (a non-profit AIDS organization), and Vezina reports that the number of women attending the festival and the culminating party has consistently grown over those years.

Even smaller, less well-known circuit parties are beginning to see the importance of women's events in their line-ups. In January of 2001, the Blue Ball Weekend in Philadelphia held the first women's event in its eleven-year history, Deep Blue, a women's tea dance. According to Special Events Co-ordinator, Jeremy Williams (pc, May 2001), the event drew several hundred women and raised over $2,000 for Philadelphia FIGHT, a local AIDS service organization. A small per centage of those women also attended the main event, the Blue Ball, at the International Cruise Terminal (at Philadelphia's Naval Shipyard), where tickets sold for up to $70.

And although they do not yet have any lesbian-specific events, The Cherry Party in Washington, DC, an internationally recognized circuit weekend, has also had a small but steady increase in lesbians participating in its three-day weekend over the past six years. Produced by the non-profit group, the Cherry Fund, it occurs each April, timed to coincide with the city's famous cherry blossom festival. The desire for more women has also led to a shift in the fund-raising efforts for the event. According to Bruce Namerow (pc, April 2001), the Fund's vice-chairman, they added the Mautner Project for Lesbians with Cancer to their list of beneficiaries last year in an effort to reach out to the lesbian community.

DESTINATION: PALM SPRINGS

As much as the White Party Miami has been dubbed by the press as the 'crown jewel' of men's circuit events, the Dinah Shore Weekend in Palm Springs could be called the 'ruby in paradise' for women, drawing approximately 8000 women to the desert each spring. The transformation of this event over the years has shown how the demographics of the lesbian population, and their tastes, have changed.

Founded by singer and television personality Dinah Shore in 1972, the Colgate Dinah Shore Professional Women's Golf Tournament (as it was then known) was one of the first important money-winning tournaments for women golfers. Until this tournament, women were competing for far smaller purses than the men. As an avid golfer herself, Shore created a tournament that would help women golfers receive the same deserved recognition in their sport that the men enjoyed (Friesema, 1999, see *http://www.gfriends.com/archive/gf799/pages/feature3.htm Girlfriends Magazine* online archives).

Although Shore was not gay herself, because golf was one of the few sports in which women were competing professionally at the time, the sport had a large lesbian following. Each year at the tournament, more lesbian events began to spring up, much to the chagrin of the Ladies' Professional Golf Association, which chooses to ignore the lesbian festivities, and in no way wants to be associated with them. Nabisco Dinah Shore Tournament director Mike Galeski told *Girljock* editor Roxxie: 'Whatever else is going on in town is in no way connected to the golf tournament' (Roxxie, 1998).

Then, as promoters Mariah Hanson, Sandy Sachs and Robin Gans came in with larger upscale parties and booking blocks of rooms at area hotels at $150 apiece, the weekend exploded into the large lesbian gathering it is today. In 1990 Hanson brought her Los Angeles-based production company down to Palm Springs and took over an entire hotel rather than a wing. 'I made sure that all of the parties were within walking distance and added a lot more style and pomp', Hanson (pc, February 2001) recalls. She booked the Palm Springs Museum for the first big event: 'Of course, we were never allowed to throw a party there again. The girls climbed on the roof and danced in front of the lights with their tops off with these eighty-year-old guards chasing them. That was a show all in itself!' The next year, Hanson joined forces with Sachs and Gans of Girl Bar, the popular Los Angeles lesbian nightspot, and they took over a ballroom to do a state-of-the-art party. Hanson says, 'and from there, it's history. It just evolved into this very unique and much anticipated weekend.' Four night-time dances and two pool parties are now part of the event line-up, with 1500 women attending the infamous Splash pool party alone. With the advent each year of more high-profile corporate sponsors such as Captain Morgan rum, Absolut vodka and Coors beer, the Dinah Shore is now very similar to a male circuit event.

Sandy Sachs (pc, February 2001) notes that her friendship with the man many call the 'Circuit Master', Jeffrey Sanker, had an influence on the Dinah Shore: 'Robin and I have always been comfortable hanging out with guys, and we like the circuit parties, we like the big stuff. It was because of our participation with Jeffrey, our close friend for 15 years, that we actually brought some of that element to the Dinah Shore.' Sanker's signature events include the annual White Party in Palm Springs, Snowball (during White Party week in Miami) and One Mighty Party during Gay Days at Disney World. Sachs says: 'We have been modeling after each other. Most of the women's parties I've gone to – they don't get the big circuit kind of feel. Whereas when you come into Dinah Shore, you would think you are at a boy party, and we're really proud of that.'

Over the years, the golf tournament has become secondary, as other parties and events have been added on. Sachs admits, 'I don't know anybody who goes to the golf tournament, I don't think I've ever been. I even forget that there is a golf tournament.' And when the weekend first started, it was a Friday–Saturday event, which has now expanded to Thursday–Sunday. Sachs explains: 'We've added more parties, although we've definitely kind of reached the ceiling. They're pretty much set on Thursday–Sunday, or we get the three-day crowd that comes in Friday and leaves Monday.'

While the event has expanded over the years and added more glamorous parties, the age range of the participants has generally remained stable at twenty-one to thirty-five. Still, Sachs notes some humorous observations by some of the long-term party-goers who feel a sense that the party is attracting younger women:

We still drag some of our old broad friends out there, but even they go, 'God they're just so young.' As people become 40 and up you see less and less of them. You'll see them at maybe one party, maybe, early. They're the ones who are there at nine o'clock, and are like 'Where is everybody?' And we're like, 'It's nine o'clock; we just opened, they're taking a disco nap.'

Besides becoming larger and more glitzy over the years, Dinah Shore has also developed into more of a darling for various corporate sponsors such as Budget Rent-A-Car, PacBell, Subaru and Naya Water. 'I think corporate sponsorship of the gay and lesbian community is certainly more forthcoming than it was when I was first banging on doors', says Hanson:

We've introduced the idea of corporate sponsorship of the lesbian community to a lot of corporations. It was always the men's community that was being sponsored, and I do think that there is more of an awareness today in corporations than there used to be. They find the market very viable and want to invest in it to create loyal customers.

Other events around the country such as WomenFest Key West and Monterey Women's Weekend are all also on the same path as the Dinah Shore, albeit a few years behind. Some women argue that the events are not nearly as large or as upscale as to be called a circuit party, but they are well on their way. Womenfest started in 1993 with 500 women and in 2000 drew up to 3700 lesbians, (pc, Quinn, 2001) while the Monterey Weekend started in 1995 with 900 women and is up to 1500 each year (pc, Hanson, 2001).

NEW GIRL ON THE BLOCK

In addition to women attending and reshaping already established events, new party weekends are popping up such as Aqua Girl Weekend, which is held in Miami each spring. Created as a stand-alone event originally called Sweet Charity in 1999 by promoter, Alison Burgos (pc, February 2001), Aqua Girl is particularly interesting because for the first time a non-profit charity, the Dade Human Rights Foundation (DHRF), produced the event in the same way other non-profits around the country produce male circuit parties. DHRF is well known for the popular male circuit event Winter Party, held each March. By putting their sponsorship and volunteer resources behind Aqua Girl, DHRF drew 2000 lesbians from the United States and abroad to the event just in its first year. With a weekend line-up of events that included everything from chic cocktail parties to an outdoor pool/beach event, the structure of the weekend was very similar to the Winter Party Weekend. DHRF has purchased the trademark of the event from Burgos and will be producing it again each year.

'DHRF was interested in establishing a women's fund', remembers Burgos, 'and they were a big supporter of the first event, (Sweet Charity). I asked them, if we make the DHRF Women's Fund the beneficiary, I would be willing to turn this weekend into the "sister" of Winter Party. I gave them the rights to the weekend, so that it would grow and prosper into what I want it to become.' So the DHRF Women's Fund was established to educate, empower and unite the women's community in South Florida by recognizing, educating and supporting lesbian health and rights issues.

Burgos estimated that approximately 30 per cent of the women attending in 2000 were from outside Miami, and that the number would only increase in the following years. 'I think our community as a whole has evolved quite a bit', Burgos explains:

I think we're becoming much more comfortable and sophisticated as a power-ful group. You see Olivia Cruises, which have tripled the number of cruises they have each year. There are a lot of women's weekends that are popping up that meet the needs of different women. I think the lesbian community is coming into its own. These professional women, who work hard and play hard, want to be able to do something fabulous like come to a glamorous town like South Beach.

While the women's community tends to get pigeonholed as having less discre-tionary income than the men due to the lack of parity in incomes, the gap might be narrowing as is illustrated in events like Aqua Girl and Dinah Shore. 'Usually men make more money', says Burgos:

It's true whether heterosexual or homosexual. The boys are always willing to spend more money than the women, and they don't think anything of spending $100 to go to a dance party. There's just no way I'm going to get girls to do that, but women are definitely getting out there and spending more money. They want to have a good value, and they want to have a good time. They are willing to fly across the country and go on a cruise or to Palm Springs. It costs some money, Dinah Shore, you're looking at $170–$180 a night for a hotel room in the middle of the desert, but thousands of women are willing to do it because it's a great time.

Even with a first-time event, Burgos found that the response from sponsors was extremely positive:

I found that places like MAC Cosmetics, Bicardi, Guess Jeans, Kenneth Cole, Naya Water, Budweiser, Corona, Sky Vodka, especially companies like MAC and Guess who are taking their first forays into the lesbian community, were super supportive, were really excited about reaching our market. Especially when I talk about the fact that we have a higher disposable income because there are less children, when I talk about the brand loyalty that is so strong in our community, marketing directors at ad agencies and corporations around the country are getting that.

For 2001, organizers drew around 3000 women and changed the structure of the event, adding a lesbian art exhibit and a Sunday brunch. Cindy Brown, Aqua Girl 2001 producer, notes: 'We did this to appeal to women who wanted more social/cultural opportunities outside of a party. As we get established, and make some money, we will expand further with perhaps a comedy night or bring some form of the concert and golf outing back.' They raised over $25,000 for the DHRF Women's Fund and conducted a survey at the events to determine the wants and needs of women in terms of community and what services and programmes would appeal to them. 'The results will not only help to shape future Aqua Girl weekends', explains Brown, 'but will help to determine the direction of the Women's Fund.'

In an interesting twist, DHRF's Winter Party actually adopted some tactics from Aqua Girl at its 2001 weekend. 'This year's Winter Party adopted Aqua Girl's Pool Party which was the most successful event outside of the actual Winter Party itself', notes Brown. 'There are plans to make Winter Party more like Aqua Girl with events that have more to offer than just loud music and sweaty men.'

WHAT'S IN A NAME?

Despite all of the positive aspects of these gay and lesbian events, the term 'circuit party' has earned a tarnished reputation over the years, leaving many people hesitant to use those words. Efforts to create communities and raise money for non-profit organizations are often overlooked, as many male circuit events are criticized by the press and community leaders for lacking politicism, encouraging drug and alcohol abuse, and providing settings for casual and unsafe sex.

In fact, Mariah Hanson of Dinah Shore even goes so far as to say: 'I wouldn't call the Dinah Shore a circuit party. I don't think it's modeled after the boys circuit events at all. There's certainly not the presence of drugs at our events that are at the guys events.' But her business partner Sandy Sachs counters:

> The Dinah Shore Weekend is definitely a circuit party. I tell you why Mariah is hesitant to use the word circuit party, it's because corporate sponsors are shying away from the word 'circuit'. Circuit parties also have a very strong affiliation with drug use, and what's happened is that a lot of corporate sponsors don't want to have any sort of association with that. It kind of depends on who you're talking to and how they define circuit party. If you're talking to someone who is doing the party favours [drugs], that's what they equate with the circuit party. If you talk to other people who go because they just like to be around lots of people and they like the big DJs, then that's a different interpretation.

And it's not only the organizers of women's events who are hesitant to use the term, as many male event organizers are also shying away from it as well, due to not only sponsors staying away but also beneficiaries. Recently in Atlanta, the Change of Seasons circuit party, now in its fourth year, donated its proceeds to the Atlanta Humane Society after several local gay and AIDS groups turned down money from the event. Linda Ellis, the executive director of one of the Atlanta-based groups who turned down the funds, YouthPride, told *Southern Voice*: 'It's a discomfort that we have with taking money from events or establishments that wouldn't be a good place for a good number of our youth' (Erikson, 2001). Lark Bennett recalls: 'It's interesting because when I was on staff with White Party at CARE Resource, we were never allowed to embrace the circuit name as well. But to me, if it walks like a duck, talks like a duck, it's a duck at the end of the day.'

The discomfort with more than just the label of 'circuit party' caused the New York-based Gay Men's Health Crisis (GMHC) to discontinue its relationship with the huge Fire Island Morning Party in 1999, due to the highly publicized controversy over drug overdoses and arrests at the popular event. GMHC, the nation's largest AIDS-care and service organization, had organized the dance event in previous years on the beach of the Fire Island Pines, and nearly 5000 people paid $100 each to attend the final party, raising nearly half a million dollars for the group. But in a statement released by GMHC, the organization said it was cancelling the party because: 'regrettably, over the past few years the Morning Party has become associated with alarming levels of recreational drug use, despite GMHC's many attempts to discourage drug-taking at the event' (Barillas, 1999, from *http://www.datalounge.com/datalounge/news/record. html*).

With the shift to the male circuit model of partying comes concerns that lesbians will pick up these bad elements along with the good. But promoters say that at any dance event, gay or straight, there will be drug and alcohol use as well as a sexually charged atmosphere – it's a party after all. Bennett says:

> It's the same answer whether it's a men's party or a women's party for me, issues of drug abuse and alcohol abuse have to do with issues of self-worth – that's an individual issue. Now there are people who go to extremes, but they can go to extremes at a party; they can go to extremes in their own home. If you've got a problem, it's going to manifest itself in a grocery store. I don't think being at a party is going to fuel it any more.

Sachs also notes that the men and women do party differently:

> There's no drug use really at Dinah Shore. The testament to that is that our parties are over at 3 o'clock. End of story. We couldn't get them to stay until four or five even if we gave them all Red Bull [a guarana-based energy drink popular at clubs]. They get tired, they go home, and they go to bed. The boys are up and up and up . . . and we all know why.

However, recent research on lesbians and alcohol abuse, does show that lesbians are more likely than their heterosexual counterparts to use alcohol and to seek treatment for alcohol-related problems. According to a pilot study called *Sexual Identity and Drinking: Risk and Protective Factors* conducted by researchers at the University of Illinois at Chicago in 2000, 17 per cent of lesbians reported they were in recovery for alcoholism, while only 2 per cent of heterosexual women reported they were in recovery (Fox, 2000, from the *Blade* online archives, 20 October).

It also found that 47 per cent of lesbians, compared with only 16 per cent of heterosexual women, reported that they have wondered at some point in the past whether they might have a drinking problem. In addition, 18 per cent of lesbians, and only 2 per cent of heterosexual women, reported seeking treatment for alcohol-related problems. Lesbians were also more likely than heterosexual women (25 per cent compared with 16 per cent) to report a twelve-month abstinence from alcohol, but none of the lesbians were lifetime abstainers.

As for sex, whereas men seem to be more focused on immediate gratification at these events, women are a little slower on the approach. Sachs explains:

> There are some definite hook-ups; It's really fun to watch the progression. Friday, everybody is kind of checking everybody else out, and by Sunday everybody's hugging and kissing, coupled off. It takes longer than for the boys because that's the number one reason the guys are at a circuit event. Girls, they're going to go with their girlfriends or meet some new people, be in a really nice hotel in a really nice resort area, where they can be comfortable. Guys are going to get laid.

A study by the Centers for Disease Control and Prevention seems to back up these concerns about circuit parties by showing that rampant drug use and risky sex *can be* commonplace at these events. The study, published in the *American Journal of Public Health*, was based on a survey of 295 gay or bisexual men in San Francisco who attended at least one circuit party in the previous year (Garbo, 2001). Although this is a limited study in its scope, 95 per cent of the respondents said they used a psychoactive drug at the last circuit party they attended and 61 per cent used three or more. Ecstasy was the most popular drug (75 per cent had taken it), followed by Ketamine (58 per cent) and alcohol (56 per cent). In addition, 29 per cent reported having multiple sex partners during the circuit party weekend, and among those men, 24 per cent reported having unprotected anal sex. 'As a whole, these findings suggest that a substantial drug culture permeates the circuit party environment, a drug culture that is distinct from broader communities of gay and bisexual men' (*Advocate*, 2001).

BREAKING DOWN BARRIERS

Now in 2001, as lesbians look about for travel destinations, they are finding themselves presented with more options than even just ten years ago when the first men's circuit parties began to take off. No longer are they forced to choose from a limited selection of events that may not mirror their own preferences for an ideal vacation. If current trends continue, the lesbian community should see an increase in acceptance at male-oriented events with more parties targeted towards them, as well as more women's events striving towards the circuit party model. Barriers are breaking down across gender lines as gay men and lesbian women look to each other and try to learn what elements create events that are not only glamorous and exciting but also truly build community.

REFERENCES

Advocate (2001), 'Study: Drug use, risky sex put circuit party attendees at risk for HIV', 15 June (see *www.Advocate.com* and search for circuit party).

Barillas, C. (1999), 'GMHC cancels Fire Island morning party', *Datalounge*, 4 January (see *www.Datalounge.com* and search for Fire Island).

Erikson, E. (2001), 'ATL gay, AIDS groups turn down money from circuit party', *Southern Voice*, 19 April (see *www.southernvoice.com/southernvoice/news* and search for circuit party).

Fox, K. (2000), 'Lesbian health update: lesbians at risk for alcohol abuse', *New York Blade News*, 20 October (see *www.nyblade.com* and search for lesbian health).

Friesema, S. (1999), 'Short circuit', *Girlfriends Magazine*, 17 August (see *www.girlfriendsmag.com* and search archive).

Garbo, J. (2001), 'Drug use puts circuit party attendees at risk of HIV', *Gay Health*, 11 June (see *www.GayHealth.com* and search for circuit party).

Lee, V. (2001), 'Tee party', *Guardian*, 7 May.

Palmer, K. S. (2000), 'Gay consumers in the driver's seat: Subaru's new ad campaign is among those signaling to homosexual buyers', *Washington Post*, 4 July, C1 (see *www.washingtonpost.com* and search archives).

Roxxie (1998) (ed.), *Girljock: The Book*. San Francisco, CA: St Martin's Press (Roxxie, 'All Dinah Shore golf action') (see *www.stonewallin.com* and *www.girljock.com* for further details about girljocks).

Stein, A. (2000), 'Lesbian-themed advertising turns heads – or goes over them', *Tribune*, 15 November: 15.

Young & Rubicam (2000), *The Single Female Consumer*. New York: Young & Rubicam, Intelligence Factory Research Report, July.

Personal communications

Lark Bennett, February 2001.
Cindy Brown, May 2001.
Alison Burgos (Aqua Girl), February 2001.
Mariah Hanson, February 2001.
Bruce Namerow (Cherry Fund), April 2001.
Katey Quinn (Womenfest), June 2001.
Sandy Sachs, February 2001.
Robert Vezina (BBCM), April 2001.
Jeremy Williams (Blue Ball), May 2001.

WEBSITES

Advocate magazine: *www.Advocate.com*
Circuit Noize (a guide to the circuit scene), Online version: *www.circuitnoize.com*
Current US lesbian issues: *www.LesbiaNation.com*
Girlfriends magazine: *www.girlfriendsmag.com*
Information on current US gay and lesbian issues: *www.Datalounge.com*
Information on health matters affecting gay men and lesbian women: *www.Gay Health.com*
Information on lesbian sportswomen: *www.girljock.com*
New York Blade (US newspaper covering gay and lesbian issues): *www.nyblade.com*
Project examining representations of gay men and lesbian women in the media: *www.commercialcloset.com*
Southern Voice (US newspaper covering gay and lesbian issues): *www.southern voice.com*
Stonewall Inn (Publishers of lesbian and gay books): *www.stonewallinn.com*

PART 3

Sexual Behaviour, Risk and HIV Prevention

CHAPTER 10

Gay Men, Holidays and Sex: Surveys of Gay Men Visiting the London Freedom Fairs

STEPHEN CLIFT, CARRY CALLISTER AND MICHAEL LUONGO

INTRODUCTION

In November 1995 the UK Health Departments published a revised strategy for HIV and AIDS health promotion, based on current knowledge of HIV transmission in the UK (UK Departments of Health, 1995). The key concern of this document was to emphasize the importance of targeting prevention initiatives in a precise way towards communities known to be at greatest risk of HIV infection. In future, the document stated: 'Campaigns will continue to maintain awareness of HIV in the general population but greater emphasis will be placed on developing national and local health promotion directed at vulnerable groups' (UK Departments of Health, 1995: 5). Five groups were specifically identified. Of these, two were associated with homosexual sex ('gay men' and 'bisexual men, and other men who have sex with men') and a third associated with travel outside the UK ('men and women who travel to, or have family links with, high-prevalence countries where the predominant mode of transmission is sex between men and women'). It is clear that travel as a risk factor associated with HIV was linked to heterosexual sex. To some this was, and still is, justifiable given the epidemiological evidence showing that a higher percentage of HIV infections among heterosexuals in the UK were probably acquired outside the country. However, the apparent implicit assumption that travel and HIV risks is not an issue that requires consideration in relation to gay and bisexual men is questionable. It is clear, for instance, that in the early stages of the HIV/AIDS epidemic among gay men in Europe, the majority of cases were among 'men who had had sexual contacts with men who lived in the United States' (Conway *et al.*, 1990). In addition, the significance of travel in the development of the epidemic among gay men in the United States itself, has been clearly documented (Gould, 1993; Rotello, 1997). Furthermore, as the contributions to this volume amply demonstrate, many gay men have travelled, and continue to travel, widely throughout the world for holidays, and opportunities for sex in holiday settings are often enhanced. This is true for gay and straight tourists alike (Clift and Carter, 2000).

The lack of specific attention to travel and gay men in the UK strategy document probably reflected the fact that in the UK, epidemiological data for HIV infection among gay and bisexual men are not broken down with respect to whether the infection is presumed to have occurred within or outside the UK. In addition, at the time the strategy document was written, research evidence on HIV risks among gay men in the context of travel, was rather meagre and diverse in quality (Clift and Wilkins, 1995). Furthermore, very little if any academic attention had been given to patterns of gay travel and tourism, the factors affecting it, and gay men's experiences and behaviours on holiday (a notable early exception being Holcomb and Luongo, 1996).

This chapter reports on a series of projects undertaken in the UK by the authors to study the tourism patterns and experiences of gay men and assess whether unsafe sexual behaviour in holiday settings was an issue of concern that needed to be a focus of specific prevention initiatives. The findings from the first study, which centred on Brighton, a resort town on the south coast of England with a large gay community, have been reported in detail elsewhere, and will be summarized here (see Clift and Forrest, 1998; 1999a, b; 2000a, b; Forrest and Clift, 1998). More attention will be given to subsequent surveys carried out at the Gay and Lesbian travel fairs in London in 1997–8. Further survey work, conducted to support the development of a national travel-HIV prevention campaign for gay men, is discussed by Scholey (Chapter 11, this volume) and is not considered here.

THE BRIGHTON SURVEY

In this project, just under 600 men provided information on their experiences of holidays and sexual activity by means of a self-completion questionnaire.[1]

Approximately half of the sample was recruited in bars and clubs in central Brighton during two weeks of fieldwork in August 1996, and half through a postal survey conducted with the assistance of a local lesbian and gay magazine *Gscene*. The questionnaire included questions on destinations visited over the previous five years, holiday motivations, attitudes towards sex on holiday and sexual behaviour and risk on up to two holidays taken in 1996 prior to the survey. Information on demographic and biographical characteristics and aspects of sexual history (e.g. HIV status, previous sexually transmitted infections [STIs]) was also gathered. The only question considered in any way sensitive by a few respondents was one asking for details of income! The key findings from this survey can be summarized as follows. Gay men reported visiting a wide range of destinations outside the UK over the previous five years, with over 40 per cent visiting Amsterdam, Paris and the United States. Well-known southern European gay destinations had been visited by varying proportions of men: Gran Canaria (32 per cent), Ibiza (23 per cent), Sitges, near Barcelona (14 per cent) and the Greek island of Mykonos (8 per cent). Among men having holidayed during 1996 up to the time of the survey, the five most commonly visited countries outside of the UK on the first or only holiday were the United States (14 per cent), Gran Canaria (8 per cent), Holland (Amsterdam) (8 per cent), France (Paris) (7 per cent) and Spain (Sitges/Barcelona) (7 per cent).

Over 70 per cent of gay men rated 'comfort and good food' and 'rest and relaxation' as very important aspects of holidays, whereas only just over a third rated 'opportunities to socialize with gay men' and 'gay culture and venues' as very important. Furthermore, just under a third rated 'opportunities to have sex' as very important. Gay men's attitudes towards sex on holiday appeared to be fairly polarized. Just under half of the sample agreed there are more opportunities for sex on holiday, but just over a third disagreed. Similarly, 39 per cent agreed they were more sexually active on holiday, while 42 per cent disagreed. More interestingly, 11 per cent agreed they found it easier to forget about safer sex on holiday and 10 per cent agreed they were more likely to take sexual risks on holiday compared with at home.

Just over a quarter of men reported experience of a sexually transmitted infection during the previous five years (29 per cent), and of these 17 per cent believed they had contracted an infection while on holiday. With respect to HIV status, 9 per cent of men described themselves as 'definitely positive'.

For the first or only holiday in 1996, 48 per cent reported sex with one or more new partners, and among these, 61 per cent experienced penetrative sex (as the 'active' or 'passive' partner, or both). Among men who were active in

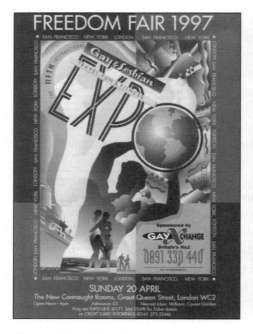

Figure 10.1 The London Freedom Fair Surveys 1997 and 1998. *Source*: Stephen Coote, organizer Freedom Fairs 1997/98.

penetrative sex, 90 per cent reported using condoms consistently (i.e. 10 per cent reported some unsafe sex), whereas among those who were receptive partners in penetrative sex, only 79 per cent reported consistent condom use by their insertive partner(s) (i.e. 21 per cent reported some unsafe sex).

Three factors were associated with reports of unprotected anal sex on holiday: (1) agreement that holidays increase opportunities for sex and enhance risk; (2) neglecting to take condoms on holiday; and (3) being HIV-positive. These links are tentative and need to be interpreted cautiously, however, since in the sample as a whole, the numbers of men who were HIV-positive, who did not take condoms, and who engaged in unsafe sex, were all fairly small.

THE LONDON FREEDOM FAIR SURVEYS

Travel fairs aimed at gay men and lesbian women were held in Earls Court, London during 1997 and 1998 (see Figure 10.1). These fairs brought together principal UK gay tour operators and travel businesses; the gay press, which regularly publishes travel features (e.g. *Gay Times*, *The Pink Paper*, *Boyz*); publishers of gay and lesbian travel guides (e.g. *Ferrari*), and other businesses catering for the gay market (e.g. *Zipper*).

A stall was set up at both fairs for the purpose of recruiting participants for a survey on gay tourism and sexual behaviour. All men showing interest in the display of materials on the stall were invited to participate in the survey, and very few men refused to take part. No systematic system of sampling was employed, and as a result it is not possible to claim that the sample achieved was representative of the visitors to the fairs. It was possible, however, to compare the findings from the two samples achieved during the 1997 and 1998 fairs, and to compare the findings from this survey with the results from the earlier survey in Brighton.

A short self-completion questionnaire was used in the survey, based on the longer questionnaire used in the earlier Brighton project. Men were asked to give details of their most recent holiday abroad, and were given a list of possible activities and experiences during their holiday (e.g. making friends with other men, experiencing local culture, drinking alcohol) and asked: 'to what extent were the following experiences part of this holiday?' A three-point rating scale was provided: 'great extent', 'some extent' and 'not at all.' Questions were also included on whether sexual activity with new partners took place on holiday, whether penetrative sex occurred and whether condoms were used consistently. Information was also gathered on previous history of sexually transmitted infections, HIV status, age, whether respondents were in a 'committed relationship' and the number of new sexual partners they had had 'this year at home'.

Characteristics of the sample

Just under 300 usable questionnaires were completed, 186 gathered in 1997 and 109 in 1998. Comparisons between the two samples on age, place of residence, partnership status, sexually transmitted infections in the last five years and HIV status revealed no statistically significant differences. In addition, only one significant difference emerged among the variables related to the last holiday abroad, with respondents in the 1997 sample more likely to report 'resting and relaxing' on holiday than those in 1998. In general, therefore, it was considered reasonable to combine the two samples for further analysis. Table 10.1 reports sample characteristics for the combined sample.

Table 10.1 Freedom Fairs 1997 and 1998: sample characteristics

	No.	%
Age (no. = 295)		
17–29	79	27
30–39	140	48
40+	76	26
Place of residence (no. = 293)		
UK	260	89
outside UK	33	11
Committed relationship (no. = 291)		
yes	157	54
no	134	46
Sex partners at home 'this year' (no. = 295)		
none	92	31
1–3	84	29
4+	119	40
Sexual infections in last five years (no. = 294)		
yes	51	17
no	243	83
Had HIV test (no. = 291)		
yes	190	65
no	101	35
HIV status (no. = 285)		
definitely negative	131	46
probably negative	96	34
unsure	30	11
probably positive	3	1
definitely positive	25	9

Most recent holiday abroad

Respondents were asked to give details of their most recent holiday destination abroad (country and city). Men on holiday at the time of completing the

Table 10.2 Regions visited for last holiday and most popular country/island destinations

	No.	% of total sample
Region visited (no. = 295)		
Europe	147	50
North America	56	19
Asia	29	10
UK	18	6
Australia/New Zealand	16	5
Africa	15	5
South and Central America, Caribbean	7	2
Middle East	6	2
World tour	1	<1
Most popular countries/islands (no. = 183)		
United States	51	17
Canary Islands	31	11
Spain/Balearic Islands	26	9
France	23	8
Holland	15	5
Australia	13	4
Greece/Greek Islands	12	4
England	12	4

questionnaire (i.e. in London) were asked to regard it as their most recent holiday. Table 10.2 reports the region of the world visited for a holiday and the eight most popular countries/island groups visited. Within countries and island groups, the most popular specific destinations are generally regarded as significant gay resorts or cities, i.e. Gran Canaria (22), Amsterdam (12), London (12), New York (9), Key West (7), Mykonos (6), Sitges (7), Paris (5), Sydney (5), Ibiza (5) and Berlin (4).

Lengths of holidays described varied from one to 90 days, with 35 per cent lasting up to seven days, 41 per cent between eight and fourteen days and 24 per cent fifteen days and over. Just under a third of men went on holiday alone (32 per cent), 38 per cent went with a partner or family members and 30 per cent went on holiday with friends.

Table 10.3 Gay men's experiences during their last holiday abroad

To what extent were the following experiences part of this holiday?	Great extent %	Some extent %	Not at all %
Comfortable surroundings and good food	59	37	5
Rest and relaxing	52	43	5
Beautiful landscapes	49	35	16
Seeing well-known sights	45	39	16
Seeing local culture	40	45	14
Using alcohol	37	48	14
Good night life	36	46	18
Socializing with other gay men	25	53	22
Gay culture and venues	25	48	27
Seeing wildlife and nature	18	32	50
Visiting art galleries, antiquities, etc.	18	40	42
Being more cautious about sex	16	26	58
Feeling less inhibited sexually	16	37	47
Making friends with other men	16	56	28
Feeling more adventurous sexually	12	28	60
Having a holiday romance	10	15	75
Getting away from gay culture	10	33	58
Visiting sex clubs/saunas	9	25	66
Seeing safer sex promotion material	9	32	59
Poor service and accommodation	6	22	72
Using drugs	6	16	79
Being sick or ill	2	8	90
Experiencing homophobia	1	6	93
Paying for sex	0	4	96

Holiday experiences

Respondents were asked to indicate the extent to which 25 possible activities and experiences had featured in their most recent holiday. Table 10.3 reports the percentage distribution of answers to these items, with experiences ranked according to the proportion of men answering 'great extent'. A number of significant age differences emerged from the data. The youngest group were less likely to have seen 'wildlife and nature' (χ^2 = 13.4, p<0.01); men in the two older groups combined, were more likely to have paid for sex (χ^2 = 4.6, df=1, p<0.01); and men were less likely to consume alcohol to a 'great extent' as they got older (χ^2 = 16.0, p<0.005).

Interrelationships among the various aspects of gay men's holiday experiences were analysed by means of principal components analysis followed by varimax rotation. An initial analysis revealed eight components with eigen values greater than one, although three of these components were defined by strong loadings from only two items and the final component by only one (paying for sex). Examination of a plot of eigen values revealed a levelling-off of values at the fourth and fifth components followed by a 'scree' from the sixth component onwards. This suggested that no more than five components should be retained for rotation. Five, four and three component solutions were examined and the three-component solution was judged to be the most satisfactory and interpretable. Table 10.4 reports the three-component solution, with loadings below 0.3 omitted in the interests of clarity. Interestingly, the first two components emerging from this analysis of holiday *experiences* are very similar to the first two dimensions of holiday *motivations* reported by Clift and Forrest (1998).

Do holiday experiences vary by destination visited?

The range of destinations visited by gay men is clearly very large, and even the most popular destination attracted only a small proportion of the total sample. As a result, it is very difficult to conduct any precise analysis of gay men's holiday experiences or behaviour on holiday in relation to specific destinations. It is possible, however, to categorize destinations based on their description as 'important gay cities' in the international gay guide *Spartacus*. In the sample, 238 respondents gave sufficient information about their holiday destinations for them to be so categorized, and of these 134 (56 per cent) were 'gay' and 104 (44 per cent) were 'not gay'. Destinations for 57 men could not be categorized due to lack of specific information.

It is important to note that destinations not described as an 'important gay city' in *Spartacus* may have a thriving gay scene which a visitor could access. Equally, gay tourists visiting a well-known gay destination might readily avoid contact with local gay culture if they so wished. Nevertheless, as the results in Table 10.5 indicate, the reported experiences of men visiting the two categories of destination were markedly different, and do indicate that men visiting

Table 10.4 Three components of gay men's holiday experiences during their last holiday

	Components		
	1	2	3
Gay social life and sex			
Socializing with other gay men	0.72		
Making friends with other men	0.69		
Gay culture and venues	0.60		−0.34
Good nightlife	0.59		
Feeling less inhibited sexually	0.55		
Being more adventurous sexually than at home	0.51		
Seeing safer sex promotion material	0.49		
Visiting sex clubs/saunas	0.43		
Being more cautious about sex	0.37		
Using alcohol	0.37		
Having a holiday romance	0.34		
Using drugs	−		
Paying for sex	−		
Culture and sights			
Seeing local culture		0.72	
Seeing dramatic or beautiful landscapes		0.71	
Seeing well known sights		0.66	
Visiting art galleries, antiquities, etc.		0.59	
Seeing wildlife and nature		0.54	0.39
Comfortable surroundings and good food		0.46	
Resting and relaxing		−	
Holiday problems			
Being sick or ill			0.64
Poor service and accommodation			0.62
Experiencing homophobia			0.55
Getting away from gay culture		0.31	0.53

significant gay destinations are very likely to participate in the local gay scene. This suggests that the gay character of the destination may well have been an important factor motivating destination choice.

Table 10.5   Experiences of men visiting destinations which are 'gay' and 'not gay' (only items showing significant differences reported)

To what extent were the following experiences part of this holiday?	Great extent	Some extent	Not at all	
Gay culture and venues				
gay	40	55	5	$\chi^2 = 62.9$
not gay	11	43	46	p<0.00001
Good night life				
gay	52	39	9	$\chi^2 = 34.6$
not gay	19	51	31	p<0.00001
Socializing with other gay men				
gay	35	59	6	$\chi^2 = 34.4$
not gay	17	49	34	p<0.00001
Getting away from gay culture				
gay	1	23	76	$\chi^2 = 33.9$
not gay	17	39	44	p<0.00001
Seeing safer-sex promotion material				
gay	11	47	43	$\chi^2 = 30.3$
not gay	6	17	78	p<0.00001
Visiting sex clubs/saunas				
gay	15	24	61	$\chi^2 = 10.4$
not gay	3	27	70	p<0.01
Using alcohol				
gay	44	45	11	$\chi^2 = 7.8$
not gay	27	55	18	p<0.05
Making friends with other men				
gay	21	56	23	$\chi^2 = 6.1$
not gay	11	54	35	p<0.05
Seeing wildlife and nature				
gay	8	24	68	$\chi^2 = 28.5$
not gay	24	41	35	p<0.00001
Seeing dramatic or beautiful landscape				
gay	33	40	28	$\chi^2 = 28.2$
not gay	64	30	7	p<0.00001

Table 10.6 Details of gay men's sexual activity on holiday

		No.	%
New sexual partners (no. = 294)	yes	132	45
	no	162	55
	missing	1	
Number of new partners (no. = 122)	one	41	34
	two or three	44	36
	four or more	37	30
	missing	11	
Penetrative sex with new partners (no. = 131)	yes	63	48
	no	68	52
	missing	2	
Number of penetrative partners (no. = 58)	one	22	38
	two	16	28
	three or more	20	35
	missing	7	
Consistent condom use with partners (no. = 50)	yes	42	84
	no	8	16
	missing	15	

Sex with new partners on holiday

Respondents were asked about sexual activity with new partners during their last holiday: whether they had been sexually active; whether penetration had taken place, and if so, whether condoms had been used consistently. The results obtained are reported in Table 10.6, and revealed a pattern very similar to that previously found in the Brighton survey. Just under half of the men surveyed had been sexually active, and just under half of these had experienced penetrative sex. A majority of men used condoms consistently, but 16 per cent reported inconsistent use.

In order to explore factors associated with sexual activity and penetrative sex on holiday, a series of univariate analyses using chi-square tests were conducted. These analyses revealed that a large number of biographical, contextual, behavioural and experiential factors were associated with sexual activity with new partners on holiday (see Clift *et al.*, 1999, for further details). Sexual activity on holiday was associated with the following factors:

- *biographical*: being single, being more sexually active at home, having a history of STIs in the last five years;
- *contextual*: visiting a gay destination, holidaying alone or with friends, experiencing gay culture/venues, having a good night life, visiting a sex club or sauna, *not* visiting art galleries, etc., *not* getting away from gay culture;
- *behavioural*: using alcohol, using drugs, paying for sex, being more cautious about sex, socializing with gay men, making friends on holiday;
- *experiential*: feeling more adventurous, feeling less inhibited sexually, seeing safer-sex promotion material.

A more restricted range of factors was associated with reported penetrative sex on holiday:

- *contextual*: holidaying alone or with friends;
- *behavioural*: using alcohol, using drugs, larger number of sexual partners;
- *experiential*: feeling less inhibited sexually.

No analysis was carried out for 'safe vs. unsafe' sex, as the incidence of reported unsafe sex was too low for tests to be appropriately conducted.

DISCUSSION

Sampling issues

It is widely acknowledged that obtaining information from representative samples of gay men, and men who are sexually active with men, is very difficult if not impossible. It is necessary, therefore, to gather data from men who are accessible in a variety of contexts or networks, or more generally via the gay press. Generalizing from the results from such samples is always problematic, and the most one might claim is that the findings *may* reflect a wider constituency of gay and homosexually active men. In the present study, the sample was clearly an opportunistic one, drawn in a non-random way from much larger numbers of men visiting the one-day gay and lesbian travel fairs in 1997 and 1998. Clearly, any conclusions drawn from the survey must be qualified by an acknowledgement of sample limitations.

Nevertheless, the fact that data were gathered over two years using the same questionnaire, offered the opportunity to compare the two independently gathered sets of data. These comparisons were reassuring in demonstrating substantial similarities across virtually all questions asked, with a 'statistically significant' difference emerging for only one aspect of holiday experience. Thus, the two groups were very similar in terms of age, partnership status, sexual behaviour, whether tested for HIV antibodies, HIV status and history of sexually transmitted infections. They were also very similar in their reported holiday experiences. It was also possible to compare the Freedom Fair sample with previously studied samples where similar or identical questions were asked, and again the similarities were more striking than the differences. For example in the Brighton survey, 49 per cent of men were in a committed relationship, compared with 54 per cent in the Freedom Fair sample. Similarly, 63 per cent of the Brighton sample reported having had an HIV antibody test, compared with 65 per cent in the London sample.

Gay men's holiday destinations

In the present survey, almost half of all last holiday destinations were in Europe, with Spain and the Spanish islands (the Balearics and the Canaries) being the most popular destinations, followed by France, Holland and Greece and the Greek islands. Just under a fifth of holidays were also taken in the United States. This pattern of holidaying predominantly in southern Europe and in the United States, reinforces findings from the earlier survey in Brighton. In that research, for the first or only holiday taken in 1996, 50 per cent had visited destinations in Europe (with Spain and the Spanish islands, France and Holland being the most popular destinations) and 12 per cent had visited the United States. In both studies, the most popular specific destinations given are described by *Spartacus*, the international gay travel guide, as important gay cities. In the present survey, over half of the destinations visited (56 per cent) could be regarded as 'gay' and the remainder (44 per cent) as non-gay.

These data are important in documenting where gay men travel to for holidays and the extent to which the gay character of the destination appears to be an attractive feature. It appears that approximately half of gay men travelling abroad visit gay destinations and half do not. Important 'gay' destinations will have either a substantial local gay population, or will attract considerable numbers of gay tourists, and so any visitor interested in meeting other gay men for sex, will have ample opportunity in such destinations. Furthermore, men travelling to such destinations may well be moving into a social environment in which levels of HIV infection and other sexual infections are higher than in their home environment. In addition, their levels of sexual activity may be higher than they would normally be at home over the same period. Both factors could lead to an increased level of infection risk. On the other hand, gay men travelling from localities where local gay communities are less visible, the commercial gay scene smaller or non-existent, and levels of sexual infections lower, to larger and more vibrant gay spaces may be more likely to come across safer-sex information and be more vigilant about possible risks from sexual contact with new partners.

Gay men's holiday experiences

In order to explore the characteristics of gay men's holidays, a list of 24 activities and experiences were presented and men asked to indicate whether they had been part of their last holiday abroad. The approach adopted was a modification of that used in the Brighton survey where men were asked how important sixteen issues were in planning a holiday. Interestingly, however, there was considerable overlap in the findings. In the Brighton survey, for instance, 'comfort and good food' and 'rest and relaxation' were the most widely endorsed motivational factors, and in this survey, the items most widely endorsed were 'comfortable surroundings and good food' and being able to 'rest and relax'. Similarly, in the Brighton survey, approximately a third of men regarded socializing with gay men and opportunities for sex as important in planning a holiday. In this survey, between a quarter and a third of men reported that gay culture and socializing with gay men had been an important part of their holiday, and over a third of men had visited sex clubs or saunas on holiday. Interestingly, most men reported experiencing no homophobia on holiday, with only 7 per cent saying they had come across this to some or a great extent.

Not only was the profile of answers similar across the two surveys, but the broad components of holiday motivations and holiday experiences identified by factor analysis were very similar too. In the present survey, the first two factors identified, 'gay social life and sex' and 'culture and sights' were very close in character to the first two factors emerging from the Brighton survey. In the Freedom Fair study, however, a wider range of experiential items were included than in the earlier study, and consequently a larger number of items defines the gay life and sex factor – including the items 'visiting sex clubs/saunas' and 'using alcohol'.

The similarities in the first two dimensions of holiday motivation and holiday experience emerging from the Brighton and London surveys, serve to suggest a two-dimensional model of gay tourism. Men vary firstly in the extent to which they seek 'gay' holidays which offer opportunities for meeting other men and having sex, and secondly, in the extent to which they are interested in more obviously 'touristic' holidays which offer new experiences and sights (culture, history and environment, etc.). The two dimensions appear to be independent of one another, which suggests four gay tourist types: some men seek both sex and culture in the context of holidays, others tend to focus on one or the other, and for some neither assumes particular importance. The later group may be men who tend to pursue special interests on holiday such as skiing and other sports, an issue not addressed in the London survey. Of course, it may be that different issues come to the fore with different holidays and at different times. Given that the data from the London survey related to the last holiday abroad we can only say that men's experiences on that holiday appeared to vary along these two dimensions. This is not to say that men might not vary from holiday to holiday in the factors affecting their travel decisions and their patterns of activity and experience on holiday. This is an issue requiring further research.

Holiday experiences in 'gay' and 'non-gay' destinations

It is reasonable to expect that men who visit 'gay' destinations for a holiday are likely to be seeking social and sexual contact with other gay men, whereas those choosing to visit non-gay destinations may be less interested in such contact. It is not surprising, therefore, to find marked differences in the activities and experiences of men visiting the two kinds of destination. 'Gay culture and venues' for example, were experienced to a 'great extent' by over 40 per cent of visitors to gay destinations, compared to 11 per cent of visitors to destinations that were not gay. Conversely, 64 per cent of men in non-gay destinations reported 'seeing dramatic and beautiful scenery' compared to 33 per cent of men in gay destinations. Similar patterns were found in the Brighton survey, with holiday motivations relating to gay social life and sex being expressed more commonly among men who had visited important gay destinations in the last five years (e.g. Gran Canaria, Sitges and Mykonos), than those who had not visited such destinations (Clift and Forrest, 1999a).

Sexual activity on holiday

In the present survey, 45 per cent of men reported sex with a new partner or partners during their last holiday. This is very close to the figure of 48 per cent found from the Brighton survey. A number of factors were significantly associated with sex on holiday: not being in a committed relationship; having more sexual partners at home; and a history of sexually transmitted infections over the previous five years. Each of these factors was also related to having sex with new partners on holiday in the Brighton survey. Holidaying in a gay destination and being on holiday alone or with friends was also associated with sex on holiday with new partners, again in line with the Brighton findings. In addition, most of the holiday-experience items loading on the first 'gay social life and sex' dimension emerging from the factor analysis, were significantly associated with sex on holiday. This again is very consistent with the finding from the Brighton survey of a significant association between being motivated by gay social life on holiday, and reported new partners.

In the London survey, 48 per cent of sexually active respondents reported penetrative sex, which compares with 60 per cent in the Brighton survey. A significant relationship emerged for the number of partners on holiday, with only 33 per cent of men reporting one partner having penetrative sex, compared with 73 per cent of those with four or more partners. A similar association was found in the early survey in Brighton. This suggests that the more sexually active men are on holiday the more likely they are to experience penetration.

Reassuringly, in this survey, the number of men reporting unprotected anal sex was low (i.e. 16 per cent of men reporting penetration). Interestingly, this figure is similar to that found in the Brighton survey (15 per cent). This suggests that only a relatively small number of gay men in the late 1990s were having unprotected sex on holiday. These figures are much lower than the estimates of the levels of unprotected sex during holidays/travel found in studies of heterosexuals (Bloor et al., 1997, 1998; Clift and Carter, 2000).

CONCLUSION

The present study was conducted in the context of two recent travel fairs in London aimed at the lesbian and gay market. The field-workers set up a stall at the fairs, with an attractive display, and invited men passing by to complete a short, simple questionnaire about their last holiday abroad. The questionnaire was based on one used previously in a survey of gay tourism centred on Brighton (Clift and Forrest, 1998; 1999a, b; 2000a, b; Forrest and Clift, 1998), but extended to include a list of holiday experiences and behaviour, including references to alcohol and drug use and visits to saunas and sex clubs – issues not addressed in the earlier survey.

The survey was well received, and men visiting the fairs were very willing to complete the questionnaire. The setting of travel fairs is thus a good one in which to conduct research of this kind, and further work could be more ambitious in attempting to recruit larger numbers of men into a more comprehensive survey addressing not only previous travel experiences, but future plans too (see Stuber, Chapter 4 and Roth and Luongo, Chapter 5 this volume). Men could also be recruited into a longer-term study, and interviewed before and after travel and holidays, to explore more fully motivations and expectations prior to travel, and experiences and behaviour afterwards, when memory for events and especially for sexual activity would still be fresh.

The most important aspects of the present survey relate to gay men's reports of their sexual behaviours and risks while on holiday, and the factors associated with these activities. The general pattern which emerged was very similar to that previously reported from the Brighton research. In particular, the incidence of unprotected sex was reassuringly low, with only eight men out of the total sample of 294 reporting penetration without consistent use of condoms (i.e. just under 3 per cent). Nevertheless, this represents 16 per cent of men reporting penetrative sex, a percentage very close to that previously reported from the Brighton survey (17 out of 110, or 16 per cent). The findings from both surveys reinforce the continuing need for safer-sex promotion initiatives aimed at gay men, and target campaigns reminding them of the risks of unprotected sex on holiday (see Scholey, Chapter 11, this volume).

NOTE

1. Thanks are due to Simon Forrest for assistance in the design of the questionnaire and the collection of data during the 1997 Freedom Fair.

REFERENCES

Bloor, M., Thomas, M., Abeni, D., Goujon, C., Hausser, D., Hubert, M., Klieber, D. and Nieto, J. A. (1997), *Feasibility Study for Co-ordinated Community Action on the Improved Targeting of HIV/AIDS Prevention Campaigns among International Travellers: Final Report.* Cardiff: School of Social and Administrative Studies, Cardiff University of Wales.

Bloor, M., Thomas, M., Abeni, D., Goujon, C., Hausser, D., Hubert, M., Klieber, D. and Nieto, J. A. (1998), 'Differences in sexual risk behaviour between young men and women travelling abroad from the UK', *The Lancet*, 352: 1664–8.

Clift, S., Callister, C. and Luongo, M. (1999), *Gay Men, Holidays and Sex: Findings from Surveys Conducted at the London Gay and Lesbian Travel Fairs.* Canterbury: Canterbury Christ Church University College.

Clift, S. and Carter, S. (eds) (2000), *Tourism and Sex: Culture, Commerce and Coercion.* Leicester: Pinter.

Clift, S. and Forrest, S. (1998), *Gay Men, Travel and HIV Risk.* Canterbury: Canterbury Christ Church College.

Clift, S. and Forrest, S. (1999a), 'Factors associated with the sexual behaviour and risk of gay men on holiday', *AIDSCare*, 11 (3): 281–95.

Clift, S. and Forrest, S. (1999b), 'Gay men and tourism: motivations and holiday destinations', *Tourism Management*, 20: 615–25.

Clift, S. and Forrest, S. (2000a), 'Tourism and the sexual ecology of gay men', in S. Clift and S. Carter (eds), *Tourism and Sex: Culture, Commerce and Coercion* Leicester: Pinter.

Clift, S. and Forrest, S. (2000b), 'Gay tourism, sex and sexual health promotion', in J. Horne and S. Flemming (eds), *Masculinities: Leisure Cultures, Identities and Consumption.* Eastbourne: Leisure Studies Association.

Clift, S. and Wilkins, J. (1995), 'Travel, sexual behaviour and gay men', in P. Aggleton, P. Davies and G. Hart (eds), *AIDS: Sexuality, Safety and Risk.* London: Taylor & Francis.

Conway, S., Gillies, P. and Slack, R. (1990), *The Health of Travellers.* Nottingham: Department of Public Health Medicine and Epidemiology, University of Nottingham and Nottingham Health Authority.

Forrest, S. and Clift, S. (1998), 'Gay tourist space and sexual risk behaviour', in C. Aitchison and F. Jordan (eds), *Gender, Space and Identity.* Brighton: Leisure Studies Association.

Gould, P. (1993), *The Slow Plague: A Geography of the AIDS Pandemic.* Oxford: Blackwell.

Holcomb, B. and Luongo, M. (1996), 'Gay tourism in the United States', *Annals of Tourism Research*, 23 (3): 711–13.

Rotello, G. (1997), *Sexual Ecology: AIDS and the Destiny of Gay Men.* New York: Dutton.

UK Departments of Health (1995), *HIV and AIDS Health Promotion: An Evolving Strategy.* London: Department of Health.

CHAPTER 11

Going Far this Holiday? A UK HIV-Prevention Intervention with Gay Male Travellers

RICHARD SCHOLEY

INTRODUCTION

My attitude changes. It's fresh faces, fresh meat, fresh trade. Quite easily available depending on where you go. Yeah, you don't know them, they don't know you. You don't have to face them over tea and cakes and a chat. I think I'm more sexually active when I'm on holiday (gay man, fifty, HIV-negative, quoted in Clift and Forrest, 1998: 58).

In narratives of the early years of HIV in the West one individual finds himself unfairly (and erroneously) labelled 'Patient Zero': the source of North America's AIDS epidemic. Sexual contact with this one man featured as a common link in early epidemiological investigations into the outbreak of HIV infection on the North American continent in the late 1970s and early 1980s. 'Patient Zero' clearly must himself have been infected by someone, yet he has the misfortune to play the symbolic role of the 'Typhoid Mary' of HIV/AIDS.

The man, Gaetan Dugas, was a French Canadian airline steward, a sexually active gay man whose ability to travel extensively made it possible for him to play a pivotal role in the early spread of HIV through North America's gay male communities. His almost iconic presence in the history of AIDS is a powerful illustration of how gay sex, travel and HIV have been linked since the very earliest days of the HIV epidemic. Once HIV infection was established in the gay metropolises of North America, gay male tourists travelling between North America and Western Europe were in turn to act as unwitting conduits of HIV transmission into Europe. Early cases of HIV infection documented in, among other places, Germany, the UK and Denmark involved local gay men who had travelled to North America (Conway *et al.*, 1990). Similarly, gay male tourism between the West Coast of the United States and Australia played a key role in introducing HIV into Australia's gay communities.

The rapid global sexual spread of HIV in the late 1970s and early 1980s was hugely aided by the growing amount of international tourism and intercontinental air travel. Tourism that includes sex, be it homosexual or heterosexual, and travel for business or holidays continues to play its part today in new HIV infections around the globe.

A UK TRAVEL CAMPAIGN FOR GAY MEN

In recognition of this, the UK Department of Health decided in 1997 to fund, among the range of HIV prevention activities it finances, an intervention targeting gay men travelling abroad. It chose a partnership of agencies called CHAPS (Community HIV and AIDS Prevention Strategy) to produce and deliver this intervention. The CHAPS partnership is funded by the Department of Health and comprises around a dozen community-based organizations across England and Wales involved in health promotion with gay men or people with HIV. CHAPS partners include the principal gay men's health/HIV-prevention agencies in London, Manchester, Birmingham and Leeds, as well as Terrence Higgins Trust regional centres in Brighton and Bristol. Also included is the Network of Self-Help HIV and AIDS Groups. CHAPS is co-ordinated by the UK's leading HIV charity, Terrence Higgins Trust. The SIGMA research agency is also involved in the partnership ensuring that CHAPS activity is research-informed and evaluated (Weatherburn *et al.*, 2001).

CHAPS remains the chief mechanism by which gay men can be reached in very large numbers across England and Wales. This is thanks to the extensive systems CHAPS partner agencies have in place for making contact with gay men in their locality. Although not the first travel-related HIV-prevention piece of work aimed at UK gay men (Gay Men Fighting AIDS had previously undertaken initiatives on travel and HIV-prevention, see Figure 11.1), in its scale and reach the CHAPS travel intervention has been the most significant; it was also the most rigorously researched, both before, during and after production.

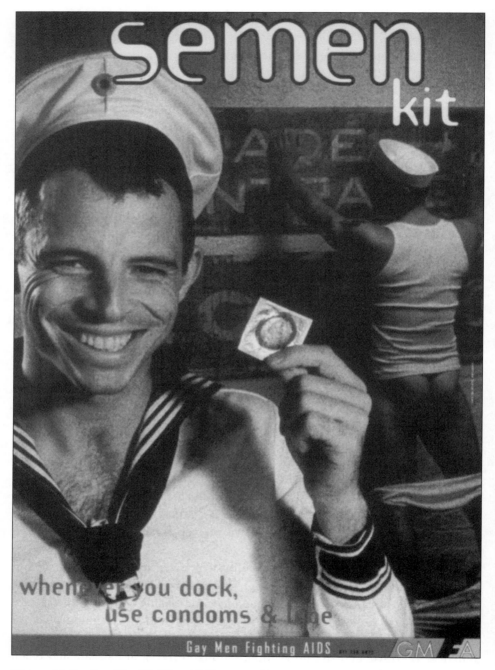

Figure 11.1 Gay Men Fighting AIDS: semen kit postcard. *Source*: Jamie Taylor, Gay Men Fighting AIDS, London.

The research base for the campaign

The travel intervention was made up of a substantial evidence-based element. The Centre for Health Education and Research (CHER), based in Canterbury Christ Church University College, was commissioned to ensure the CHAPS travel work was conducted on a sound research and evidence-based footing. Part of this role involved an investigation into issues around gay men, HIV and travel. Information was gathered in 1998 about the holiday and sexual behaviours of 236 gay men through a questionnaire survey of men from London and northwest England (see Clift et al., 1998 for details). This supplemented CHER's earlier study of similar behaviours among just under 600 men in the English south coast town of Brighton (see Clift and Forrest, 1998; 1999a, b; 2000a, b).

In addition to research with gay travellers, CHER also contacted health professionals, especially doctors in sexual health clinics, to gain the perspective of those working directly with gay men around their sexual health. Travel agents and tour operators specializing in the gay market were also canvassed about gay men's behaviour on holiday and how travel industry representatives might support any HIV-prevention work aimed at their client base (Callister and Clift, 1999).

In addition, face-to-face interviews and focus groups were held with well over a hundred gay men. Face-to-face interviewing was conducted with men in gay bars (and on one occasion in a gay male sexual health clinic), while men were recruited to the focus groups by outreach workers from CHAPS partner agencies leafleting gay venues in their cities.

This face-to-face contact gave gay men the chance to identify and discuss their own issues, which then informed the development of the CHAPS travel initiative. Men were asked what would be important for them to see addressed in a travel campaign aimed at them. HIV and safer sex did not feature prominently, nor did health in general (although some men asked about vaccination requirements). A minority of men reported wanting to know more about condom availability and the policies of foreign countries regarding HIV-positive travellers. Of greater interest were attitudes abroad (cultural and legal) towards gay men, including police attitudes, legal restrictions on sex between men (including outdoor sex) and pornography. Men were also interested in general attitudes in the local population regarding 'gay-friendliness' or tolerance, how 'gay-orientated' a locality is and how to find local gay life.

It was possible through this direct contact with the target group to hear and incorporate their experiences and perceptions of sexual risk and safety in holiday settings, as well as their views on the effectiveness of 'safer sex' promotion. Men were also specifically encouraged to comment on text and design at key stages in the development of the campaign. Finally, after the end products had been launched, the impact on its audience was gauged by further interviews with gay men conducted by the SIGMA research agency as part of their ongoing evaluation of CHAPS activity.

Responsibility for the development of the travel intervention lay with the gay men's team within Terrence Higgins Trust's health promotion division. Co-operation with CHER aimed to ensure the campaign materials were, as far as possible, in keeping with available research evidence and the opinions of gay men and health professionals as noted in the researchers' fieldwork.

Both research documents produced by CHER (the earlier Brighton study and the CHAPS survey a year later) offered valuable pointers into what the issues were around gay men, travel and HIV. Findings from the two studies were broadly in line with each other, with common narratives recurring (see also Clift *et al.*, Introduction, this volume).

A key finding from the CHAPS survey was that many men believed themselves to be a greater risk of HIV away from home – or considered others to be so. Men had a variety of justifications for believing this. Some described the atmosphere on a 'gay holiday' as being highly sexualized, which they felt encouraged sexual behaviour and sexual competitiveness. Patterns of drink and drugs consumption would alter, with no work to do, time for drinking and clubbing expanded. Local factors allied to this were cited as playing a role, such as larger alcohol measures and cheaper prices, longer legal drinking hours, unfamiliar drinks and drugs with different qualities than back home.

A frequently repeated script involved the disinhibiting effect that comes with being on holiday, in particular being away from peers, with 'no one watching' or likely ever to see you again. Travelling alone is a significant feature of gay men's holiday experience, with 20–25 per cent of men doing so in the two CHER surveys that informed the CHAPS travel campaign.

They're abroad, they're a bit wrecked and they start doing things that they wouldn't normally do at home. Mainly because your own inhibitions go down . . . Because people don't know you, you certainly feel as if you can behave in a way that is different to the way you normally behave . . . It's just amazing how much people change on holiday . . . Just two weeks of letting rip and being a completely different person. It's how they want to live but wouldn't dare to live at home because they are going to have to actually face these people the next day. Whereas when you're on holiday you don't have to face them again (gay man, thirty-four, HIV-positive, quoted in Clift and Forrest, 1998: 6).

As the above statement testifies, certain destinations gave some men a real or imagined sense of expanded freedom regarding expression of gay cultural or sexual identity. For some, the local milieu was the focus of this liberalizing effect; for others a liberal space was constructed with little or no reference to this wider local environment. Either way, 'permission' for behaviour that transgressed personal and social norms was experienced, including those relating to sexuality or drugs and alcohol:

> Before I actually started going abroad, over the last few years, I would have never dreamt of going into a darkroom if there was one in this country because of being seen by somebody who knows me. But when you're abroad I think your inhibitions drop. Whereas you just don't care because they see you for two weeks and then you're gone. And I think a lot of people do have the same attitude, where, oh yeah, nobody knows me, I'll let myself go a bit (gay man, twenty-nine, HIV-negative, quoted in Clift and Forrest, 1998: 59).

> I mean, people who have never travelled before, they're out to the pub at nine o'clock and by midnight they're off their fucking trolley. And things in Gran Canaria are instant . . . 42 bars in the Centre, all gay bars, and I'd say about 60 per cent have darkrooms and your inhibitions go while you're on holiday. I've seen it before and I'll see it again . . . I see it happening in the cruising areas and I see it happening in the darkrooms and safe sex goes out the window . . . (gay tour operator, quoted in Clift et al., 1998: 60).

Additional reasons given for believing there was increased HIV risk on holiday included encountering unfamiliar sexual environments, such as backrooms and cruising areas, communication difficulties arising from sex with non-English speakers and holiday locations in areas of high HIV prevalence among gay men. Men also related how they had an expectation of having more sex and with more men on holiday than at home (nearly 40 per cent report this belief in the surveys). Indeed, the research shows that at least one half of men had one or more new sexual partners on holiday and one-third exceeded their annual 'at home' total of sexual partners during just one trip (see Clift and Forrest, 1999b).

The CHER research identified a range of factors that appeared to influence men's sexual behaviour on holiday. Men could have more time for sex and more potential sexual partners. They might experience a change in sexual environment (especially for men less experienced with backrooms and outdoor sex sites). They were likely in European resorts to come up against language barriers with sexual partners. In all locations it would be possible to consume more alcohol and drugs, the nature of which could differ from what they might be familiar with. They could feel disinhibited due to being away from their usual peer group and encounter increased willingness of sexual partners to have unprotected sex compared with home.

These factors could coincide with perceptions of HIV prevalence/risk that could contribute to sexual risk-taking. A man, for example, from a high-prevalence area of the UK could judge, possibly incorrectly, some locations as lower-prevalence, especially in the absence of high-profile HIV-prevention activity. Conversely, a man from a UK low-prevalence area could find himself in a location with a far higher chance of meeting sexual partners with HIV. Both scenarios, for uninfected and infected men alike, have potential for judgements around HIV risk being rendered less reliable than at home.

Other significant findings to emerge from the research included the relatively high proportion of men who believed they had previously contracted a sexually transmitted infection (STI) on holiday (17 per cent in the Brighton survey). In addition, over one in ten men surveyed described themselves as HIV-positive and these men were considerably less likely to use condoms in holiday settings. Despite problems accessing condoms and lubricant in many resorts, a significant number of men had not taken condoms or lubricant away with them. Many men also reported having sex under the influence of drink or drugs. However, despite all of the above factors, the data suggests that men's sexual risk-taking on holiday was likely to reflect their sexual risk-taking at home. 'I mean, I tend not to be too much different. I drink a little more but I wouldn't say I get into any riskier practices but I do tend to have a slightly more blasé attitude towards it' (gay man, thirty-four, HIV-positive, quoted in Clift and Forrest, 1998: 62).

This last finding suggests that gay men on holiday may be no more likely to have unprotected anal intercourse (UAI) on holiday than they do at home. However, men perceive they are at greater risk of HIV, because of the reasons already outlined. The increased numbers of sexual partners and rates of STI acquisition certainly could lead to greater risk of HIV. The more sex an uninfected man has, the greater chance it will be between an uninfected man and an infected one. Although greatly reducing HIV transmission, the more episodes of even protected intercourse, the greater the likelihood a condom will fail, with the potential for HIV infection (CHAPS research shows 13 per cent of men using condoms for insertive anal sex report condom failure over the previous year). And the greater the chance of sexually transmitted infection, the more likelihood HIV transmission will happen – in light of the proven role of STIs as co-factors in HIV transmission (Weatherburn *et al.*, 1999).

The campaign: aims, audience and materials

CHER's data very much shaped the content of the CHAPS travel work, both in terms of the target group and the initiative's aims and objectives. These were as follows:

- to raise awareness of HIV and other STI transmission and prevention, and raise awareness of sexual health services;
- to encourage men to take with them and use correctly appropriate condoms and lubricant;
- to give information for men with HIV about travel and sexual health.

The target audience was gay-identified men travelling to the destinations prioritized. CHAPS took the decision at the outset of its formation to aim its prevention activity at homosexually active men who see themselves as gay. Research shows that in the UK men who accept a gay identity, are closer to the HIV epidemic, more likely to engage in sex which involves risk of HIV infection and, more likely to become HIV-positive, compared with behaviourally bisexual men and men who have sex with men but who do not identify as 'gay' (Hickson *et al.*, 2001).

It was clear that men with HIV must also be included in the target audience. The intervention could not be one aimed solely at uninfected men with a view to keeping them uninfected. Staff at sexual health clinics were also keen for HIV-positive travellers to be included. Addressing both the uninfected and infected – often simultaneously – is a key characteristic of much CHAPS prevention work, and is now considered a mark of good practice in primary HIV prevention (i.e. that which seeks to stop new infections). With a significant proportion of gay male travellers diagnosed with HIV, and with such men engaging in unprotected anal intercourse to a greater degree than uninfected men, the campaign had to be relevant to men of both HIV statuses.

Once the campaign's aims and objectives had been agreed, the decision was made to divide the target audience according to the type of holiday that they were planning. It was felt that the issues were sufficiently different across a range of destinations to warrant separate but linked elements of the travel campaign. The destination areas prioritized were

- southern European beach resorts popular with UK gay men (Ibiza, Gran Canaria and Sitges in Spain, and Mykonos in Greece);
- mainland European cities popular with UK gay men (e.g. Berlin, Paris, Amsterdam);
- long-haul destinations popular with UK gay men (cities in North America and Australia).

These three geographical groupings accounted for the top eight destinations reported by men in CHER's 1998 report (see Clift and Forrest, 1999a, and Clift *et al.*, Introduction, this volume).

Leaflets

The main element of the travel campaign consisted of three leaflets dealing with the three most frequently visited types of location. 'Some like it hot!' covered European beach holidays, 'European Union made easy' addressed European city breaks and 'Go West! Or off to Oz?' focused on long-haul vacations (see Figure 11.2). Content and imagery for all three were subjected to pre-testing focus groups with gay men, carried out by CHER and SIGMA research agency. As well as highlighting men's needs around knowledge (such as STI facts or condom-availability abroad), pre-testing checked that language and tone of the leaflets' messages were comprehensible and acceptable to the target audience.

Pre-testing threw up some interesting tensions. An early draft of 'Some like it hot!' contained statistics about the scale of HIV epidemics in southern European countries compared to the UK (many such countries have HIV-prevalence rates many times greater than the UK). Men reacted very well to this information and were surprised at the extent of HIV infection in these countries. A minority of men, however, interpreted inclusion of the figures as a sort of warning against sex with men from these countries or had concerns about comparing one country's HIV epidemic with another's. Reaction from several HIV-prevention professionals was strongly against inclusion of international comparisons of HIV epidemics. They feared these facts could be interpreted in a xenophobic way, or saw use of them as a resort to 'shock tactics', an approach out of favour with current HIV-prevention thinking in the UK. The relevance of the figures was doubted, as in southern Europe in particular they reflected the predominantly heterosexual nature of those countries' epidemics. As with all statistics, they would also rapidly become out of date. Given these reservations, the section looking at HIV prevalence across countries was dropped from the final leaflet.

Certain issues were common to each of the three destinations. For example: information on STIs and advice for HIV-infected travellers:

Travel insurance
- Standard travel insurance, even when sold by gay travel firms, won't cover you for HIV-related illness, though it will cover you for accidents or stolen luggage.
- You can get travel insurance that will cover HIV-related illness.
- The Terrence Higgins Trust Helpline has details of suitable travel insurance policies.

('Some like it hot!' Leaflet)

Other issues were more specific to individual locations. Examples of the latter would include language barriers (for European destinations), lack of free condom and lubricant distribution in southern Europe, restrictions on people with HIV entering the United States and incorporating changes in time-zones when taking HIV medication (for long-haul destinations). Differences in recreational drugs between destinations was another factor addressed (the higher profile of Crystal Meth in North America and the strength of cannabis on sale in Amsterdam being two examples alluded to in the relevant leaflets):

Three drugs in particular are more common on the scene in North America than at home. They are:

GHB, called 'G' in America ('liquid Ecstasy'). You drink it. Mixing it with other drugs or alcohol can cause you to collapse.

Ketamine, called 'K' or 'Special K' (a heavy-duty anaesthetic in liquid form or in pills mixed with other drugs). It can leave you unable to move for several hours.

Crystal Meth, called 'Crystal' (refined Speed). Available as a powder, pills or chunks, it can be snorted, swallowed or injected. If a hard-on's still possible, it can lead to long sex sessions, with split condoms or damage to the genitals increasing the risk of HIV being passed on. It's highly addictive and continued use leads to violent behaviour and mental health problems.

('Go West! Or off to Oz?' leaflet)

Advice specific to European travel around health insurance (the E111 reciprocal medical care scheme) was included in the two leaflets covering holidays in Europe. The more cautious American HIV-prevention messages around oral sex risk was a further example of an issue associated with a particular destination:

Figure 11.2 Three leaflets for the CHAPS HIV-prevention intervention campaign for gay men. *Source*: Richard Scholey, Terrence Higgins Trust, London.

Some American men and HIV organisations judge sucking to be riskier than we do in the UK and other countries. You may notice condoms are recommended for sucking. This is because:

- US organisations tend to stress the very safest type of oral sex, rather than encouraging 'safer' sucking.
- This might be to protect themselves from being sued by people claiming they got HIV though oral sex.
- HIV being more widespread in America makes some people more cautious about what they do sexually.

('Go West! Or off to Oz?' leaflet)

Each leaflet contained reminders to take appropriate condoms and lubricant on holiday, as well as a section on STIs and their treatment. Referral details for where to have HIV and sexual-health questions dealt with were also given. However, it was felt important the HIV prevention and sexual-health content

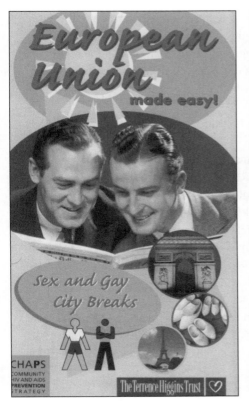

was counterbalanced by other content that was either humorous or of practical use to the reader. For this reason, among features included in the leaflets were items such as foreign phrases of a gay-themed or sexual nature, numbers for gay information lines in a range of cities and physical and sexual safety advice for those inexperienced in using backrooms:

Backrooms are a part of the scene in many European cities. Whether new to backrooms or not, here are some tips:
- It's OK to talk in there, to say 'no' or ask for sex to be safe
- Pickpockets like backrooms too. Leave wallets, keys, etc., with a friend or put them in your sock or shoe. But take your condoms and lube in there with you!
- Staying nearer the door makes it easier to get out if you need to. In a tightly packed crowd, you might not have the control you'd want over who does what to who.

- The more men you have sex with in a backroom (or anywhere), the more chance you'll pick up sexually transmitted infections.
- Do drink and drugs affect your judgement around safer sex? Pace yourself with both. You + backrooms + booze or drugs = how safe a combination?
- Some men have unprotected sex in backrooms, uninfected men and men with HIV.

('European Union made easy' leaflet)

Also included was advice on Customs, health insurance and travel tips for men with HIV, including warning of US entry restrictions for people with HIV (something not widely known among British gay men). Sources of further advice were signposted for men with HIV about US travel restrictions (and the Terrence Higgins Trust helpline was briefed specifically on handling calls on this issue). Incorporating these elements was designed to increase the appeal of the leaflets by making them useful in a practical sense:

Easy entry?
- Canada, Australia and New Zealand don't have entry restrictions if you have HIV and are just going for a holiday. Visas aren't needed for UK passport holders travelling to Canada and New Zealand. Visas are needed for Australia.
- USA Immigration restrict entry to travellers with HIV. The form UK passport holders fill in on arrival in the US ('visa waiver forms') asks if you have a 'communicable disease'. HIV is on the list of such diseases. Entry into the US can be denied if you say you have HIV or if things in your luggage (such as HIV drugs) give officials reason to believe you have HIV. For advice about travel and taking HIV drugs with you, speak to your local HIV organisation, the THT helpline or other people with HIV who've been to the US.

('Go West! Or off to Oz?' leaftlet)

The look of the leaflets and accompanying publicity was shaped by a desire to break with traditional imagery associated with gay men and holidays. The use of contemporary semi-naked, well-muscled 'Adonis' figures would have been entirely expected. As one travel agent remarked when discussing imagery that could prove effective: 'Not just a picture of a big sexy guy with a hard-on glowing there saying "keep it safe on holiday". I think that doesn't really work . . . It was really effective in the beginning when it was shocking but now it's a bit boring really' (Clift *et al.*, 1998: 55). The design agency's creative solution was to use archive images from the 1950s, giving a playful, 'camp' feel to the travel material.

262

When striking imagery could not be found for the long-haul leaflet, particularly suitable images were kindly donated by the Athletic Model Guild. Employing images from a bygone era allowed us to show semi-naked men without appearing to propagate the 'body beautiful' gay male culture of the present – a culture which alienates some men and is seen as oppressive or damaging by others. However, following feedback on the first two leaflets from those distributing them in London gay bars, the front cover for the third leaflet (long-haul) was specifically chosen for its more sexual feel so as to increase the leaflet's overall appeal (see Figure 11.2).

Promoting the campaign

The leaflets appeared in stages, with initial print runs of 60,000 per leaflet followed by a reprint (incorporating changes in telephone codes and the Terrence Higgins Trust logo), with all three brought together in a wrap-around wallet for distributors wishing to provide the set of three. Individual leaflets and the wallet enjoyed extensive advertising, promoting both their availability (in gay venues or over the telephone from Terrence Higgins Trust) and a key campaign message about taking condoms on holiday ('buy before you fly').

The advertisements have enjoyed widespread year-round placement in the UK gay press in recognition of established holiday patterns (Gran Canaria's popularity in winter, Sydney's Mardi Gras in February, etc.). Ads were placed in some non-gay magazines and many general gay press publications (e.g. *Boyz*, *Pink Paper*, *Axiom*, *QX*, *Metropolis*, *Attitude*, *Gay Times* and *DNA*) but also in the HIV-positive press (e.g. *Postive Nation* and *Positive Times*) as part of a strategy to target men with HIV. An ad was also placed in *Spartacus*, the international travel guide for gay men.

An element to the distribution of the travel leaflets was the involvement of (primarily gay) travel agents selling holidays to the target group. Initial negotiations showed a willingness on behalf of many such businesses to play a role in HIV-prevention activity. Subsequently, eight of these travel firms agreed to send out appropriate leaflets to men booking trips abroad. The bulk of copies, however, have been distributed in gay bars in cities represented in the CHAPS partnership.

Trying to involve tour operators and owners of holiday accommodation in distribution of safer-sex material presents certain challenges. The question that poses itself is: to what extent, if any, can commercial travel operations be expected to carry out health-promotion activity? It is difficult for health-promoters to monitor any input agreed with travel businesses even if their co-operation is (in theory), secured. Only a minority of gay men use gay holiday companies or accommodation, and accurately targeting gay holidaymakers is problematic – *in situ* what controls exist to ensure material goes to gay men and not others? Some travel operators and gay men interviewed in focus groups felt that by being given safer-sex material or condoms they were being identified as gay and as planning sex – something which annoyed them. Some men find it inappropriate and intrusive to be given sex-related literature or condoms with their travel documents or on arrival in a hotel.

As health-promoters in the home country it is probably a more effective use of our efforts to ensure that men set out for abroad with the knowledge (and condoms) they need ahead of their holiday: something that is both achievable and preferable to relying on travel businesses to do this for us. Placing adverts in gay travel guides and the brochures of gay travel companies is one route that the CHAPS campaign has pursued that involves the industry. Its appeal is that it does not rely on industry representatives to deliver an intervention, nor does it risk antagonizing gay men.

Pre-testing with men during the development process saw the leaflets rated as 'very useful, helpful and appropriate . . . easy to read and very straightforward'. Men appreciated the tone adopted in the leaflets and were grateful they were not being lectured: 'It's factual and I don't feel I'm being preached at. It's not silly and jokey but at the same time it's not patronizing. It's just clear, simple information.' Another man remarked: 'It didn't only tell the reader to always use a condom like so many of the other leaflets' (Clift *et al.*, 1998).

Evaluation and future developments

CHAPS materials are also evaluated by researchers once they have been in circulation to see how many men have seen them and what effect they have had on the target audience. SIGMA research agency evaluated the travel leaflets with men at Gay Pride-style community events across England, and the results were published in early 2001 (Weatherburn *et al.*, 2001). An average of 17 per cent of men had come across one or more of the travel leaflets – a figure in line with recognition data for other HIV-prevention leaflets surveyed at the same time. Far more men had seen the press adverts publicizing the availability of the leaflets. Most men reacted positively, appreciating the humour, design, information and the fact they were easy to read.

It is clear that for many gay men travel abroad involves entering an 'altered state', even before the first alcohol or drugs are taken! Many men report strong feelings of liberation, relaxation and freedom from restriction. The psychology of the holidaymaker seems often to involve an escape from rules and restraint, reputation and responsibility; in other words, the very things which 'safer sex' is traditionally seen to rely upon. It is in the tension between the routine of home and the release of the new environment that risk is situated. The personae and performances witnessed in the holiday setting bring a compelling and not yet fully understood dynamic to a sexual experience far removed from that which is mundane and domestic. If the erotic means the desire for distance and differ- ence, a need to connect with the unknown and unknowable, then what more potent arena for this eroticism than the oasis in time and space represented by the holiday?

The travel leaflets marked the first stage of the CHAPS campaign for gay male travellers and an attempt to connect with gay men and their journeys out of self to places far away from the ties of HIV, sexual restraint and self-control. The early years of the new millenium mark a new stage of the campaign. Whatever form it takes, it will ensure that for UK gay men holidaying abroad, health, HIV and safer sex, but also pleasure, remain firmly on the travel map.

REFERENCES

Callister, C. and Clift, S. (1999), *The Business of Gay Tourism*. Canterbury: Canterbury Christ Church University College.

Clift, S., and Forrest, S. (1998), *Gay Men, Travel and HIV Risk*. Canterbury: Centre for Health Education and Research.

Clift, S. and Forrest, S. (1999a), 'Factors associated with the sexual behaviour and risk of gay men on holiday', *AIDSCare*, 11 (3): 281–95.

Clift, S. and Forrest, S. (1999b), 'Gay men and tourism: motivations and holiday desti- nations', *Tourism Management*, 20: 615–25.

Clift, S. and Forrest, S. (2000a), 'Tourism and the sexual ecology of gay men', in S. Clift and S. Carter (eds), *Tourism and Sex: Culture, Commerce and Coercion*. Leicester: Pinter.

Clift, S. and Forrest, S. (2000b), 'Gay tourism, sex and sexual health promotion', in J. Horne and S. Flemming (eds), *Masculinities: Leisure Cultures, Identities and Con- sumption*. Eastbourne: Leisure Studies Association.

Clift, S., Forrest S., Callister C. and Luongo, M. (1998), *Travel-related HIV Prevention Work for Gay and Bisexual Men: final report on research to inform the development of a leaflet-based safer sex promotion campaign aimed at gay men travelling to southern European gay resorts on holiday*. Canterbury: Centre for Health Education and Research.

Conway, S., Gillies, P. and Slack, R. (1990), *The Health of Travellers*. Nottingham: Department of Public Health Medicine and Epidemiology, University of Nottingham and Nottingham Health Authority.

Hickson, F., Reid, D., Weatherburn, P., Stephens, M., Henderson, L. and Brown, D. (2001), *Time for More: Findings from the Gay Men's Sex Survey 2000*. London: Sigma Research.

Weatherburn, P., Bonell, C., Hickson, F., and Stewart, W. (1999), *The Facilitation of HIV Transmission by other Sexually Transmitted Infections during Sex between Men.* London: Sigma Research.

Weatherburn, P., Reid, D., Keogh, P., Hickson, F., Henderson, L., Branigan, P. (2001), *Advertising Awareness: Evaluation of CHAPS National HIV Prevention Adverts and Leaflets Targeted at Gay Men – 1996 to 2000.* London: Sigma Research.

WEBSITES

Terrence Higgins Trust: *www.tht.org.uk*
Gay Men Fighting AIDS: *www.demon.co.uk/gmfa/*

Appendix:
Gay and Lesbian Travel Resources Guide

MICHAEL LUONGO

Anyone unfamiliar with the gay tourism market needs to be aware of some of the resources available to the gay traveller – both electronic and printed. Though by no means comprehensive, this section will review some of the most important. Whether researching the gay travel field as a tourist, business interest, or academic field of study, it is important not to rely on one form of medium, or only one resource within that medium, as each has its own bias. In some cases, that is due to advertising pressures, the restrictions of the medium itself, and simply, the variety of gay travel options which are impossible to define concisely in only one volume or website.

Reflecting that extensive gay tourism marketing efforts began in the United States, most of these resources are geared to the American market. Still, a good search engine and the listings within the print media will allow one to find information relating to even the most obscure location.

WEBSITES

As it has for many industries, the Internet has revolutionized gay travel both in the way that destinations and tour operators can advertise, as well as the ease with which gay and lesbian travellers can access this information.

The Internet is ideal for its immediacy and ability to link the world from one remote location to another. Unlike print media, it can be instantly updated providing full current details at low cost. However, the value of a website is only as good as its information. It is very difficult to provide current information for locations that are not visited frequently or where advertisers do not assist in the updating. Thus, websites generally will provide travellers with the best information for the United States, Canada, Europe and Australia.

The 'QT' in *QTMagazine.com* stands for Queer Travel. Articles cover destinations, or profile key people in the gay travel industry. Recent profiles included David Rubin of David Tours, a luxury gay tour company, and Michael Fricke, National Sales Manager to the Gay and Lesbian Community for American Airlines. The site is heavily advertisement-driven, and allows visitors to book trips directly with tour companies. The site was once independent, but is now a part of GSociety Inc., which was created by the combination of *Gaywired.com*, *Lesbianation.com*, *QTMagazine.com* and other media entities.

OutandAbout.com is the website for the print newsletter *Out & About*, begun by Billy Kolber-Stuart and David Alport. At one time its own private entity, *Out & About* entered into a content syndication relationship in 1999 with *PlanetOut.com*, and eventually merged in April of 2000. *OutandAbout.com* contains some free articles, but more detailed information, called Masterfiles, is available for paid downloads. In theory, the site is less influenced by advertising than other sites because it is subscription-based. Co-founder Kolber-Stuart says: 'Our move into electronic info delivery is a natural extension of our original goal – to provide useful timely travel info.' Article themes often include the gay scene of a region, such as Asia, city updates for frequently visited locations such as New York and San Francisco, as well as seasonal themes such as beach resorts in the summer and ski destinations in the winter.

The San Francisco-based *PlanetOut.com*'s travel section works largely in conjunction with *Out & About*. They will have free information on specific destinations, some of which might be available only for a fee on *OutandAbout.com*. However, garnering this information via *PlanetOut.com* is more time-consuming, and does not provide opinionated critiquing. There is a calendar of forthcoming events and tours around the globe, and visitors can book trips through the site. There is also a large selection of information available for the lesbian traveller. *Gay.com* is a part of the *PlanetOut.com* and *OutandAbout.com* electronic media conglomerate.

Cruisingforsex.com is not a travel website *per se*, but clearly is of use to the gay traveller. The site lists locations of all kinds, in nearly a hundred countries, where men can have sex with men. The site began in 1996 and has expanded to become one of the most-visited gay websites in the world, with nearly 1.5 million hits a month. The site's information is created by its own users who provide tips from cottages, parks and saunas and other public-sex environments. In some cases, this website provides the only listings of locations to meet other gay men in countries with little or no commercial gay infrastructures. The website is supported primarily by pornographic advertisers, but does contain links to mainstream advertisers such as *amazon.com*. The site includes destination articles often with a sexual nature. *Cruisingforsex.com* also fills a gap in sexual information for destinations as other gay travel information sources have mainstreamed. (Ironically, Keith Griffith, the creator of the site, is a gay US Southern Baptist Republican.)

Gayexplorer.com provides information on particular destinations and events along with links to tour companies. Travel-related merchandise is also for sale on the website. Users will find a database of destination articles by gay travel writer Andrew Collins, the creator of *Fodor's Gay Guide to the USA*, the first gay travel guide produced by a mainstream publisher.

Travelgayzette.com contains both destination pieces and hard news articles pertaining to gay travel. Some recent critical articles included an incident where two gay men were thrown off a plane for kissing, and the 'de-gaying' of Key West. Other articles cover gay and lesbian tour companies.

The Canadian-based site *Gaytravelexperts.com* advertises various tour companies' trips. The site lists vacations by type, with a legend indicating whether tours are gay men only, lesbian, or mixed gay and straight. Sections give advice on currency abroad, health and HIV and other travel-related information. The site also links to other gay travel sites.

Purpleroofs.com lists gay- and lesbian-friendly accommodation throughout the world, as well as apartment exchanges through its sister site *gayhometrade.com*. The site gives price details on each accommodation, as well as descriptions of its clientele, including whether mixed gay and lesbian or mixed gay and straight. In some cases, visitors who mention the website's name when making direct reservations receive a discount. Information for contacting accommodation directly is provided, and the site also includes many budget choices. The site also lists information for gay-friendly tour companies throughout the globe. *Purpleroofs.com* is not all-inclusive, and tends to concentrate on smaller properties.

Gaytravel.com provides information on various destinations throughout the world. By clicking on the map of the world, viewers can find articles giving overviews of an entire nation or city, or focusing on a select business. Site visitor postings provide direct advice and recommendations for bars, clubs or hotels, or overall impressions of a destination. Once visitors join as members, they can book trips through the site and join in live chat about destinations and vacations.

Most travel websites have a definite bend towards gay male, and not lesbian, travel. In these cases, the travel sections of lesbian-oriented websites provide the best information. *Lesbianation.com* for instance provides a travel section, often focusing on adventure travel. Each of the major portals, such as *gay.com* and *PlanetOut.com* also provide specifically lesbian travel information.

Lesbiantravel.com is a property of *gaytravel.com*, but does not offer lesbian-only travel information. They are currently looking to launch a lesbian travel centre on the site, however, and were conducting a survey to determine visitors' needs. As of the printing of this book, the authors knew of no websites aimed solely at the lesbian travel market.

Many other websites exist as adjuncts to already popular gay and lesbian travel publications and guidebooks. For instance, *Damron.com* serves to promote the popular Damron's guides, and *odyusa.com* is the site for Odysseus travel guides. *Ourworldmag.com* and *guidemag.com* supplement these travel magazines, and *FunMaps.com* offers downloadable maps for gay resorts and destinations, serving a similar function to its print versions. Other sites, such as *alysonadventures.com*, promote tour companies and their trips to gay destinations.

IGLTA.com is the website for the trade-oriented International Gay and Lesbian Travel Association. The site provides little for the lay gay traveller for planning a trip, but it does provide links to many gay travel websites.

The website *gaybritain.org* is run by the British Tourist Authority, and while any traveller would find it useful, it bills itself as 'The official site for Americans travelling to Britain'. It provides comprehensive information and lists of gay and lesbian events in London, Brighton, Manchester, Glasgow and other British cities. It also has a good balance between men's and women's material.

Based on *gaybritain.com*, one might think that simply using code words such as 'gay' or 'queer' with the name of a destination would yield gay travel sites. For example, *Queerlondon.com* is a gay website covering the London scene. *GayLondon.co.uk* offers similar information. This rule does not hold true in many cases. Many such sites are on hold or incomplete, such as *gaymanchester.com*. *Gaynewyork.com* provides hotel information for the city, but does not list any gay hotels. Oddly, in some cases, putting the words 'gay' or 'queer' in with the name of a city will bring up porn websites aimed at heterosexuals.

Even the most seemingly comprehensive websites do not provide updated information for less frequently visited gay destinations such as South America, Africa or Asia. In these cases, locally created websites where the webmasters reside in the midst of the environment they are describing are best. Very good South American information for example comes from sites such as *GayPeru.com*, a Lima-based website, *gaybrasil.com*, or *riogayguide.com*, a Rio-based travel-site which is a spin-off of the locally produced *ipanema.com* mainstream website, or *gaychile.com*, based in Santiago. The downside of many of these locally produced websites, however, is that while English predominates on the web, as each nation develops its own web identity, this is changing. This might ultimately make it difficult for travellers to use the web to access current information.

An ideal international website is *GayGuide.net*. Maintained in Budapest, Hungary, it links nearly 400 gay guide websites throughout the world. Most are locally created, providing very accurate information, though some pages are rewrites of material found in Western guidebooks. Webmasters producing the sites can be contacted via email (though the language may be an issue) and many of the sites allow direct booking into hotels. This is one of the most comprehensive sites of its kind, and even less well-known destinations will have several links.

Some international websites in smaller countries tend to be all-purpose gay sites, providing travel information as one part of a broader portfolio of offerings. One example is that of J-FLAG, the Jamaican Forum of Lesbians All-Sexuals and Gays, whose complicated URL is <<*http://village.fortunecity.com/garland/704/*>>. The site provides legal, political, inspirational material and reviews of books of gay-black interest. For people wishing to visit Jamaica, there is an advertisement for the tour company Gay Friendly Jamaica, and contact information for gay-friendly hotels.

Even sites not originally designed as travel websites now prove useful to travellers. Such is the case with *thaiguys.com*, the website for the Thailand-based magazine *Thai Guys* (mentioned in Sanders, Chapter 2, this volume). One of the lead click-though icons is for securing a hotel in Thailand. Other travel links include articles on other Asian destinations, gay travel maps of various Asian cities and a link to Utopia Tours highlighting its Asian destinations. Still other article links feature books on Thailand such as a historical guide to 1920s Siam – the old name for Thailand.

Thomas Roth's company, Community Marketing, runs a variety of websites with information of interest to both the gay traveller and gay travel suppliers. The main site, *www.mark8ing.com* provides information on special events such as the Gay Travel Expo, discussed in the interview with him in this book (see Luongo and Roth, Chapter 5).

The site *gayjet.com* provides articles on various destinations, other news, as well as a calendar of gay and lesbian events around the world, with 5 per cent of its profits returned to the community. Visitors can directly book on the site, or hunt for the lowest airfares on other websites. The site *gaytravelnews.com* provides similar information. Like Roth's company, *Witeck-combs.com*, the website of Witeck Combs, provides information for companies interested in breaking into the gay and lesbian travel market.

Tour-based websites include *alternative-holidays.com*, of the London-based Alternative Holidays which takes over Club Med resorts for exclusively gay holidays. *RSVP.net* is the website for the RSVP cruise company, providing information on their cruises, along with links to other sites. Similarly, *olivia.com* provides information for the lesbian cruise company Olivia Cruises.

In 1994 New York City hosted the Gay Games, and in 1998, the Games went to Amsterdam – the first time they had ever moved from North America. The 2002 Gay Games are planned for Sydney, Australia. The website *www.gaygames. com* provides more information on these games, whilst *www.sydney2002.org.au* provides information on the Sydney event.

Most websites are concerned with promoting travel, but it is important that gays and lesbians have some understanding of the legal situation in the country they are visiting. *ILGA.org*, the website for the International Lesbian and Gay Association has a world legal survey serving just such a purpose. Whilst acknowledging the difficulties in maintaining information culled from so many sources (often after translation), the site is comprehensive. When available, information is broken into detailed categories such as HIV immigration policy, or issues specific to the transgendered. *IGLHRC.org*, the website for the International Gay and Lesbian Human Rights Commission, provides similar information, but not in as much detail. This information is perhaps most important for gays and lesbians travelling to countries not known as gay destinations. However, nations can differ internally, with less urbanized areas being particularly dangerous for openly gay and lesbian travellers. There are US states where it is technically illegal to be gay or lesbian, and it still remains illegal for HIV-positive travellers to enter the country without special permission. When arranging trips, particularly to destinations not usually part of a gay holiday, visitors should double-check such information.

PRINTED REFERENCES AND SOURCES

The economic promise of the Internet collapsed in the year 2000, and now a key issue among websites is consolidation. Gay websites are not immune to this world of mergers, and many of the previously mentioned sites are combining resources to remain financially viable. In some cases, the same information will be presented from one site to another with only minor variations. Ideally, travellers seeking information about gay destinations would use as many sources as possible. Like any other guide, each website has its own biases. To that end, traditional books and magazines are still highly useful and relevant sources of travel information before and during a trip.

Damron's is one of the oldest resources available to the gay and lesbian, having been established by Bob Damron in 1964. The company is now in its third generation of ownership, under the direction of Gina Gatta. The main publication is *Damron Men's Travel Guide*, formerly known as *Damron's Address Book*. The company now produces several travel guides for both lesbians and gay men, including *Damron Women's Traveler*, *Damron Accommodations* and *Damron Road Atlas*.

Odysseus is based out of Long Island, New York. The year 2001 represented its 15th edition. While international, it tends to be best for North America, and highlights only the most important European locations. *Spartacus International Gay Guide*, published by Bruno Gmünder, is also international but best for Europe. It is particularly detailed on Germany, where it is based. It does, however, provide excellent information for the United States' largest cities. The history of this book spans more than 30 years. Both books provide the best detail for the places in which their advertisers are based: but the general problem with broad international guidebooks is that they are not always able to offer 'less gay' locations.

Ferrari Guide Books owe their roots to the publication of a local gay directory for Arizona in the 1970s. Over the years, the company expanded internationally and now produces four major books: *Gay Travel A–Z*, *Men's Travel*, *Women's Travel* and *Inn Places*. More information is available on their website *ferrariguides.com*.

The 1996 *Fodor's Gay Guide to the USA* by Andrew Collins was the first gay guidebook published by a large mainstream house. In contrast to *Damron's* and *Spartacus* which tend to list as many gay-oriented sites as possible, *Fodor's Gay Guide* provides detailed and critical information on select destinations. As a mainstream book, it does however, specifically exclude most sex-oriented businesses. The book has been republished several times, and extended into a city series. Other books have followed suit; for example *Frommer's Gay & Lesbian Europe*, by David Andrusia (first published in 1997), and *Access Gay USA*, by David Appell (Harper Information, 1998).

Out & About Gay Travel Guides series by Billy Kolber-Stuart, David Alport and David Strange combined the efforts of Hyperion, a mainstream publishing house with an already established gay travel company. As well, as the market has expanded for gay travel, some gay travel books have broken beyond merely discussing destinations. *The Gay Vacation Guide: The Best Trips and How to*

Plan Them, by Mark Chesnut (Citadel Press, 1997), provides reviews of various forms of gay vacations, mentioning obscure items like square-dancing tours, to aspects of destinations like Miami Beach. Many books also became very specific to a place, such as the *Rainbow Handbook Hawaii* by Matthew Link (see Chapter 3, this volume, on Hawaii). In the UK, the Gay Men's Press publishes a series of gay pocket guidebooks called *Scene*, each focusing on a different city or country or region such as Paris, Berlin and Scotland.

Other gay guidebooks are of a more academic nature, concentrating not on bars, clubs and hotels, but on historic sites of gay interest. Among these is *Stepping Out*, by Daniel Hurewitz. Published in 1997 by Owl Press, it provides walking tours of various New York neighbourhoods with a focus on where gay events occurred or famous gay people lived. A much earlier book is *The Pink Plaque Guide to London*, by Michael Elliman and Frederick Roll. Published by the Gay Men's Press in 1986, it provides the addresses of buildings associated with famous gays and lesbians in British history.

Magazines

In the United States there are several gay travel publications. The first was *Our World*, launched in 1989 in Florida. Published monthly, this gay glossy provides details on destinations, tours and other information of interest to gay and lesbian travellers. The newsletter *Out & About* was launched in 1992. Subscriber-based, it does not advertise within its pages, but does so in separate travel-packet mailings. While both publications will mail to any international subscriber, they also provide PDF subscriptions online, (*ourworldmag.com* and *outandabout.com*).

The Guide is published out of Boston and is a cross between a magazine and a guidebook. Comprehensive in its overview of individual cities, it also provides detailed maps along with its articles. Unlike most of the other travel magazines, it covers sexual issues along with other aspects of a destination, and includes travel classifieds (*www.guidemag.com*). *Circuit Noize* provides information on circuit parties around the world and is published quarterly (*www.circuitnoize.com*). The magazine mixes articles about parties, drug-use and spirituality.

The newest of the gay travel magazines is *Passport Magazine*, a division of *Q Communications*, a San Francisco-based company. A bi-monthly, the magazine had its debut in early 2001 (*www.passportmagazine.net*).

Travel maps

As gay destinations are often neighbourhood-based, they are ideal for the production of comprehensive scene maps. Columbia FunMaps is perhaps the oldest gay travel map company and owes its existence to an even earlier company bought out by Alan Beck, the publisher. This US-based company produces maps for more than 60 destinations worldwide, concentrating on the United States, Canada and Europe. They were the producers of the official maps of the 1994 Gay Games, New York, and the 1998 Gay Games, Amsterdam (*www.funmaps.com*).

The German company Friends – the Gaymap, was launched in 2000 and concentrates on maps of Europe (*www.gaymaps.ws*). Other companies produce maps regionally, such as the Italian company, Echo Communication of the *Up City* series. They also produced the official map for Rome's World Pride (*www.upcity.it*).

Index